Justice for Judges

The Bitter Experiences

Justice for Judges

The Bitter Experiences

V.P. Srivastav

Manas Publications
New Delhi-110002

MANAS PUBLICATIONS
(Publishers, Distributors, Importers & Exporters)
4819,Varun House, Mathur Lane,
24, Ansari Road, Darya Ganj,
New Delhi - 110 002 (INDIA)
Ph.: 3260783, 3265523, 3984388
Fax: 011 - 3272766
E-mail: manaspublications@vsnl.com

First Published 2002

ISBN 81-7049-070-7

Typeset at
Manas Publications

Printed in India at
R.K. Offset, Delhi
and Published by Mrs. Suman Lata for
Manas Publications, 4819, Varun House,
Mathur Lane, 24, Ansari Road, Daryaganj
New Delhi 110002 (INDIA)

Preface

In historical retrospect, the colonial rule in India was least concerned with the welfare of the people in general and much less with the justice to them. It is a pity that even after four decades of independence the problem in the field of judicial administration and justice to the common people remains on our agenda, although the human instinct and human desire have been manifested. The judiciary, particularly the supreme court has played a positive role in affirming the individual rights of citizens, the federal and secular constitutional structure, and governmental accountability but fails to provide the cheap and obtainable justice to the of common people.

To my mind, for a successful democracy, the existence of a free judiciary becomes a must. Without an independent judiciary, the system may be termed "democratic centralism", which is practically equivalent to despotism or dictatorship. In any healthy democratic state, the independence of the judiciary is sought to be maintained through certain norms in appointing Judges along with an independent procedure for removing them from office. Furthermore, their salaries and allowances are not changeable at the whim of the executive or the legislature. But above all, a free judiciary can only exist in a political system in which democratic principles are truly believed in and acted upon by all alike -executive, Legislatures and the citizenry at large. Reciprocally, the judiciary in a democracy should have the courage to protect its independence and deliver impartial judgment free of fear of repercussions on career and prospects. It is a good sign that our judiciary has set the examples of its independence by way of pronouncing the judgement without fear whatever it may be.

Today the problem is not of laws or even of effective laws but of their strict enforcement and implementation. A man is said to be known by the society he keeps, a legal system is known by the laws that work. **Sir John Salmond's** view that law is a body of principles recognised and applied by the state in the administration of Justice is not for wrong. It is no denying the fact that there is a big gap between the people of India and our judicial system. Eighty percent of the people of India live in villages. They are illiterate and poor and for them the various fundamental or other rights guaranteed to the individuals by the constitution and laws of India are meaningless. Every person of common understanding reacts on the issues of present judicial system and feels that this present system was given to us by the former English rulers who made the judicial system with a bias in their own favour. On one hand, this judicial system suffers a defeat on its procedure which is so complex and difficult that it creates the doubt and fear in the mind of the people and on the other hand it creates delay in decision without being cheap and easily available to the common people. Whether denial of Justice is made due to delays, complexities or high costs, we have to remember that a nation to be strong needs not only a strong army but also a strong system of justice. **Henery Sidgwiek** has rightly pointed out that the most decision factor to measure rank of a nation in political civilization and therefore its strength, is justice, as defined by law, which is actually realised in its administration of justice with as much honesty and discipline as we require them in armed forces. Therefore, so long as we do not actually provide Justice to the masses, our right to call ourselves civilized will remain doubtful.

So the responsibility of judiciary for the protection of individual rights and dignity is very high and the judiciary has to play an unbiased role in providing the justice to all. In this process I wanted to pinpoint the limited sentencing powers of the judiciary. Just to meet the aspiration & welfare of the public, it is required that the sentencing powers should be reviewed and a discretionary powers should be introduced so that the court can provide sentence according to facts and circumstances of the each case.

In the present book, there are a collection of sixteen articles which try to examine various situations, issues and problems and demands meaningful academic interactions. The contributors have also given the practical suggestions to improve the present structure of Indian Judiciary and its administration. If besides entertaining the reader, this book succeeds in creating and entightened awareness, its mission would be fulfilled. I may humbly add that I would look upon the constructive criticism of my readers with gratitude as such interaction would ultimately enhance the aims and objective of this book.

V.P. Srivastav

Acknowledgments

I take the opportunity to record my deep sense of gratitude to my parents who are always a constant source of inspiration to me at every stage of the book. Without their blessings, it would have been difficult for me to produce this work successfully. The commissioning and editing of the set of original articles on Indian Judiciary is a genuinely collaborative process which makes these acknowledgments much more than mere formality. At first, my thanks go naturally to all the contributors of this volume for devoting their valuable time and more than it for their commitment and patience.

I am grateful to all my colleagues in the faculty of law, Delhi Police Training College, Jharoda Kalan and the Directorate of Prosecution, Tis Hazari for their kind and consistent cooperation in this endeavour. My frank discussions with them greatly helped me in anaylsing the problems in the right prospective. Besides this, I would like to give my sincere thanks to all the members of the copyright office who have spared me for several months to complete the book.

I wish to add my gratitude to all my friends and colleagues particularity Sh. Suresh Chand, Spl. officer (Book Promotion) and Sh. A.C. Singh, Asstt. legal Adviser. Deptt. of Revenue who have sincerely helped me at different stages and get the materials amended whenever required.

My sincere thanks to Sh. R.C. Rustogi M/o Human Resource Development, Deptt. of Education who has helped me and extended his services for typing whenever I needed.

I express my sincere thanks to Shri V.K. Garg of MANAS PUBLICATION for taking up the publication job in right earnest and bringing the book out besides so many odds.

My wife Smt. Anita Srivatav and my children Master Tanmaya and Baby Garima, deserve my special thanks for all that they had suffered ungrudgingly while I was busy in editing this book. Besides, they allowed me to devote my time in writing by sparing me from household work and continued encouragement.

Above all, this work is an obligation to God almighty whose grace and blessings I pray would remain the divine force behind my endeavours.

Contents

1

Gender Equality: Turmoil or Triumph?

*- Justice J.N. Bhatt**

Gender based discrimination represents the ugly face of society. This issue is global with varying degree and very old. Really, it is a travesty of all canons of social justice and equity that women who constitute half the world's population and who work two-third of world's working hours should earn just one tenth of the world's property and also should remain victims of inequality and injustice. This anomaly, is, now, being openly questioned and the underlying discrimination is seriously challenged. As human development moves centre-stage in the global development debate, gender equality and gender equity are emerging as major challenges. Gender discrimination, though amongst the most subtle, is one of the most all-pervading forms of institutionalized deprivation.

The term 'sex' and 'gender' are often used interchangeably in everyday life, but in sociological literature they are frequently differentiated. The term 'sex' is applied to those distinctions between men and women that are based on biological differences, such as anatomy, physiology, hormones and chromosomes, and in this respect people are female or male. The term 'gender' is applied to the cultural aspects of male and female roles, in other words the behaviour, personality and other social attributes that are expected of males and females. These social attributes become the basis of masculine and feminine roles. Sexuality

* Judge, Gujarat High Court, Navrangpura, Ahmedabad (Guj.)

and the different capacities of men and women in the reproductive process are particularly likely to be thought of as giving 'natural reasons' for gender divisions in society.

The question of gender equality is a very old and burning problem. Twenty years ago in Mexico, the First World Conference on Women inspired a movement that has helped to reduce gender inequality worldwide. Illiteracy among women is declining, maternal mortality and total fertility rates are beginning to fall, and more women are participating in the labour force than ever before. However, much remains to be done. Persistent inequality between women and men constrains a society's productivity and ultimately slows its rate of economic growth. Although this problem has been generally recognized, the evidence available of the need for corrective action is more compelling today than ever.

The principles of gender equality and gender equity have been basic to Indian thinking. The 19th and early 20th centuries saw a succession of women's movements, first around social issues and later around the freedom struggle itself. The Constitution of India adopted in 1950 not only grants the equality of women, but also empowers the State to adopt measures of affirmative discrimination in favour of women.

The principle of gender equality is enshrined in the Indian Constitution in its Preamble, Fundamental Rights, Fundamental Duties and Directive Principles. However, there still exists a very wide gap between the goals enunciated in the Constitution, legislation, policies, plans, programmes and related mechanisms on the one hand and the situational reality of the status of women in India on the other.

References to the equality between women and men in the Constitution are to be found in the following:

1. Part III of the Constitution which guarantees the Fundamental Rights of men and women. In particular, Article 14, 15 and 16 Part III of the constitution which guarantee rights to equality and elaborate on the concept of equality underpinning these rights.

2. Article 325, which guarantees that all shall have the right to vote irrespective of sex.

3. Part IV of the Constitution, the Directive Principles of State Policy, which are fundamental guidelines for governance, although not enforceable in a court of law.

4. Some Constitutional amendments, which also refer to women, such as the 42nd Amendment to the Constitution, which contains a clause referring specifically to women, declaring that: It shall be the duty of every citizen of India: (e) to renounce practices derogatory to the dignity of women. The 73rd Constitutional Amendment also provides for the reservation of one-third seats in all tiers of local government for women.

Although guaranteed equally to men and women, there are several ways in which the structure of the family and the existence of several inequitable social customs and practices serve to deprive women of these rights. In particular, discrimination occurs within the family, where norms regarding women's secondary status are reinforced in children from birth. Son-preference is one of the key aspects underlining social values that view girls as burdens. Women are viewed as dependents within the family and face severe restrictions on their mobility, a fact that further impedes their ability to gain access to education, economic opportunities, to move freely and settle anywhere, to form unions or groups and so on, which are all fundamental freedoms under the Indian Constitution. Freedom of speech and expression is often denied to women within the family, and women are kept out of the decision-making processes both within community and State institutions. Cultural norms regarding appropriate behaviour for women often reinforce images of docility, passivity and subservience, severely curtailing the exposure and confidence women require to participate on an equal footing with men in public life. Practices like female foeticide, infanticide and the constant if not increasing incidences of violence on women, also constitute consistent assaults on women's right to life and personal liberty.

The Constitution guarantees several Fundamental Rights in addition to the rights to equality and non-discrimination discussed earlier. Some of these Fundamental Rights include:

- Protection of life and personal liberty [Article 21]
- Freedom of movement [Article 19 (d)]

- Right to choose an occupation and pursue a lawful vocation [Article 19 (g)]
- Right against exploitation, traffic in human beings and other forms of forced labour [Article 23 (i)]
- Right to form associations and unions [Article 19(c)]
- Right to freedom of speech and expression [Article 19(a)]

In conclusion, it must be emphasised that the Constitution of India provides the only explicit guarantee of women's right to equality in the country. There is no other legislation explicitly or specifically prohibiting discrimination against women in specific areas. The Constitution provides the equality standard. However, the way the Constitution is interpreted and acted upon in some case-law reveals not only the bias of the judiciary, but the normative approach to gender equality that underpins much of State action in India, which views women as persons deserving protection, rather than promoting women's rights. Violations of women's rights continue in practice, aided by the legal system, which is slow, often expensive (despite the existence of legal aid cells which are supposed to provide women with free legal services if required) and often procedurally biased against women, who face restrictions on their mobility and access to resources. Further, public institutions or authorities are not specifically regulated by laws prohibiting discrimination, and there is no code that lays down guidelines for equal opportunities or nondiscrimination that institutions can follow. While employers are bound by laws regarding maternity benefits, provision of creches and so on, the only other law that binds public institutions concerns the matter of custodial rape, where the minimum sentence has been set for a higher period than that of non-custodial rape, and where the burden of proof rests on the perpetrators.

The concept of rights, particularly economic and social rights, has been markedly absent from the Indian government's activities and approaches to gender equality. There is a lack of effort to secure basic economic rights for women in the family, in relation to property, income and shelter, prerequisites for women's right to dignity and a measure of autonomy. Assets that have been created out of public resources for poor households have been largely granted to male heads, while the responsibility for the social costs of child care, household maintenance and survival-oriented productive tasks are laid on women's shoulders. The Government of India largely considers the household to be the basic unit or structure in development assistance, despite evidence to show that intra-household inequalities take a great toll on women and girl children, inhibiting their access to basic rights in development such as good health, education, freedom of movement and the right to autonomy. However, there are indications, which will be elaborated below, that in some policy areas and programmes, the Government has been willing to invest in processes that empower women and emphasize their rights.

One of the fundamental obstacles to promoting gender equality in development remains at the community level, where attitudinal biases often prevent women from realizing their rights. The Government has done little to take on board these obstacles, apart from occasional land irregular campaigns around single issues like dowry, girl-child education, amniocentesis, and so on. Police education campaigns are restricted to occasional posters and TV spots, but are neither consistent nor backed up by strong and clear action by the State. Their impact remains less than effective, particularly since there is little action taken against advertising or campaigns that are gender-discriminatory.

The National Human Rights Commission (NHRC) was set up in 1993, as a statutory body to which individuals and interested parties could make complaints on human rights violations in the country. The NHRC has explicitly stated that women's rights will be a part of its concerns. As yet, the NHRC has taken up no specific issue of violation, though it has attempted to address single instances of state violence on women. It is yet to take a significant interest in women's rights. Part of the problem arises out of the division seen between the National Commission for Women and the NHRC; although a member of the Women's Commission is represented on the NHRC, it is often assumed that the Women's Commission will deal primarily with women's rights violations. The NHRC's ability to function as an autonomous body is yet to be established. Like the Women's Commission, its establishment has been criticized as a move on the part of the State to appear accountable without providing these bodies with sufficient autonomy to push through decisions or recommendations that may appear contrary to State interests. The Law Commission, the Minorities Commission, the Commission for Scheduled Tribes and Scheduled Castes are broadly mandated to look at women's issues. Barring the Law Commission, which has participated actively in recommending gender-just legal change, the remaining Commissions have shown little concern for women's rights in their functioning.

The causes of gender inequality are complex, linked as they are to the intra-household decision making process. However the decisions are made, the intra-household allocation of resources is influenced by market signals and institutional norms that do not capture the full benefits to society of investing in women. Low levels of education and training, poor health and nutritional status, and limited access to resources depress women's equality of life and create hurdles in economic efficiency and growth. Regional perspectives play a very important role in the realm of gender equality.

It is therefore essential that public policies work to compensate for market failures in the area of gender equality. These policies should equalise opportunities between women and men and redirect resources to those investments with the highest social returns. Of these investments, female education, particularly at the primary and lower-secondary level, is the most important, as it is the catalyst that increases the impact of other investments in health, nutrition, family planning, agriculture, industry, and infrastructure. Women themselves are agents for change because they play a key role in shaping the welfare of future generations. Public policies cannot be effective without the participation of the target group, in this case women, who make up more than half of the world's people. Their views, therefore, must find a place into policy formulation.

The causes of the persistent disparity and inequality between men and women are only partially examined, explored and understood. In recent years attention has focused on inequalities in the allocation of resources at the household level, as seen in the fact that boys receive higher shares of education, health and food expenditures in comparison with girls. The decision making process within households is complex and is influenced by social and cultural norms, market opportunities and institutional factors. There is considerable proof that the intra-household allocation of resources is a key factor in determining the levels of schooling, health and nutrition accorded to household members. Regional factors also have contributed in gender equalities.

Bias has been defined as a particular influential power that ways the judgement, the inclination, or propensity of the mind towards a particular object. In judicial parlance, justice requires that the judges should have no bias for or against any individual in making their judicial decisions and that their minds should be perfectly free to act as the law requires.

Whilst bias may take various forms in the judiciary, bias on account of a particular gender should have no place in it. Bias in any form is anathema to a judge. It is therefore recognized that, wherever bias is perceived, the public considers the judicial system as having failed to adhere to the highest standards of impartiality and fairness. The rule of law obtains validity or ratification by society because of its commitment to equality for all citizens irrespective of race, colour, creed or sex.

Less than ten years ago, terms such as 'judicial gender bias' or 'gender bias and the courts' were unheard of. Today, the systematic discussion of gender bias is not only part of the most national judicial education system, but it has also received national and international recognition. Pervasive gender bias in the courts, which was virtually invisible as recently as the 1980s, has become apparent and is plainly visible on record. Research conducted into this matter by social scientists and researchers in the legal field has documented judicial gender bias and its profound effect on judicial fact-finding and decision making. Even though such progressive empirical studies were originally uncoordinated, a disquieting picture has emerged in numerous areas of the law, which shows that gender bias exists in all areas, operating sometimes to the advantage of men and more often and more seriously to the disadvantage of women.

If gender bias is identified in all its nuances and hues, that would be a large step in dealing with this dilemma. It is not special treatment for women or for men that is called for; instead, what is needed is a sensitivity to the ways in which unexamined attitudes about men and women lead to the unintended result of biased decision making. Only when this sensitivity is achieved, and is reinforced by curiosity, analysis and openness, will the litigants be able to explain their circumstances to a court that is both willing to learn and to judge to achieve a gender neutrality in its judicial system, which is both vital and important to the ultimate achievement of justice in its purest and highest form.

Violence and its perpetuation are often related to conflicts of caste, class, ethnicity, communalism, fundamentalism and terrorism. And all these factors cumulatively have a negative impact on women. Other forms of violence are trafficking in women and girls and custodial violence perpetrated by law enforcement agencies. Violence is reprehensible in all contexts.

The Amendment in the Indian Penal Code and the introduction of Section 304-B or 498-A), important amendments in IPC on custodial deaths and amendments in the Indian Evidence Act are not sufficient to check increasing domestic cruelty and violence. Therefore, legal literacy and awareness programmes must be evolved for the enhanced development and empowerment of women. In principle, India is deeply committed to the object of elimination of all forms of discrimination against women and is one of the signatories of the convention on the said subject.

As per the report of review of New Internationalist "Women: A World Report", there has been progress in the field of gender equality since 1985, but less than what was expected. The report illustrates how women's ability to bear children means they are expected to take responsibility for domestic work worldwide. A woman in a Pakistani village, for example, spends around 63 hours a week on domestic work alone. In spite of the importance of such work, housework is invisible and undervalued. Calculations demonstrate that if the services provided free by a housewife in the USA in 1979 had been purchased with wages at market rates, they would have cost $ 14,5000 a year. On this basis, unpaid work done in the industrialised countries contributes 25-40 percent of the GNP.

It is significant to consider that, if women paid each other to do their housework, the GNP would nearly double. It is not of course that we wish to value all work and caring in monetary terms, but it does seem that because such work is undervalued, women's abilities and contribution throughout society and throughout the world also tend to be undervalued. It is interesting that, in parts of the world where cash and wages have not penetrated, women and men tend to do relatively equal amounts of work.

Three fifths of the world's population lives their lives by the rhythm of the seasons. The remaining two-fifths of us - about 1 billion people - are hitched to the machines that run modern society. Women predominantly work in service jobs - reflecting their traditional role of caring and cleaning. In 1985, women's wages were consistently lower than men's were, ranging from 73 per cent in the countries of northern Europe to less than 50 per cent in Japan and Korea. Overall, women employed in the rich world did an average of three hours less paid work per week than men, but over 17 hours more unpaid domestic work. Even in United States, the figures are alarming. There are numbers and statistics like measured mile-markers, flashing along a dawn drive toward a still distant reckoning. There were 301 women state legislators in 1969, 908 in 1981; and 5,765 female elected officials in 1975. And yet those 908 legislators are only 12 per cent of the members of the State legislative bodies. Only 19 of the 435 members of the US House of Representatives are women, only two of the 100 senators.

The numbers mark the distance travelled and the distance yet to go. Eighty per cent of all women who work hold down "pink-collar jobs" and get paid about 66 cent of a man's dollar. Seventy per cent of all classroom teachers are women, yet for the same job, they make an average of $ 3,000 a year less than their male colleagues. More than a third of all candidates for MBA degrees are women; however, only 5 per cent of the Executives in the top 50 American companies are women. Where once even recently, there was nothing, all those statistics and all their corollaries now show that there has been something; some progress forged for women over the past decade of challenge and confusion. Perhaps those numbers are really a crude scale for a new geography, exploring the wide gulf between something and satisfaction.

Across the world, as many as one thirds of all households were headed by women. Migration was a major cause of this. In many of the poor world's cities, men far outnumber women - leaving large numbers of women managing alone in rural areas. Divorce is rising all over the world. On top of this, 75 per cent of the health care for elderly people was provided by women at home. Clearly, traditional family structures are under strain across the planet.

While women represent fifty per cent of the world's population; yet, they perform nearly two thirds of the working hours, receive only one-tenth of the world's income and less than one per cent of the world's property. There are grave inequalities between nations and also serious inequalities within nations; however, women everywhere lack position and power and are over- represented amongst the poor.

Gender relations need to be measured in the context of participation in, and sharing of, the important decision-making process that results in the above inequalities. Such a measure would help identify the differing degrees of inequality in terms of age, income levels and geographical location. For governments and concerned citizens seeking to redress these inequalities, indices are a means of determining the issues on which they must concentrate, and provide feedback on the effectiveness of their actions. Clearly, then, the accuracy of any measure of gender inequality needs close scrutiny.

I refer in particular to a recent event: the initial euphoria generated a few months ago - mainly by men - over the proposed reservations for women of one third the total seats in Parliament and in Legislative Assemblies. A constitutional amendment was tabled, and it was even insisted that it should be put to the vote as early as possible. But cold feet soon developed. The excitement bubbled over as quickly as it had started and dissolved into nothingness, exhibiting what the CJI has so accurately described (in the Preface to the Volume on "Gender and Judges") as "the general male chauvinist attitude that is unwittingly nurtured by us". That is why judicial verdicts, especially from the highest court, can move mountains. They frequently do.

For instance, before 1990, no married woman was entitled as of right to be appointed to the Indian Foreign Service. She required special written permission from the Government before her marriage was solemnized and could be made to resign if the Government was satisfied that "her family and domestic commitments were likely to come in the way of the efficient discharge of her duties". Along came one Ms. Muthamma, a brilliant member of the Indian Foreign Service. She came with the complaint that as a result of the Service Rules she had been denied promotion to Grade I in the Indian Foreign Services: a grade which would have entitled her to be appointed Ambassador.

The judges found in the rules what they described as "transparent discrimination" against women. But what is of interest and importance is than an enlightened member of the Bar, the then Solicitor General of India, appearing for the Union of India, volunteered to review the rules and the seniority of Ms. Muthamma. The court, whilst pronouncing the marriage rule invalid, said that it wished to impress upon the Government.

"The need to overhaul all service rules to remove the stain of discrimination without waiting for ad hoc inspiration from writ petition or gender charity".

Ms. Muthamma got her promotion and distinguished herself as India's Ambassador serving in several countries abroad.

What we want today is evidence of a visible absence of gender bias in all decision-making. Not the sort of judicial gender charity exhibited in the Air India case some years ago. In the early eighties air hostess claimed parity in retirement age, under the statutory regulations, when they attained 35 years or on marriage, whichever was earlier, but this was extendible at the discretion of the Managing Director to 45 years. Male air pursers retired at 58.

The court said that the conferment of discretion on the Managing Director to extend the date of retirement of air hostesses from 35 to 45 years was arbitrary, and decreed that air hostesses would henceforth retire at 45 years. The obvious differentiation of 45 years for females and 58 years for males was simply wished away as neither arbitrary nor discriminatory. Five years later, counsel for the airhostesses asked for a reconsideration of the previous decision (of 1982) but the judges said, "We do not feel persuaded to accept this request". An attempt was then made to extend the date of retirement of air-hostesses - this time on the basis of the fact that British girls recruited by Air India abroad retired at 55 years, whereas those recruited in India had to retire at 45, but the effort failed and an assurance was taken from counsel that even British girls recruited by Air India would retire at 45 years. These are but two instances of what Justice Krishna Iyer, in the Muthamma case, characterized as "gender charity".

But if we are to rid ourselves of patronizing attitudes, we must be conscious of an innate gender bias, especially amongst the male population in this region. Yes, even amongst judges. We can learn to improve only if we first want to learn.

How do you get rid of such attitudes and approaches? For one thing, by adopting the direct Krishna Iyer approach more frequently.

In Muthamma's case this great judge just hacked through the Foreign Services Recruitment Rules - expressing in cold print his wonderment as to how sex prejudice against Indian women pervaded Indian Service Rules even 30 years after freedom was won. He wrote:

> If a married man has a right, a married woman, other things being equal, stands on no worse footing. This misogynous posture is a hangover of the masculine culture of manacling the weaker sex, forgetting how our struggle for national freedom was also a battle against women's thralldom. Freedom is indivisible, so is Justice. That our founding faith enshrined in Article 14 and 16 should have been tragically ignored vis-a-vis half of India's humanity, viz., our women, is a sad reflection on the distance between the Constitution in the book and the Law in

action. And if the Executives as the surrogate of Parliament, make rules in the teeth of part-III, especially when high political office, even diplomatic assignment, has been filled by women, the inference of die-hard allergy to gender parity is inevitable.

"Diehard allergy to gender parity". Strong words necessary to express judicial indignation. We require more of this from the judiciary to shake people out of Gender Bias.

Has our attitude been too paternalistic and out of touch with realities? Is it in tune with fast changing social conditions and values? All this will be discussed under different sub-topics.

Strategies and Actions Points for the Future

If the benefits from investing in girls and women are so great and can be quantified, why do households and employers underinvest in women? The main reason is that, as discussed above, markets fail to capture the full benefit to society of investing in women and girls. Where the market fails or is absent, government must take the lead. Public policy can contribute, directly and indirectly, to reducing gender inequalities. For example:

1. Modifying the legal and regulatory framework to en sure equal opportunities.
2. Ensuring macroeconomic stability and improving microeconomic incentives.
3. Redirecting public policies and public expenditure to those investments with the highest social returns.
4. Adopting targeted interventions that correct gender inequalities at the microlevel.
5. Organising, at the grass roots, women into self-help groups at the local or 'anganwadi' level. These women's groups should be helped to institutionalise themselves into registered societies and to federate at the town level. Such societies should bring about synergistic implementation of all the social and economic development programmes by drawing resources made available through Government and non-Government channels, including backs and

financial institutions, and by establishing a close interface with the Panchayats and Municipalities.

A national action plan for translating the policy into a set of concrete actions should be drawn. Such action plans should include the following:

1. Committing resources for women in key sectors relating to education, vocational training, employment and income generation, health and support services, gender sensitization programmes and information dissemination.
2. Setting time targets to achieve the mandates, strategies and action points of such policies.
3. Fixing responsibilities for the implementation of action points.
4. Formulating structures and mechanisms to ensure efficient implementation, monitoring and reviewing of action points.
5. Widely disseminating information on all aspects of legal rights, human rights and other entitlements of women, through specially designed legal literacy programmes and rights information programmes.
6. Reviewing curricula and educational materials to include gender education and human rights issues.
7. Using different kinds of mass media to communicate social messages relating to women's equality and empowerment.

Several initiatives have been taken to improve the status of women. From Mexico to Copenhagen, on to Nairobi and finally to Beijing is merely two decades of contemporary social history. However, if one looks at the history of the struggle for women's rights, both in India and around the world, it constitutes one of the most eventful and momentous in recent times. India's search for an organisational structure to co-ordinate efforts towards gender equality and gender equity began with the establishment of the Central Social Welfare Board in 1953. A Department of Women and Child Development was set up in 1985 under the newly created Ministry of Human Resources Development. There has been a subsequent growth of many new institutions to interact with and add to the existing network. Amongst these, one of the most significant is the setting up of the National Commission for Women by an Act of Parliament in 1990.

The 73rd and 74th Constitutional Amendment Acts of 1993 constitute a watershed for the advancement of Indian women. They ensure 1/3 of the total elected seats and positions of Chairpersons in rural and urban local elected bodies to women. About 1 million women are estimated to emerge as leaders at the grass-roots levels in rural areas alone. Of these, 75,000 are to be Chairpersons.

In spite of a series of actions, singular policies, new programmes and some achievements, certain critical areas call for immediate attention. Some of them could be highlighted as follows, keeping in mind differences in regional factors and perspectives:

1. Inadequacy of institutional mechanisms for the advancement of women.
2. Persistent and institutionalised discrimination against the girl child.
3. Feminization of poverty.
4. Gender blindness in macro-economic policies.
5. Invisibility of women's contribution to the economy and environmental sustenance.
6. Poor participation by women in decision making structures and processes.
7. Gender gaps in literacy, education and health.
8. Growing trends of violence against women.
9. Barriers encountered by women in accessing legal entitlements.
10. Gender biased social norms.
11. Negative portrayals and perpetuation of gender stereotypes by mass media.
12. Adverse regional perspectives and problems, affecting the goal of gender equality and equity.

A few measures for the administration of laws can be taken, including some changes in the provision of a substantial penal and evidentiary nature.

1. To introduced relating to domestic violence i.e., to enact the Domestic Violence Act which will ensure the physical safety of women as well as prevent them from being thrown out of their maternal home, with the power to the Family Court to grant injunctions to protect a `battered wife', even though the house was inthe name of husband's sole name and it belonged to him without her having a share in it.
2. For better investigation and inquiry into the cases of unnatural deaths, the Coroners Act, 1871 asoperative in Bombay, should be made applicable inother areas. This should enable an independent authority with judicial powers to probe into the cause of an unnatural death.
3. More female police personnel should be inducted so as to be available in situations relating to the unnatural deaths of women. A man-woman police combination is likely to produce better results in such investigations.
4. In the interest of more responsible and efficient investigation, no officer below the rank of Assistant Commissioner or Assistant Superintendent of Police should handle the case of an unnatural death.
5. Punishment for abetment to suicide should be raised to a minimum of 7 years, as in the case of dowrydeath. This is desirable in view of the fact that police treat most unnatural deaths as suicides, and the accused persons are prosecuted for abetment of suicide, which attracts a lesser punishment.
6. Under section 113-B of the Evidence Act, a very heavy burden is cast on the prosecution to get the benefit of the presumption; a nexus to be established between the dowry issue and fatal violence. The section may be made more liberal by dispensing with the burden of proof that the violence was in relation to dowry demand.`
7. Early appointment of dowry prohibition officers, as envisaged in Dowry Prohibition Act, is highly desirable for their likely utility in the prevention, Investigation and prosecution of dowry related crimes.

8. Compulsory and free education up to middle school standards for all girls; and prohibition of labour of the girls child up to the age of sixteen.
9. The offence under the Dowry Prohibition Act and under section 498A of the Indian Penal Code should be made of compoundable nature, with a view to affecting a healthy reconciliation between the parties. The court needs to be invested with a discretionary power to ask for an undertaking from the husband that he will not proceed with his demand for dowry and that he will be faithful to his wife and to the obligations of the marital tie. Suitable amendments should be made to implement this provision under the Code of Criminal Procedure of 1973 and Dowry Prohibition Act, 1961.

Women continue to be in marginal employments and low levels of skills, their contribution being largely invisible. The prevailing social construction of gender largely relegates women to the inside sphere. Reproduction and responsibilities of nurturing, management of a fragile environment, and low paid or unpaid but heavy work responsibilities in agriculture, animal husbandry and other traditional sectors, creates a syndrome of gender stereotypes, marginalisation, alienation and deprivation. One may be reminded of one of India's greatest poets, Rabindranath Tagore, who expressed the pain and inequality of the situation more than half a century ago:

"O lord why have you not given women the right to conquer her destiny?
Why does she have to wait head bowed,
By the roadside, waiting with tired patience,
Hoping for a miracle in the morrow?"

Making women equal partners in the national development process and equipping them to make informed choices in order to equalise their self-worth through empowerment are goals to which the Government must be committed. There is a long way to go, but the endeavour must be ceaseless. The disparity and inequality emerging on account of regional perspectives must be seriously examined, analyzed and then controlled by appropriate plans and programmes.

Bibliography

1. *Indian NGOs Report, Discrimination against Women.*
2. *National Police for Women,* 1996.
3. *Discrimination against Women.*
4. *Public Policies Matters.*
5. *Towards Gender Equality.*
6. *Advancing Gender Equality.*
7. *Women's Charter for Effective Equality.*

2

Judiciary on Trial

*- Giri Raj Shah**

The judiciary itself is on trial, a fact that alone compels an inspection and a self-assessment of its working. It is being flayed by its luminaries like Justice Krishna Iyer and H R Khanna who have raised an accusing finger against judges involved in the allotment of housing sites or those with casteist leanings. Not only retired judges and the common people, but also many conscious serving judges and people who believe in moral values have exerted their strong views against judicial misdemeanors and ostentatious styles of living and functioning. It is common knowledge that the ordinary citizen is interested in speedy justice and not in image building in public interest judgements or populist judgements, as is the fashion of the day. It is unfortunate that nothing has been done to clear the huge backlog of pending cases.

Independence of the Judiciary

Jefferson had declared that the independence of judiciary was itself a threat to democracy. This view was shared by one of the most distinguished legal luminaries, Justices Hormas Brandies, Cardozo and Frankfurtes. It was Jefferson's view that in a democracy there is more jurisdiction for the Legislative and Executive than for judiciary, because the decision of the popular branches is subject to popular referendum and that of the judicial is not. According to Justice H R Khanna: "There can be no conflict between the State and the judiciary because the judiciary is a part of the State. The Constitution has defined the sphere of activity of each of those three wings

* Inspector-General of Police, (Training), U.P. Police, Directorate of Police Training, 4th floor, Indira Bhawan, Lucknow- 226001, U.P.

of the State. . . the trouble arises when overactivists in one wing try to encroach upon what is essentially within the domain of the other wing."[1]

Super Parliament

It is alleged that the judiciary, particularly the Supreme Court, has been trying to function as a sort of Super Parliament and has thus sown the seeds of confrontation between the judiciary and the State. However, it should be borne in mind that the mere exercise of the power of judicial reviews of the action of the Executive and Legislative by the judiciary should not be construed as confrontation. The judiciary must restrain its power only to the limits of interpretation and should not use it as interference.

The resulting conflict has been most evident over the years in the student debate on Fundamental Rights vs. Directive Principles of the Constitution. The Supreme Court has constantly thwacked attempts on the part of the Legislative and the Executive to ensure the supremacy of the Directive Principles of State Policy over the Fundamental Rights of individual citizens. Many laws enacted to advance socio-economic policies and programmes of the Government have been struck down by the court, on the grounds that they violated Fundamental Rights.

A Necessary Restraint

In the words of Lalit Bhasin: "The nation's elite, by and large, realise that the power of judicial review is a necessary restraint against the abuse of Legislative or Executive power." To the political activities who cry 'Power to the People', implying that the power of judicial review shall not cover parliamentary Legislation, Lord Acton gives a complete answer: "The fate of every democracy of every Government based on the sovereignty of the people depends on the claim it makes between those opposite principles: absolute power on the one hand, and, on the other, the restraint of legality and the authority of tradition. It must stand or fall according to its choice, whether to give supremacy to the law or to the will of the people. Whether to constitute a moral association maintained by duty or a physical one kept together by force."

At times, legislation "plainly missed the fire," as Lord Macmillon said in reference to acts enacted after independence, and to a few instances from the Income Tax Act, the NDPS Act and a score of other legislative activities that have cropped up from time to time as ad hoc measures. However, Lord Diplok, commenting on the statement of Lord Macmillon, rightly asserted: "If, as in this case, the courts can identify the target of Parliamentary Legislation, their function is to see that it is hit, not merely to record that it has been missed."

The Problem

Since the written Constitution, any law made by Parliament or a State Legislative would be ultravirus, if it is repugnant to any of its express provisions or is beyond the legislative competence of the legislative concerned, the matter being in the Union list or the State list, as the case may be. The power of the court to strike down such laws on the grounds that they violate the constitutional provisions is perfectly legitimate. But the question that arises is whether the courts should also have the authority to strike down constitutional amendments that are valid and carried out in accordance with the procedure set out in the Constitution itself? Such arrogation of powers to itself by the Supreme Court is not understandable, because the courts are not contemporary institutions like Parliament. Judicial reviews of the reasonableness of the Legislation means the testimony of the whole social powers by the single standard of law.

Behind our commitment to the text of the Constitution, there lurks a brooding remnant of distrust for popular government. This is the formulation of the popular belief in contemporary judicial supremacy. This phenomenon was thus described by Justice Desai: "The third centre of power, the judiciary, to whom is it accountable? The Constituency - God forbid, the word has become anathema to some persons - of the judiciary, is the consumers of the justice, the people of India. The Constitution appears not to have derived any mode or method of accountability for the lumb. A centre of power not accountable to the repository of power may become oblivious to the expectation of the people for whose benefit the power is conferred and enjoyed." Therefore the question arises whether there should be an apex body to control and supervise the functioning of the judiciary vis-a-vis Executive and Legislative.

Self Restraint

No court, not even the Supreme Court, can be expected to decide dispassionately matters where judges themselves are involved, either as parties or indirectly. The Supreme Court has itself reiterated that any action taken in violation of natural justice is null and void and one of the cardinal and basic features of natural justice is that justice should not only be done but it should be explicit to have been done. If there is an apex body, all such cases can be referred to it.

In addition to dealing with matters pertaining to the judges and judiciary, this apex body should also decide about the constitutional validity of constitutional amendments. Such issues can be taken up by the said apex body, this taking out string of the theoriticism.

The most important safeguard for the judiciary is the exercise of self-restraint.

References

1 *The Illustrated Weekly of India*, "What all our Judiciary" April 29, 1987.

3

Judiciary, Judicial Activism and the Media

*- Dr. M. Sridharacharyulu**

The judiciary is one of the important pillars of democracy. It has more onerous responsibilities than two other important estates, the Executive and the Legislature. In fact, it is the judiciary and the institution of justice that helps the orderly functioning of parliamentary democracy and the exercise of powers by the various wings of administrative machinery.

Supreme Court cracking the whip and the broom used by the judiciary is all-pervasive, whether it is saving the Taj Mahal from industrial pollution or supervising the CBI's investigations into political and administrative crime.

It is the abdication of responsibility by Parliament and the Executive that has forced the judiciary to take over. If the interventions of the judiciary is judicial activism, is not the administrative 'inactivism' a reason for it? Looking at the issue from a different angle, judicial activism is inspired by the public, who knock the doors of justice, and thus the so-called judicial activism is basically citizens' activism. By exercising the right to freedom of expression and assuring the representation of the common citizen, the press has raised some particular issues, conducted risky investigation and exposed serious omissions, sometimes going to court with PILs. The lion's share of citizens' activism is that of the press, the fourth estate. When the administration fails to respond, the citizen looks to the press for communication, and turns to

* Journalist & Law Lecturer, Pendekanti Law College, Himayathnagar, Hyderabad (A.P.)

the judiciary for a remedy. The Constitution has provisions for both the estates, freedom for the press, and the power of active review, coupled with a watchdog function for the judiciary.

Former Chief Justice of India, A M Ahmadi, explained the current phase of activism in his Zakir Hussain Memorial Lecture in February 1996[1], when he said that the "courts would never have resorted to [activism], had the other two democratic institutions functioned in an effective manner". Justice Ahmadi was critical at the manner in which Parliament was conducting itself lately. In fact, it is worth noting that there has been a perceptible decline in the performance of Parliament. One particularly disturbing phenomenon, which has become quite a regular feature, is the holding up and the paralysing of the entire proceedings of the Houses of Parliament by groups of members, who walk into the well of the House and disrupt normal activity; this inevitably leads to walk-outs and sometimes many days pass without business being transacted. Another worrying feature is the decline in the level of debate within the Houses in terms of both quality and content.[2]

Justice Ahmadi's comments, therefore, are apt, and the frustrated majority agrees with him. Justice Krishna Iyer said it more bluntly. In an interview to ***Outlook***[3], answering a question on activism leading to judicial despotism, he said: "When the Executive betrays the people, viewed in the light of constitutional promises, there are two corrective agencies. The first is Parliament, which has the constitutional authority to correct the Executive. But if Parliament, because of the arithmetical deficiency of the opposition and the majority arrogance of the Treasury benches, wobbles or stands paralysed, there is a jurisprudential vacuum. In such a situation of vacuum, some constitutional machinery must move into action. . . Had the Executive been more responsive and responsible, the court would have hesitated to tread territory which does not normally belong to it. That is why you can never call it a judicial invasion of the Executive power."

Since the judiciary is part and parcel of the society as a whole and since the persons who man the administration of justice are none other than the same persons from the community, it is difficult to imagine better standards and higher moral values only in the judiciary. The people as a whole should therefore have overall control, in accordance with democratic principles. Hence an enlightened and conscious citizen should ponder over the need to reform every system, including the judiciary, to be more useful to the public in general and the democratic institutions in particular.

The delayed dispensation of justice is one of the main maladies confronting the fabric of our republic. If by delay justice is denied, it is conversely buried if hurried. With its defective structure and unquestionable powers devoid of any accountability, the judiciary, or for that matter, any system can play havoc with the set-up. Our constitutional framework provides for a fairly good amount of independence to the judiciary to act as a watchdog over the other two estates. To retain such independence the judiciary is rightly enjoying an enormous amount of power too. The power to punish anyone for contempt of court without a complaint by any other person is one such privilege available to the judiciary. The recent suspension of Vinay Chandra Misra, the Chairman of the Bar Council of India, from practicing as an advocate for his contemptuous remarks on the Allahabad High Court Judge is an example of the *suo moto* powers of court to punish for contempt. The problems created by the contempt jurisdiction came to be highlighted when the Supreme Court affirmed that Mr. E M S Namboodripad was guilty of contempt of court simply because he made the general allegation that judges belong to a certain class and suffer from class bias.[4]

To quote from the article "Courts and the Press: The Areas of Controversy" from the book *Contempt of the Court and the Press*, published by Indian Law Institute and the Press Council of India:

"Judges and courts in India are under considerable pressure. They are anxious to preserve their image as the protectors of justice and have used the contempt jurisdiction to protect themselves from controversy and to create and sustain respect for their work. Conscious that the contempt jurisdiction is arbitrary, the judges have often declared that they will use the contempt jurisdiction sparingly and wisely . .[5]

Who implements these declarations? It is something like a moral duty to use the legal powers with restraint. Can this happen? If somebody says that the contempt jurisdiction was misused or not used wisely or arbitrarily exercised, will that not be a fit case for contempt, because those who decide the guilt are the judges themselves? Judges are very reluctant to give up their power to punish for contempt and experiment with other methods whereby their dignity and status can be assured. It is also true that litigants, judges, politicians and others use the law of contempt of court to further their own ends. This law is quite different from other laws. The contempt of court power was given to judges by themselves, not created by the Executive or the Legislature. Judges created the contempt jurisdiction and claimed it was a natural adjunct to their adjudicating work. In a trial of complaints about contempt, the complainant and the judge are one and the same. This is against the principle of natural justice. It was evolved as an extremely strict law; yet, while other trials take years of time, a trial for contempt runs fast beyond expectations. In addition, practically no defense is available to a person once he is deemed guilty of contempt of court.

There is a demand for an investigative process to examine allegations and complaints by and against the judiciary; contempt of court should be made an offence as part of the ordinary law of the land, to be tried according to the ordinary process. A separate defense of justification and fair comment should be permitted provided it is shown that the comments were made in the public interest.

The media and citizens have a fundamental right to free speech and expression under Article 19(1)(a) of the Constitution. However, such freedom is subjected to limitations on reasonable grounds, mentioned under Art. 19(2), which takes care of social interests and the dignity of the judiciary. When every Executive action is being challenged in the court of law, it is in the need of society to be aware of the proceedings, observations and conclusions of the judges relating to the Executive actions under challenge. The openness of public trial is one of the essential features of the judiciary, which gives the people a right to know and in a way imposes a duty on the media to report the proceedings for the knowledge of the public in general. This duty is again limited by the need to protect the dignity of the court of law. Hence, 19(2) includes "contempt of court" as a ground, based on which a limitation can be imposed on freedom of speech.

The ground of contempt of court was included in Article 19(2)[6] to ensure the independence and dignity of the judiciary and due administration of justice. The Supreme Court under Article 129 and the High Court under Article 215 have been vested with the power to punish a person for contempt of the Supreme or the High Courts as the case may be. The Supreme Court upheld the constitutional validity of the contempt of Court law, as it is in conformity with Article 19(1)(a). At the same time, the Supreme Court has laid down certain norms regarding publications in newspapers. They may be summarised as follows: "National interest requires that all criticism of the judiciary must be strictly rational and sober and proceed from the highest motives without being coloured by partisan spirit or tactics. The judiciary cannot be immured from criticism. But when that criticism is based on obvious distortion or gross misstatements and made in a manner which seems designed to lower the respect for the judiciary and destroy public confidence in it, it cannot be ignored. The court must harmonise the constitutional values of free criticism and the need for a fearless curial process and its presiding functionary - the judge. To criticise the judge fairly, albeit fiercely is no crime, but a necessary right. Where freedom of expression subserves public interest in reasonable measure, public justice cannot gag it. But if the court considered the attack on the judge or judges scurrilous, offensive, intimidatory or malicious beyond condonable limits, the strong arm of the law must strike a blow on him who challenges the supremacy of the rule of law by fouling its source and stream."[7]

In a 1983 case, National Textile Workers Union vs. P R Ramakrishnan,[8] a contemner made serious allegations which were published in the press against the judges of the Madras

High Court. Holding him guilty, as he could not justify his remarks, the Supreme Court observed that, while commenting on matters pending in courts, the press should keep in mind that the parties to a case have as much right to get redress at the hands of court uninfluenced by external pressure as the press has its right to publish news comments.

The Second Press Commission also observed that the press does have the right, which is also its professional function, to criticise and advocate. "The whole gamut of public affairs including the administration of justice is the domain for fearless and critical comment. But the public function which belongs to the press makes it an obligation of honour to exercise this function only with the fullest sense of responsibility. However the judges are human. . . since judges, however stalwart, are human, the delicate task of administering justice ought not to be made unduly difficult by irresponsible publication."[9]

While underlining the indispensability of a "free and healthy press" to the functioning of a true democracy, the Supreme Court cautioned the press to be careful and not to publish improper, mischievously false or illegal reports. The contempt proceedings were initiated when news items, published in the *Sunday Tribune* and *Punjab Kesari*, on alleged allotment of petrol outlets from the discretionary quota of the Petroleum and Natural Gas Ministry to two sons of a senior judge of the Apex Court and two sons of the Chief Justice of India, were found to be patently false.

Holding that the freedom of the press is not absolute and unfettered, Supreme Court Justices Kuldeep Singh and Faizan Uddin said, *In re* Harijaj Singh and *In re Vijay Kumar cases*[10], "Journalists must be conscientious in disseminating information which must be dispassionate, objective and impartial. . . Journalists have greater responsibility towards the society to safeguard public order, decency and morality."

Justice Kuldeep Singh advised the above mentioned journalists to take necessary care in evaluating the correctness and credibility of the information published by them, in respect of an allegation of a very serious nature having great repercussions and causing an embarrassment to the Supreme Court. He came down heavily on irresponsible journalism, saying that "Such an irresponsible conduct and attitude on the part of the editor, publisher and the reporter cannot be said to be done in good faith, but distinctly opposed to the high professional standards as even a slightest enquiry or a simple verification of the alleged statement about the grant of petrol pumps to the two sons of a senior judge of the Supreme Court, out of discretionary quota, which is found to be patently false would have revealed the truth. . . . They cannot escape the responsibility for being careless in publishing the news without caring to verify its correctness. However, since they have not only expressed repentance on the incident but have expressed their sincere written unconditional apology, the same is accepted with the warning that they should be careful in future."

At the same time, courts should not be hypersensitive. This was stated by the Bench in the above case. "This court is not hypersensitive in matters relating to contempt of Court and has always shown magnanimity in accepting the apology on being satisfied that the error made in the publication was without any malice or without any intention of disrespect towards the Courts or towards any member of the judiciary." It also said "This Court has always entertained fair criticism of the Judgement and orders or about the person of a judge. . . Fair criticism within the parameters of law is always welcome in a democratic system." In a recent judgement, the Supreme Court said that there was a duty to correctly report judgements/orders of the Court. When the Department of Information, Government of Madhya Pradesh caused the publication of a news item distorting the judgement given by the Supreme Court, it was held that the willful distortion of the judgement amounted to contempt of court. However, the court accepted the unconditional apology by the Assistant Director of Information Department. This case was filed by Sadhvi Ritumbhara against Digvijay Singh, the Chief Minister of Madhya Pradesh.[11]

Rights have to go with duties. In the words of Kuldeep Singh, "In an organised society, the rights of the press have to be recognised with its duties and responsibilities towards society. Public order, decency, morality and such other things must be safeguarded. The protective cover of press freedom must not be thrown open for wrong doings."[12]

Judges used the contempt power to diffuse political controversy about their work; politicians and others use the law of contempt to embarrass their opponents. The press is thereby sometimes prevented from looking at matters of public concern. The contempt jurisdiction is an extremely fertile one, which has often been used by various people for various purposes. Of course, for that matter, many laws are not used for the purposes for which they are allegedly designed. The contempt law began as a convenient method to enforce the orders of the court, a fact illustrated by the recent Vasudevan case. During September 1995, half a dozen senior civil servants of the IAS cadre were convicted for contempt by different courts, three in Tamil Nadu, one in Kerala and one in Karnataka; four were sentenced to imprisonment or to pay a fine. According to reports, several thousand contempt petitions against the Government are pending disposal in various courts. It seems there are 4,000 cases pending against Karnataka Government alone. In T R Dhananjaya vs. J Vasudevan, the Supreme Court sentenced Mr. J Vasudevan, Secretary to the Karnataka Government in charge of Housing and Urban Development, to one month's simple imprisonment. There were 25 writ petitions and contempt petitions against the Government, filed by an engineer of the Bangalore City Corporation over a period of 16 years. Not only the litigant, but also the Court felt exasperated at successive attempts by the State Government to deny the engineer what was declared by the court to be his legitimate right in an order passed two years ago."[13]

If the Executives turn a deaf ear to judicial pronouncements, it is inevitable for the judiciary to invoke its contempt powers in the interest of litigants who have had a long and costly fight in a court of law. Penalising someone in authority for not implementing the orders of the court is one thing; however, trying the persons for commenting and criticising the judiciary is another. Interfering with the court proceedings directly or writing to influence the minds of judges, by what is called 'trial by the press' are some of the other areas of contempt of court. Contempt by printing scandalous material about judges is the third aspect. This consists of doing or writing something which would lower the dignity of the judges or the administration of justice. This latter area is one with which the press or the media is concerned. Any criticism of the judiciary in the media can be interpreted as contemptuous of the judiciary, and indicates very wide powers in the hands of judges. Two alternatives are available: one could plead for voluntary restraints on the press and the judiciary in the exercise of their freedom to express; or one could enforce a contempt jurisdiction. Nothing more can be said. There is need to criticise the judiciary like any other organ being commented upon; on the other hand, the independence of the judiciary must be protected even by invoking the contempt law. However, the line between legitimate comment and scandalous writing is not always easy to draw. This jurisdiction has to be sparingly used in such cases, lest it develops into yet another arbitrary power.

During 1985 the Telugu Daily newspaper *Udayam* unearthed a scandal concerning the district Court of Karimnagar (AP). It was a revealing story of institutionalised corruption covering the advocates on both sides as well as the court itself. The cases pertaining to enhancement of compensation awarded to landowners for the land acquired for submergence under the Sriram Sagar Project were dealt with remarkable speed. The cases were filed, tried, heard, argued and adjudicated on the same day, as per the record.

The real consideration was the lion's share in the proceeds, resulting out of exorbitant increase in compensation beyond reasonable imagination. After seeing the report in the newspaper, the High Court ordered stoppage of payments with immediate effect, which saved some hundreds of crores of rupees from being drained out of the public exchequer. The enquiry lead to the dismissal of the judge. The glaring truth saved the newspaper and the reporter from being subjected to contempt of court. This was not the scandalisation of the court but a true scandal involving the whole of the court, including its presiding officer. The case illustrates how free criticism of the judiciary helps weed out the black sheep, and also help the exchequer to the tune of hundreds of crores of rupees. A similar scandal in Yeluru (near Visakhapattnam) canal land acquisition has been reported by the Telugu daily *Veertha*, which raises questions against the subordinate judiciary and which is being probed.

In contempt cases, the intention should form the gist of the offence and unintentional contempt of court should not be punished. The general trend is to restrict writing and discussion in any manner, on the pretext that the trial is pending, or *sub judice*. However, a case being *sub judice* should not become grounds for restriction on free comment. As Dr. Rajiv Dhawan said, the fact that the court was seized of the matter cannot gag the general public. Intention to commit contempt or absence of good faith must be considered before finding a person guilty of contempt. Instead of punishing mediapersons for scandalising the courts, there should be a system of investigating allegations of corruption, bias and gross incompetence against judges. If the allegations are not made in good faith and with intention, the contempt jurisdiction can be invoked; moreover, the defences of justification and fair comment must be available for those accused of contempt of court. Free speech should include the right to criticise the fallacies of the administration of justice, for the betterment of democratic values and in order to uphold the rule of law under the Constitution.[14]

The power of judicial review is ever-expanding. The decisions of governors at the behest of the Centre, during the "crisis" in the ruling party in the shape of coups and splits, are now subjects of challenge before the courts of law.

While supervising the top investigative agency, CBI, J S Verma said,[15] ". . . every officer of the CBI associated with the investigation has to function as a member of a cohesive team which is engaged in the common pursuit of fair, honest and complete investigation into the crisis alleged. It is needless to say that the exercise has to be performed objectively, fairly mindful of the fact that the majesty of law has to be upheld and the rule of law preserved, which does not discriminate between individuals on the basis of their status, position or power." Such majestic comments were passed by courts, in cases where top politicians in public offices were involved.

Kuldeep Singh, J., in Common Cause v. Union of India[16], stated that "It is high time that the public servants should be held personally responsible for their malafide acts in the discharge of their functions as public servants....A Minister holds position of a trustee of public property in his charge. . . The criteria for the exercise of discretionary power in granting State largesse must be transparent, just, fair and non-arbitrary. . . Non-transparency in the system promotes nepotism and arbitrariness. . . authorities cannot enjoy absolute discretion; to pick and choose in arbitrary and discriminatory manner in allotment of retail outlets of petroleum products was malafide, arbitrary and discriminatory. Public servants would be personally liable for the same, under a tortuous liability for misfeasance in public office."

The Supreme Court personally held the minister liable for criminal breach of trust, saying "a minister is in a position of a trustee in respect of the public property under his charge and discretion. He must therefore deal with people's property in just and fair manner, failing which he would be liable for criminal breach of trust under sec. 405, 406 IPC."

Pursuant to a newspaper report on irregularities in allotment of petrol pumps, the Director of Common Cause filed a public interest litigation, which was allowed, and the Court quantified the costs at Rs. 50,000, ordered to be paid by the said Minister personally to the Director of Common Cause.

A similar order was given in Shivsagar Tiwari vs. Union of India[17] by the same judges, holding that the misfeasance in public office by public authority is an actionable tort. They held that the Minister of Urban Development was liable for allotting shops or stalls to his own relatives, employees and domestic servants, without following any policy or norms, for which exemplary damages were awarded irrespective of whether such allotments caused injury to any third person or not. This is yet another case where public accountability for administrative action was established.

Many a time, courts have intervened to uphold human rights and the dignity of life. In D K Basu vs. State of West Bengal[18], the Supreme Court held that custodial violence infringes against Article 21, the right to life. In this case, the Apex Court dealt with the abuse of police power and issued some mandatory directions for compliance by police personnel while arresting or detaining any person. It was also held that the police personnel were liable to pay compensation under public law in case of abuse of power and that this liability would be in addition to their liability under tort law and criminal law.

The Supreme Court did assume vast powers in controlling administrative discretion. Judicial activism, particularly on public interest litigation, has revolutionised constitutional jurisprudence. Persons belonging to other estates have criticised the judiciary for weakening those wings and making them feel insecure. They described the situation as "judicial tyranny" and "judicial grabbing" or "judiciacracy". Recently, the Sikkim Governor and former judge of the Supreme Court Mr. P Shivashankar criticised the judiciary for turning judicial activism into judicial possessiveness, which could lead to serious complications.[19] Various cases proved that there is a need to control Executive authority, which has a tendency to grab more and more power, thus undermining the whole system. The Jain-Hawala Scam, the CRB Scam and several other corruption cases stand out as the best illustrations of the unholy link between the Executive and economic criminals.

Another area in which the media is affected is the law of defamation. Defamation and the protection of a citizen's reputation is a valid ground for restricting the freedom of the press under Article 19(2). Mediapersons have to evolve a method to construct their criticism within the sphere that does not attract civil or criminal liability for defamation. The ambit of freedom of the press should be increased to cover comments on the performance of a public servant and public officer. It is as much a duty of the citizen to criticise as it is the duty of official to administer. The Supreme Court of United States held in the New York Times Co. vs. Sullivan[20] "The Constitutional guarantee requires, we think, a Federal rule that prohibits a public official from recovering damages for a defamatory falsehood relating to his official conduct unless he proves that the statement was made with "actual malice" that is with knowledge that it was false or with reckless disregard of whether it was false or not".

If a newspaper, in the course of its usual business, exposes a Government official, a cabinet minister or a person of higher rank, it is impossible to establish the allegation as true to a hundred percent. When the publication is based on substantially reliable information, the courts should adopt a practical approach and presume the innocence of the journalist, taking into consideration the fact that the person defamed is a public official or man in power who can suppress the evidence. The latest example is Jagmohan's case, where Mr. Laiq, a reporter of the *Indian Express*, was punished for want of proof against the former Vice-Chairman of Delhi Development Authority, especially when he was specifically pulled up by the Shah Commission for his excesses during the Emergency. The thirteen-year trial ended in the conviction of the journalist for writing against a powerful bureaucrat-turned-politician. Hence, the concept of criminal defamation requires to be reviewed and reassessed. At least the *New York Times* rule of the United States should prevail when public officials are involved in criminal defamation cases and unless the actual malice is established, the freedom of press should not be limited. In a landmark case, *Derbyshire County Council vs. Times Newspaper*[21], it was rightly held that a governmental authority or public authority was not entitled to use libel law to protect its governing reputation and that to allow it to do so would impose a substantial and unjustifiable restriction on freedom of the press. The State or authority as such, cannot agitate in a criminal court for loss of reputation, while the individuals holding office can go to civil court for damages if they feel their reputations have been compromised.

Certain contradictory decisions, hasty conclusions and unwarranted and sweeping comments undermine the dignity of the judicial system. Some of the decisions of our courts are often hasty and politicised. The most glaring is anticipatory bail granted to former Delhi Pradesh Youth Congress-I Chief Sushil Sharma by a Madras Sessions Court. A woman is brutally murdered, her body hacked to pieces, stuffed into a hotel's tandoor and burnt, and the prime accused, who has gone into hiding, gets bail. The bail was cancelled by the Madras High Court on the ground that the Madras Sessions Court had no jurisdiction to grant anticipatory bail for a crime committed in Delhi allegedly by a person not a resident of Tamil Nadu. An anticipatory bail decision can be reversed. But what happens when a hasty decision, like that in the Rajan Pillai case, takes a life? According to human rights activist V M Tarkunde, the Extradition court Magistrate Madanlal Mehta may have been affected by the rash decisions granting under-trials and prisoners the right to go to hospital even though there was nothing wrong with them. He may have thought that Rajan Pillai was another such person trying to use his money power to move to a relatively plush hospital rather than stay in a jail cell.

Various phenomena reflect the degeneration of the justice system in our society: charges of corruption; links between some advocates and some judges; the brokerage system in ambulance-chasing litigation; bias; political appointments of public prosecutors and Government pleaders, including the high office of the Advocate General and judges.

What matters in a court of law is face value - not justice nor legal knowledge. It is not argument but arrangement that works. The general rule is every party has to argue their own case. To engage an advocate is an exception. However, if a layman files his own case as "party in person", he will be looked down upon and ridiculed by advocates as well as judges. A "party in person" is not encouraged, so that the profession of black robes flourishes like a business. According to the existing situation, other than officers of the court, including advocates, no one has a place of respect in a court of law; and a client is the most disregarded person. Leave alone the right to be proved in the court, the client has no right to sit, for respect, against exploitation, for an audience or for that matter for anything. This is the most pitiable condition. The whole judiciary survives on the revenue provided to the Government only by the litigants. If advocates and judges have a nexus, it is dangerous to justice. If they are at loggerheads, clients will suffer. The latest problem is the trade unionism of advocates. They go on strikes and continuous boycott of courts, without caring for the difficulties of clients. Either in collusion or contradiction, the bar and the bench prove to be dangerous for an ordinary citizen. In addition, the status of the press in the courts is no different than that of the client. Newspapers will not be considered as valuable or worth consideration according to the law. They have no place to sit and cover the proceedings.

In spit of the fact that mediapersons are discouraged and intimidated by the judiciary and its officers, it is the duty of the press to report such intimidation. The law and law courts touch almost every aspect of a human being, ranging from human rights to ordinary consumer rights. At present, every Executive or legislative action, whether political or administrative, is being challenged in the court the very next day. As the purview of judicial review is expanding by leaps and bounds, every action of the two estates is coming in for judicial scrutiny. In a way, this situation is helping increase the powers of the judiciary. This necessitates the presence of the media to report for the benefit of society in general. Undoubtedly, a legal correspondent has become part and parcel of the reporting bureau of every newspaper, even in 'mofussil' areas. Wherever the common person of group of citizens are affected, the media should be concerned and should report the activities in and around the courts of justice, to help people think about the issue at hand and to provide them with necessary information to bring about reforms. Citizens should be enlightened about the defects of the judiciary and the media should play the role of catalyst in reforming the administration of justice, to make it more useful to society and for judicial activism to help the development of law.

When legislators are bogged down with changing their leaders as frequently as possible, they have a little time to formulate the needed laws for the people. Thus the mantle falls on the judiciary to make, or suggest making, the new laws, besides testing the constitutionality of the laws made by the Legislature. Enlightened citizenry and a conscious media can spur judicial activism further.

The whole society is interested in the successful functioning of the judiciary. Because the failure of justice leads to private justice, some musclemen or armed men start hearing disputes and selling so-called 'justice'. The money earned in this process helps them run the underworld mafia business and even win an election. Such trends may be considered the origin of the criminalisation of both politics and justice.

The role of the media is to be responsible and adventurous, even in the field of reporting about the judiciary. Despite the privileges accorded to the judiciary and the legislative, there is no need to view those bodies as above the criticism. Even the fourth estate, the press, can be questioned and commented upon for its murky role in politics and its biased and involved reporting, and this should be done in the media itself. In a democratic set-up, no institution should be spared from criticism, because criticism and appraisal of existing facts is the need of democracy.

References

1. *Report "Judiciary Takes over", Outlook, March 6,1998, pp. 13.*
2. *Ibid, p. 14*
3. *Ibid, p. 18.*
4. *E M S Namboodripad vs. TN Nambiar AIR 1970 Sc 2015.*
5. *Rajiv Dhawan, Contempt of the Court and the Press, p. 3.*
6. *"Reasonable Restrictions on Fundamental Rights" in Part-III of the Constitution.*
7. *V Mulgaokar AIR 1978 Sc 727.*
8. *AIR 1983 Sc 759.*
9. *The Second Press Commission Report, 1987, p. 52.*
10. *(1996) 6 Scc 466.*
11. *(1997) 3 Scc 662.*
12. *(1996) 6 Scc 466.*
13. *NR Madhava Menon "The Vasudevan Case", The Hindu, Hyderabad, Sept. 11, 1995. pp. 12.*
14. *Ibid no. 5.*

15. *Union of India v. Sushil Kumar Modi (1996) 6 Scc 500.*
16. *(1996) 6 Scc 530.*
17. *(1996) 6 Scc 558.*
18. *(1997) 1 Scc 416.*
19. *The Hindu, Hyderabad, Oct. 25, 1995 page 3.*
20. *376 US 254.*
21. *1 Q.B. 1992 770.*

4

Equal, Expeditious and Inexpensive Justice for India

*- Justice M.G. Chitkara**

The popular notion of justice is based, however vaguely, on a sense of equality, either distributive or corrective. Distributive justice requires equal distribution of benefits among equals and also requires equality of burdens as of benefits. The need to ensure equality of treatment for all persons is a justification for the doctrine of precedent, while justice in one sense demands certainty in the law through reliance on precedents.[1]

Certainty in law must not become certainty of 'injustice', said Maitland.[2] Justice is not synonymous with equality; equality is one aspect of it, no more. Justice is not some 'thing', which can be captured in a formula once and for all;[3] it is a process, a complex and shifting balance between many factors, including equality. As Friedrich observed "Justice is never given, it is always a task to be achieved.[4]" Professor Honore suggests that it would at least be 'refreshing' to look at justice, not so much from the Aristotelian point of view of the just man, but from that of the citizen to whom just treatment is due.[5] From a somewhat similar point of view, Cahn speaks of the 'sense of injustice[6]'. It is true that persons with grievances are those who raise the question of justice.

Justice is not possible so long as the wide gulf between the rich and hungry millions persists. A violent and bloody revolution is a certainty one way, unless there is a voluntary abdication of riches and the power that riches give, to share

* Vice-Chairman, H.P. Administrative Tribunal, Shimla - 171002 (HP)

them for the common good.[7] Among the tangible goals of social revolution are the elimination of all forms of social oppressions and national inequality, full employment, free education, medical care, state social insurance, cheap housing, rapid development of backward people and ethnic groups, crisis-free economic advance, genuine democracy that gives rise to unprecedented large-scale activity of the popular masses in every area of public life, and many other things which poverty-ridden people feel deprived of.[8] The basic objective of the revolution is to bring about a new social order, based on equality and justice, through the instrumentality of law, in order to make the Indian masses free in the positive sense, so that each individual not merely realises his self, but also examines his contribution to society.[9] The truth is that the individual is a living limb of the corporate social personality. Both individual and society supplement and complement each other, with the result that both get strengthened and benefited. The essence lies in the fact that the relation between individual and society has always been not one of conflict but of harmony and co-operation, born out of a the consciousness of a single reality running through all individuals.[10]

Justice is the greatest interest of man on earth. It is the ligament which holds civilised beings and civilised nations together. Wherever her temple stands, and so long as it is duly honoured, there is a foundation for social security, general happiness and the improvement and progress of our race. And whoever labours on this edifice with usefulness and distinction, whoever clears its foundations, strengthens its pillars, adorns its entablatures, or contributes to raise its august dome still higher in the skies, connects himself in name, fame and character with that which is and must be as durable as the frame of human society.[11] According to Manusmriti, where justice is destroyed by injustice or truth by falsehood, while the Judges look on, then they shall also be destroyed.[12]

Man's capacity for justice makes democracy possible, but man's inclination to injustice makes democracy necessary.[13] Justice is the sum of all moral duty.[14] Justice without power is inefficient; power without justice is tyranny. Justice without power is opposed because there are always wicked men. Power without justice is soon questioned. Justice and power must therefore be brought together, so that whatever is just may be powerful and whatever is powerful may be just.[15] According to Pascal, justice without force is impotent; force without justice is tyranny. Justice and inconvenience are often not on speaking terms.[16] A sound justice delivery system is a *sine qua non* for the efficient governance of a country wedded to the rule of law. An independent and impartial justice delivery system, in which the litigant public have faith and confidence, alone can deliver the goods.[17] Sir Douglas Young, in a speech delivered on June 13, 1934, said: "It is of the essence that justice should be administered speedily and impartially. Forget you are Mohammedans, Hindus, Sikhs or Christians, Zamindars or Mahajans. Remember you are judges, which is much more important".

Justice is the first virtue of social institutions. The basic aim of the legal system is to provide justice to everyone in a society.[18] But today in India, our legal system is in such a deep state of crisis that it is not able to provide justice to the common man and has failed to live up to the aspirations of the half-clad and half-hungry masses of independent India. The crisis is related to the fact that the justice provided by the traditional courts has become tardy, costly and technical. Traditional judicial courts as a forum for resolving conflicts - civil, criminal and revenue - have been blown to pieces due to inordinate delay and monumental wastage of time in deciding cases. The complexity of procedure and the prohibitive cost of litigation are not far behind as the two other major drawbacks of the present judicial system. Litigants have found themselves impaled on this unholy trident of delay, cost and complexity.[19] To quote Justice Krishna Iyer, the judicial process, of which the robes and gowns are symbols, is charged with 'administration of justice'.[20] It is, however, quite disheartening that the present system of imparting justice has badly collapsed and the people have lost faith in its objectivity. F S Nariman has rightly emphasised that the myth is that the courts of law administer justice; the truth is that the courts are agents of injustice.[21]

The gravity of the problem can be better judged from the figure of pending cases. The figures of accumulated arrears are awesome. The judicial system inherited from the British has scarcely been able to keep pace with the tremendous increase in litigation. The Law Commission, in its working paper on an alternative forum 'For Resolution of Disputes', has rightly observed that the present system of administration of justice is not suited to the needs of our people and the real remedy lies in reforming the existing judicial system by immediately undertaking some interim steps.[22]

The dawn of independence brought many golden things to the people of India. The restructuring of the judicial system at the grassroots level may be said to be one of them. It was realized by the wise founding fathers of the Constitution that the Anglo-Saxon judicial system must be reorganised as to make legal relief easily accessible, cheaper and expedient to the indigent and backward in our village. Mahatma Gandhi elaborated: "India lives in her villages and most of the countryside is smeared with poverty and social squalor. Today the poor and disadvantaged are cut off from the legal system - they are functional outlaws, not only because they are priced out of the judicial system by reason of its expensiveness and dilatoriness but also because of the nature of the legal and judicial system. They have distrust and suspicion of the law, the law courts and the lawyers for several reasons. There is an air of excessive formalism in law courts which overawes them and sometimes scares them. They are completely mystified by the court proceedings and this to a large extent alienates them from the legal and judicial process. The result is that it has failed to inspire confidence in the poor and they have little faith in its capacity to do justice."[23]

There appears a lurking respect for the system as it is administered, coupled with a fond hope that the real need is to further improve the existing system to meet modern requirements in the context of our national ethos.[24] There is also a lurking fear that the faith in this system, which is one of the paramount pillars of the function of the society, is seriously jeopardised. A sense of confidence in the courts is essential to maintain the fabric of ordered liberty for a free people. If once the people forfeit their confidence in the courts, it becomes very difficult to regain respect and esteem for the courts.[25] Edmund Burke has rightly observed: "That persons possessing a portion of power ought to be strongly and awfully impressed within an idea that they act in trust, and that they are to account for their conduct in that trust to the one great Master, Author and Founder of Society."[26] Commenting on the deterioration of the Indian legal system, the distortion of its processes and the apotheosisations of its elitist, yet illiterate personnel have often made me wonder whether brave, new Bharat should not slough off the dogmas of the colonial past and adopt innovative technology equal to the challenges of the stormy present. We must not be drowned in the Atlantic Ocean; we must swim ashore through the Indian Ocean.[27] That is why Article 40 obligates the state to organise self-governing units at the village level. Justice at the village level can be cheap, quick, local and populist,[28] and Article 39A directs the State to ensure that the opposition of the legal system promotes justice on a basis of equal opportunity and shall, in particular, provide free legal aid, by suitable legislation or schemes or in any other way, to ensure that opportunities for securing justice are not denied to any citizen by reason of economic or other disabilities.

The incorporation of Article 40 in our National Charter is itself a testimony to the fact that the Constitution-makers had in their minds a firm commitment to revive the indigenous judicial system, which could ensure people's participation in the administration of justice and make it possible to have easy access to its doors. That is why Article 40 mandates the state to decentralise the judicial system, organise village Panchayats and invest them with the necessary authorities and powers to render justice to the poor and bring it to their doorsteps.

Shri Thakur Sen Negi, in his appreciation to "Lok Adalat and the Poor", writes:[29] "Lok Adalats, the people's courts, have over the past some years, been gaining considerable momentum, importance and publicity. The concept accords with the genius of India. We, in this country, can look back far into the past history, replete with evidence of various forms of this mode of dispensation of justice. The traditional Panchayats survived the British rule in numerous parts of

India. The Panchayati Raj legislation after independence has improved as well as deformed the old home-grown and home-bred institutions bearing the name Panchayati Raj. This new wave of Lok Adalats seems to be mounting to generate a revival of much of the ancient atmosphere. With millions of arrears in the courts, from the Sub Judge and the Magistrate III Class right up to the Supreme Court, the rising costs, prohibitive to the vast majority of the people, the extending distance between the ground realities and the court verdicts, and other like defects of the judicial system left behind by the British, have, despite much good in the system, generated a grounds well among the litigants against the courts inherited from the British regime and based on Roman jurisprudence. There are, in health care, excellent medicines, but they are accompanied by side effects or followed by after effects that much diminish the good of the medicine. The Lok Adalat is a medicine in litigation with hardly any such effects. In fact, apart from easy accessibility and quicker and cheaper justice, the chief beauty of the Lok Adalat is the decimation of bitterness, because compromise is the very soul of Lok Adalat justice. If only national and international affairs were attempted to be solved and settled with the decency of the spirit of compromise and content in human nature in full play, as is supposed to be the characteristic of Lok Adalat justice, a country, a nation and in fact the whole universe would be a much more peaceful place. A day-dream it may be, but a very good one at that.

The present resurgence of the content and compromise mentality is, no doubt, a virtue of necessity, forced by the flaws and failings of the general court system in the country, but now that this feeling is at work with encouraging results, this tide has to be grasped and taken into as good and useful a future account as humanely possible."

Events in the courts have contributed to bring several important aspects of our subject to the attention of a wider audience than usual. The more the law the more the litigation since it treads on the toes of an increasing number of prospective litigants. The amplitude of interest that a citizen today expects the law to defend has widened. It is needless to say that settlement through reconciliation is better than an ultimate decision after a hard and bitter struggle, which leaves behind its own bitter consequences. In the Lok Adalat, the disposal is likely to be expeditious, at the doorstep of the litigants and at a price which the parties can well afford. Today, it is unreal to suggest that persons look to the law solely to protect their personal interests in a narrow sense. It is necessary to do no more than read the newspapers to see the breadth of the interests that today's citizens expects the law to protect - and they expect the court, where necessary, to provide that protection. Primarily, they are interested in results and not in the niceties of procedural wranglings. It is against this backdrop of emphasis on conciliation, mediation and resolution of conflicts by settlement that the necessity of Lok Adalats has been felt; what is popularly known as proper justice must be placed on the proceeding of the Panchayat Courts on the operation of the Lok Adalat and during the conduct of legal aid camps. Normative law is virtually inaccessible to the most underprivileged and vulnerable groups in Indian society. Legal illiteracy of the beneficiaries of the law thus contributes to its ineffectiveness. We have to remove the Indo-British jurisprudential blinkers, give access to the court-halls for the hundreds of millions of consumers of justice and make law-power the common person's armour.

Lok Adalats contemplate justice at the door of a common person at the earliest opportunity and without any cost. Jurisprudential norms like the role of fair hearing, presenting the case through a lawyer, adducing adequate evidence, getting adequate time to present and defend the case, deciding the case on the basis of evidence and proof etc. are certainly affected in the Lok Adalat but too mach emphasis on procedure can also create uncertainty and arbitrariness regarding the decision in the mind of a common litigant. Summary trials, evening courts, mobile courts, itinerant courts, simplification of civil and criminal procedures, cutting out the mystique of legalese and dispute settlements within the limit of law by non-formal agencies are all aimed towards the reformation of the system of administration of justice. The re-organisation and the re-orientation of the legal profession, as well as the re-orientation of its emphatics, is vital to the problems of access to justice in a country where the bar enjoys a monopoly conferred by the people through legislation, as a result of which the people suffer from penury of legal literacy and other resources.

Judges manning the constitutional courts enjoy certain safeguards incorporated in the Constitution to ensure the independence of the judiciary, a basic and unalterable feature of the Constitution. When a political party is voted to power, it seeks to implement what, according to it, is the mandate given by the Constitution and declares solemnly that it will achieve, if voted to power, the objectives enshrined in the Constitution. The political executive is always loath to surrender its power, especially in matters concerning implementation of social justice. This is the combat zone where the judiciary, while administering public interest law, is very likely to come into conflict both with the political executive and the permanent executive. It is difficult to define with any degree of precision the meaning of 'public interest'. What was conceived of as public interest at one time may cease to be so at another. Legal culture reflects the beliefs and expectations of the people towards the law and the judicial system and PIL has now become part of our legal culture.

The House of Lords in England has adopted a more conservative approach on the question of *locus standi*. Lord Wilberforce, speaking for the majority, said in Inland Revenue Commissioners vs. National Federation of Self-Employed and Small Business Ltd.: "As a matter of general principle I would hold that one tax payer has no sufficient interest in asking the court to investigate the tax affairs of another tax payer or to complain that the latter has been under-assessed or over assessed; indeed, there is a strong public interest that he should not."

In the United States, the constitutional courts ordinarily insist on strict adherence to the principle of *locus standi* in public law adjudication. In Valley Forge College vs. Americans United, an organisation established by the tax payers and dedicated to the separation of the church and the State was held to have no standing to challenge a no-cost transfer of surplus State property to religious or education institutions as violative of the First Amendments. Rehnquist, J., expressed the opinion that the plaintiffs had failed to identify any personal injury other than the psychological consequence presumably produced by the observation of conduct with which one disagrees. The right to require the Government to act in accordance with the Constitution by itself was not a sufficient ground to justify standing. The Court reiterated the view that the party who invokes the jurisdiction of the court must show that he personally had suffered actual or threatened injury as a result of the alleged illegal conduct of the defendant.

Canadian Public Law has adopted a more liberal approach. In Thorson vs. Attorney-General, a tax payer who brought a class action was permitted to challenge the legality of the official languages Act as unconstitutional. The reasoning was: "It is not the alleged waste of public funds alone that will support standing but rather the right of the citizenry to constitutional behaviour by Parliament where the issue in such behaviour is justiciable as a legal question." Irish Constitutional Law is very conservative in this regard: "Where a person who questions the validity of a law can point to no right of his which has been broken, endangered or threatened by reason of the alleged invalidity, then, if nothing more can be advanced, the courts should not entertain a question so raised".

PIL has introduced a new dimension to our public law. The legal culture incorporating public interest law has also brought about perceptible changes in the administrative culture and its effects on the judicial structure deserve to be noticed minutely. PIL has become a powerful instrument for enquiring into matters concerning the dissipation of public property by State functionaries; it has helped in the issuing of suitable directions for the release of children detained in prisons in different States, laying down guidelines regarding the adoption of Indian children by foreigners, examining the constitutional scheme at the instance of advocates regarding appointment and transfer of High Court Judges, alleviating the sufferings of construction workers engaged in projects connected with Asian Games at New Delhi, initiating steps for prison reforms, unearthing atrocious crimes like the blinding of prisoners and testing, at the instance of public-spirited citizens, the legality of the award of contracts by States.

In a recent decision, the Supreme Court held: "The present day development of this branch of jurisprudence is towards free movement both of the nature of litigation and the approach of the courts. As the sweep of PIL now encompasses not only the implementation of the directives contained in Part IV but also the entire gamut of the rule of law concept, a very great responsibility rests upon the constitutional courts. The expectations of the people are very high; any perceived infraction of the rule of law tends to become the subject matter of constitutional adjudication. Economic, social and political issues are, in great measure, subject to judicial scrutiny. Although this appears to transgress the constitutional principle of separation of powers, what was confined by the Constitution in one wing of the State cannot be encroached upon by the other, one of the justifications for the present role assumed by the judiciary is that judiciary being a part of the State, it becomes its duty to render constitutional adjudication in tune with the Directive Principles and the objectives contained in the preamble.

In discharging its high constitutional obligation, the judiciary has earned an enduring fame as the saviour of democracy, protector of the rule of Law and an effective agency for social transformation. But in this process, there is a risk of the judiciary being subjected to criticism on the ground that it has assumed the role of the legislature and the executive. Stray voices at a low key are emanating that PIL has interfered with the executive through the instrumentality of the judiciary. The Constitution is likely to assume greater dimensions and PIL is another name for 'Government by Judiciary.'

Common people in India do not have adequate economic support. They have no means to access the adjudicatory process and do not have the advantage of participating at par in the fruits of independence. Travelling distances that result in the foregoing of the day's earning, spending for marshalling evidence, engaging a lawyer and paying a court fee are some of the obvious obstacles in the way of meaningful access to the justice system. The entire legal system is resource based, hence the poor and the downtrodden are at a disadvantage if they opt for redressal of their grievances. At the very outset, they are often denied access to the system by reason of their poverty.[30] In one sense the concept of "Access to Justice" is a curious phrase because it implies that the system of justice is not in fact available to all, that there obstacles in the way. As respect for the legal system is cardinal and the provision of an effective and efficient court system is paramount, it benefits States to widen the parameters of the machinery of justice by seeking and developing such new methods of dispute settling techniques as will endeavour to make the dispute settlement mechanisms adequate in quality and accessibility.[31] The new methods of dispute settlement have many advantages, chief among them being informality, speed, swift clearing of backlog, economy, privacy, harmony and easy accessibility.[32]

The truth, sadly, is that the apparatus of civil justice has historically been beyond the reach of most, though they in turn were by no means beyond the reach of criminal justice.[33] In theory, access to the courts is available to all - just like the Sheraton Hotel. Anybody can enter; all he needs is money. However, money is a commodity rarely available to most people, who can hardly spare funds for the luxury of litigation.[34] It has to be possible for the economically weak to fight the economically strong in court; and that means the economically weak have to be enabled not just to get into court but to be able to fight, if necessary, to the bitter end - that would amount to access to the court in the real sense.[35] Courts in India cannot apply a mechanical statistical razor blade, or work a magic wand to wipe out the enormous pendancy of arrears, to make room for access and proper scope for the fresh institution.[36] Speedy adjudication is one of the pre-requisites for effective access to justice.[37] Heavy arrears and resulting delays in deciding cases block access to justice.

The law has become so complicated and the procedure in courts is so technical that very rarely is a litigant able to put forth his or her case before the court without the aid of an advocate. Litigants have to pay legal fees and incur expenses for travel; and the cost of litigation deters most people from seeking justice.[38] The reason for introducing Article 39A[39] in the Constitution was to secure equal justice for all, which is a cardinal objective of the Constitution.[40] There is no doubt that everyone is equal before the law, which treats all persons alike, irrespective of their financial needs, social and economical status. But, beneath the surface of equality, there is profound inequality in the operation of our legal system.[41]

Justice should be administered in a common sense liberal way and should be based on human values rather than on narrow and restricted considerations hedged round with hair-splitting technicalities.[42] Rendering justice is a difficult job but it is actually a divine act.[43] The dispensation of justice is an inevitable feature in any civilised society.[44] The tendency towards technicalities deserves to be depreciated.[45] The substance of justice must take precedence over its mere form and the benefits of development must trickle down to the humblest poor, the unnoticed and downtrodden masses. India being a welfare state, protecting the poor is her first obligation, with a view to giving equal treatment to all, because to do justice is a complex process and requires shifting the balance between many factors, including equality. As Friederick observed, "Justice is never given, it is always a task to be achieved."[46] Political freedom without socio-economic justice would be valueless for the teeming millions of this country. From the point of view of the average citizen of India, the premise made by the Constitution that the Government of India would guarantee socio-economic justice to all citizens marks a turning point in the modern history of India.[47]

Human beings are a mixture of bestiality and divinity. However, they cannot live on bread alone and crave for dignity, honour and justice, sometimes at the risk of starvation, dishonour and even death. Justice is substantive nourishment, not for stomach but for the human soul. As already noticed, justice should not only be done, it must appear to be done.[48] The eternal equality for equality of justice was enshrined in the Magna Carta in 1215 AD.

The universal ideology is to create a legal awareness among the lowly sections of society and to deliver the utilities of law and legal services at the doorsteps of the destitute millions by the medium of legal aid and the Lok Adalat.[49] The Lok Adalat may be considered the additional arm of the legal system and is likely to mitigate the impact of disputes and other social constraints.[50]

India, even after four decades of independence, still continues to be one of the poorest nations in the world. Half of our people working on eight crore farms in six lakh villages still live below the subsistence line. The rural labourers' plight seems timeless and unchanging.[51] Most of our people have no access to the bare necessities of life and the ranks of our unemployed are ever swelling, including the unemployed doctors, unemployed teachers, unemployed engineers and millions of other skilled and semi-skilled citizens. This unemployment, coexisting with under-utilized industrial and farm capacity, leads to a criminal waste of the national resources of people, materials and know-how. The concept of social status based on birth, caste or occupation, and distinctions drawn on that basis, militate against social unity. We talk of Vasudev Katumbakam but our Scheduled Caste brethren have no access to the privileges of the higher castes. Till now, reservations provided in Government services for the Scheduled Castes and Scheduled Tribes have not been earnestly implemented.

Human raw material in the country is as fine as can be found anywhere else on earth. Pakistanis are second to none in intelligence and the spirit of enterprise and have all the skills and capabilities to be a great economic power. How we manage to remain poor and deny access to justice to our poor illiterate and ignorant masses, is an uncomfortable question.[52]

Access to courts is moonshine if civil courts will not even entertain civil actions without payment of currently profit-making rates of court fees.[53] Undoubtedly, the income from court-fees is more than the expenditure on the administration of justice[54]. Between fees and taxes, the poor, downtrodden, daridranarayan can never reach the court, and if they do, they are overwhelmed by the mystique of legalese. The hierarchy of courts, with appeals etc., puts legal justice beyond the means of the poor. Professional services - handled by a monopoly of lawyers - are too expensive to be paid for by the poor.[55]

The administration of justice has become so obsolescent that most people regard the law as an enemy rather than as a friend. The law may not be an ass but it is certainly a snail: the operation of our legal system is not merely slow but is susceptible to shameless delaying tactics, and resort to the courts has become a lottery which takes years in drawing[56] and thus we have devalued our judiciary.[57]

Accessibility to medicines and hospitals is more or less available to all. The rich patient can, but the poor patient cannot afford costly treatments with highly priced doctors, nursing homes, medicines, scannings, X-rays etc.; but still the medical system in any civilised country provides for treatment of the poor at no or token cost, including hospitals, health centres, physicians etc. Similarly, any society, governed by the rule of law but not the rule of thumb or the rule of the jungle, must provide in its legal system facilities for a poor litigant to avail freely, or for a token cost, the legal care of his problem to vindicate his rights.[58] Access to courts being equal, expeditious and inexpensive justice has become considerably easy because of PIL. PIL, if administered cautiously, appears to suit current needs and conditions. No legal system can ever be static. As realistically assessed by Professor Harold J Laski. "Law like life, has its periods of change and its periods of conservation; it is not a closed system of eternal rules elevated above time and place. The respect it can win is measured by the justice it embodies, and its power to embody ideals of justice depends upon its conscious effort to respond in an equal way to the widest demands it encounters. Our Constitution enshrines a very noble ideal, namely, `equality'. But as a matter of fact there is great economic disparity amongst the people of the country.[59] The disparity is even greater in the distribution of wealth and the main chunk of wealth is cornered by a small section of people. Unfortunately, in spite of the high ideals enshrined in the Constitution, which aimed at making Pakistan the land of opportunity, our politicians, bureaucrats and elite have converted it into a land of opportunism.

The abnormal delay in the disposal of cases in the law courts is a big clot on the Indian judicial system. At the bottom of this system is a civil court which is easily approachable and accessible to a common person; the cost of litigation, however, is exorbitant. The procedural rules, instead of facilitating early disposal of cases, play major role in causing hindrances. The abnormal delay in the disposal of civil suits has shaken the confidence of a litigant so much so that a civil litigant gets tempted to take the help of anti-social elements to get speedy justice. The need for changes in the law to achieve speedy justice is being strongly felt for the last several years. Recently, there has been a move to establish tribunals in order to reduce the burden on regular courts and also to give speedy justice.

Tribunals have certain characteristics that often give them an advantage over the courts. These are low costs, accessibility, freedom from technicality, expeditiousness and expert knowledge. It is no doubt because of these advantages that Parliament, once it has decided that certain decisions ought not to be made by normal executive or departmental processes, often entrusts them to tribunals rather than to ordinary courts. The service tribunals, as constituted presently, are satisfactorily catering to the needs of the litigants and are not only desirable but good substitutes for the High Courts. The system has considerably reduced the workload of the High Courts and deserves to be continued. The negative approach of running down a system without making concrete efforts to streamline it is uncalled for. When many persons at all stages are actively involved, the system tends to get strengthened and employees in general have reposed greater confidence in tribunals.

With a view to avoid an unnecessary burden on the exchequer and to avoid multiplication of tribunals, it would be expedient if both central and state tribunals are amalgamated. Further, the administrative tribunals, both for central, state and other corporate sector employees should be established at every state capital. This will make the administrative tribunals a real substitute of the High Courts - not only in form and *de jure*, but in content and *de facto*. The alternative arrangements as substitutes for the High Courts ought to be efficient, but also be capable of upholding constitutional limitations. It would be well to recall the philosophy of American and Scandinavian realists like Justice

Holmes, Justice Gray, Cardozo and Llywllyn, who have repeatedly stressed the efficient functioning of the judicial system. To them, the efficiency relies on two factors: the non-judicial and the judicial. What is needed is that the judge must be well aware not only of the law but also of the ground realities of the society while implementing the law. The substitute institution - the tribunal - must be a worthy successor of the High Court in all respects. This will eliminate political interference to a great extent. Justice is the first virtue of social institutions. The basic aim of the legal system is to provide equal, expeditious and inexpensive justice to every person in society, irrespective of his caste, creed, religion, region and status.

References

1. *Mirehouse vs. Rennell (1833) 1 C1[st] & Fin. 527 at 546.*
2. *Cardozo, The Nature of the Judicial Process, p. 51.*
3. *See theories of Aristotle, Kant, Stammler, Marx and Rawls.*
4. *Friedrich 'Justice: the Just Political Act' 6 Nomosk Justice, 34.*
5. *Honor'e 'Social Justice' in Essays in Legal Philosophy (edsummers) 61 at 68-69.*
6. *Cahn, The Sense of Injustice (1949).*
7. *See M K Gandhi supra note 13, pp. 82-83.*
8. *See Krishna Iyer supra note 19, p. 39.*
9. *Binoy K Roay, Socio-Political Views of Vivekananda (1st Ed.), p. 45; also see A. Sertova, What is Revolution (1986), p. 11.*
10. *See M S Golwalkar, Bunch of Thoughts (1966) p. 20; also see Dalai Lama, Vishva Shanti — Ex Manveeya Drishtikon (1984), p. 22.*
11. *Denial Webster, quoted in All India Judges Association vs. Union of India, 1992 SSC (L&S) p at 24.*
12. *Arnold Bennet, "Thought for Today", The Times of India, March 10, 1992, p. 3.*

13. *Reinhold Niebuhr, Anand Swaroop Misra, Principles and Practices of Judicial Propriety (1986) p. 215.*
14. *Justice in the sum of all moral duty.*
15. *Blaise Pascal, see also, Krishna Iyer, Human Rights and Inhuman Wrongs (1990) p. 15.*
16. *K Rama Swamy, R K Jain vs. Union of India, AIR 1993, SC 1769, p. 1791, para 47.*
17. *A M Ahmadi, R K Jain vs. Union of India, AIR 1993, SC 1769.*
18. *Rowls John, A Theory of Justice (1971), p. 586.*
19. *Berhet Virender Singh, "Judicial Courts vs. Lok Adalats", AIR 1987, Journal Section 5.*
20. *Justice V R Krishna Iyer, Justice and Beyond (1980), p. 29, also see Upendra Baxi, The Crisis of the Indian Legal System (1982), p. 64.*
21. *F S Nariman, The Judiciary and the Role of Path Finders (1987), 3 SCC (J) 1 at 3.*
22. *For details see, Fourteenth Report of Law Commission, also see, Working paper of Law Commission of India on Alternative forum for Resolution of Dispute at Grassroots Level, connected with 114th Report.*
23. *Lok Sabha USQ No. 1752, July 28, 1989, p. 145.*
24. *See Law Commission of India's 77th Report, March11,1987,p. 10.*
25. *Burger C J, of American Supreme Court, in All India Judges Association vs. Union of India, 1922, SCC (L & S) 9, at 30 para 59.*
26. *Ibid.*
27. *Justice V R Krishna Iyer, Justice and Beyond (1980) p. 7.*
28. *V R Krishna Iyer, Social Mission of Law.*
29. *M G Chitkara, Lok Adalat and the Poor (1993), p. vii - viii.*
30. *D K Sampath, Mediation (1991), page 3.*

31. *Justice Annel M Silungwe, Chief Justice, The Republic of Zambia, "Alternative Dispute Resolution", appearing in Continuing Workshop for Judicial Officers (1991), pp. 161 to 163.*

32. *Alternative Dispute Resolution, page 164.*

33. *Lord McCluskey, "Problems of Access to Justice" adopted from the Keynote address delivered at the IBA Conference on September 26, 1988, Indian Bar Review Vol. 15 (3 & 4), 1988, page 203.*

34. *Dr. P L Mehta, Constitutional Protection to Scheduled Tribes in India: Retrospect and Prospect (1991), pp. 183-184.*

35. *Ibid, page 204.*

36. *Dr. L M Singhvi, AIR 1980, Journal Section, page 12 to 14.*

37. *Ms. Justice Sujata V Manohar, Access to Justice for Under-Privileged and Public Interest Litigation, National Law School of India, Bangalore Publication (1991), page 153.*

38. *Justice D M Chandra Sekhar, quoted in Dr. S S Singhvi, "Legal Aid Justice and Democracy", Lawyer, April 1981, vol. 13, No. 4, pp. 61-62.*

39. *Article 39-A reads: Equal Justice and Free Legal Aid - The State shall secure that the operation of the legal system promotes justice, on a basis of equal opportunity, and shall, in particular, provide free legal aid, by suitable legislation or schemes or in any other way, to ensure that opportunities for securing justice are not denied to any citizen by reason of economic or other disabilities.*

40. *Dr. S S Singhvi, "Legal Aid Justice and Democracy", Lawyer, April 1981, vol. 13 No. 4, page 61 to 62.*

41. *Justice P N Bhagwati quoted in Dr. S S Singhvi, Ibid, page 63.*

42. *State of UP vs. Mohd. Noor, AIR 1958, SC 86.*

43. *All India Judges Association vs. UOI (1992), 1 sec. 119 at 132, para 35.*

44. *Ibid., page 137, para 53.*
45. *Pratap Singh vs. Krishna Gupta, AIR 1956, SC 140.*
46. *Dias, Jurisprudence, 4th Ed. (1985), p. 66.*
47. *PB Gajendragadkar, Law, Liberty and Social Justice (1956), p.6.*
48. *Devesh Chandra Mukherjee, Legal Education for Services to the Poor (1982), p. 65. This work paper was placed at the 10th Conference of Laws of the World held at Sao Paulo, Brazil (the first time in South America) by the World Peace Through Law Centre during August 16-21, 1981.*
49. *Ibid., page 68. [this basic philosophy of legal aid, advice and accessibility was also adopted by the United Nations Conference on Human Rights held in Teheran in 1988.]*
50. *Ibid.*
51. *N A Palkhivala, We the People (1988), p. 5.*
52. *Ibid., page 6.*
53. *Justice Krishna Iyer, Social Justice - Sunset or Dawn? (1987), p.133.*
54. *All India Judges Association vs. UOI (1992) 1 SCC 119, at p. 138, para 54.*
55. *Justice V R Krishna Iyer, Social Justice - Sunset or Dawn? (1987), p. 136.*
56. *N A Palkhivala, We the People (1988), p. 354.*
57. *Ibid., p. 14.*
58. *Devesh Chandra Mukherjee, "Legal Education for Services to the Poor", AIR 1980, Journal Section 65.*
59. *N A Palkhivala, We the People (1988), p. 55.*

5

Supreme Court Journey

*- Justice R.K. Mahajan**

From 1950 to present era, is the Supreme Court ruling the country through judicial review and activism? Apprehensions expressed at the time of the inauguration of the Supreme Court of India in 1950 asked whether we should be ruled by a few judges or by elected persons.

There are three wings of the government - the Executive, the Legislature and the Judiciary. Every wing of the Government is supreme in its allocated sphere prescribed by the Constitution of India, which is in itself the most supreme. In the federal setup overseas, the Legislature and Executive discharge their duties within the allocated sphere and in case they act against the spirit of the Constitution and Fundamental Rights, their actions are declared against the Constitution and invalid. Judicial review is a basic feature of Indian Constitution. Its main role is to check arbitrariness on the part of the Government as well as to ensure that the Legislature functions within the spheres provided by the Constitution and demarcated lists in the Constitution. The Parliament cannot encroach upon the rights of the State as given in List II of the Indian Constitution except as provided in the Constitution.

The Supreme Court role in a multi-lingual, multi-religious and plural society is to reconcile the interests of different people who have different languages, customs and cultures.

* Judge, Allahabad High Court, Allahabad (U.P.)

Its role is to justly interpret to the cultural rights of the minorities enshrined in Part III of the Constitution of India and to balance the interests of different sections of the society. It is a sentinel of the liberty of the people and now, it is an active participant in the mainstream life of the nation.

The Supreme Court was inaugurated on January 28, 1950, consisting of five judges and one Chief Justice. Now the strength of Supreme Court is twenty-five judges and a Chief Justice. This section will attempt to describe the role of the Supreme Court from 1950 to 1960, 1960 to 1970; 1970 to 1980; 1980 to 1990 and 1990 onwards.

Recently, the Supreme Court's role has become aggressive and fierce; it is no longer a mere paper tiger. In view of the voices raised in certain circles of society that the Executive and the Legislature have become weak, the Supreme Court was forced, in the interests of the nation, to give direction to those two bodies to perform the duties that they have failed to perform. It is said that the Supreme Court is ruling the country and has become an administrator on account of public interest litigation.

At the time of the inauguration of the Supreme Court in 1950, the late Pandit Jawaharlal Nehru remarked:

"No Supreme Court and no judiciary can stand in judgement over the sovereign will of parliament representing the will of the entire community. If we go wrong here and there it can point it out, but in the ultimate analysis, where the future of the community is concerned no judiciary can come in the way. And if it comes in the way, ultimately the whole Constitution is a creature of Parliament. But it is obvious that no Court, no system of judiciary can function in the nature of a Third House, so it is important that with this limitation the judiciary should function."

Mr. T T Krishnamachari also happened to remark that the judiciary should not place itself as an *imperium in imperio*, and I am fully satisfied that the provisions that have been made in this Constitution will not make the judiciary an *imperium in imperio*. Of course, there is always that danger also. I would rather trust five hundred people with less than even mediocre abilities than four or five people with perhaps some claim for superior abilities but at the same time having their own personal prejudices. Therefore, it seems to me that somewhere in this Constitution there must be provision so that most of these difficulties can be removed by a Parliamentary legislation, even though it might mean that you are allowing Parliament to arrogate to itself a certain amount of jurisdiction over the courts as a relative quantum of jurisdiction will thereby be taken away from the Supreme Court and the High Courts.

Dr. Ambedkar was explicit in his view about the role of the Supreme Court:

"I do not see how five or six gentlemen, sitting in the Federal or Supreme Court, examining laws made by the Legislature and by the dint of their own individual conscience or their bias or their prejudice are trusted to determine which law is good and which law is bad."

A similar opinion has been expressed by Alladi Krishnaswami Ayyar:

"It cannot be denied that there is a danger in leaving the courts by judicial legislation so to speak to read necessary limitations according to idiosyncrasies and prejudices as may be of individual judges."

Thus, eminent persons, as well as the fathers of the Constitution of India, have expressed their fears regarding the role of the Supreme Court. The fathers of the Constitution never thought or could imagine that, with the passage of time, the centre would become weak on account of divisive forces and demands would be raised by separate identities and different sections of societies in India. The late SardarVallabbhai Patel, the Iron Man of India, reorganised more than 600 States and, after few years of the Constitution of India in 1956, Andhra Pradesh was created. During that period, demands were raised in Hyderabad for the creation of states on linguistic bases and the sub-identity basis of different communities. Other problems persist: the demands of Bodo Land, movements for the creation of Jharkhand, the issue of Kashmir and water disputes in several states. After 1967, the governments at the Centre and in the states were different and as regional parties gained strength and formed government in the states, the centre became weak. The Supreme Court went where angels feared to tread.

The Supreme Court often operates to remind different organs of the State mentioned in the Constitution of their duties and obligations and has rendered valuable services to the nation in the particular contexts prevailing in particular periods.

Recently, the Supreme Court entered into the arena of the solution of problems where the centre had failed: for example, the Mandal Commission problem, the Ayodhya problem, the Kaveri water dispute and the Election Commission problem. The Supreme Court had to intervene in the Kaveri dispute by directing the Central Government to convene a meeting of the affected States for the release of water by Karnataka to Tamil Nadu, where the fields were parched without water. It intervened in the case of the Chakma tribals, who reside in the North-East and had been directed to be evicted without a consideration of their rights. Consequently, an application for the registration of citizenship of *bona fide* Chakmas is to be considered under Article 21.

In the case of the Election Commission, it was found that the Chief Election Commissioner had become aberrant in interpreting the Constitution and ignoring the two Election Commissioners under Article 324 of the Indian Constitution. The Chief Justice of India, Justice A M Ahmadi, and companion judges put the errant behaviour of the Chief Election Commissioner in order by delivering a judgement that the majority opinion would prevail in the matter of decision. It further observed that the institution is more important than the individual.

In the case of Manipur Speaker Bodababu, the Supreme Court issued directions for obeying its order; and IAS officer Vasudevan Nayyar of Karnataka Cadre was sent to prison for not obeying the order of the Supreme Court.

Recently, for the first time in Indian judicial history, the Supreme Court assumed the role of supervising the investigation in the Hawala case, which had been filed with respect to politicians who had a direct nexus with criminals and mafia gangs. The Supreme Court is currently monitoring the investigation and has signalled that, if the government does not move, the Supreme Court will move. Later on the Supreme Court's intervention made the Government file a charge sheet against certain politicians, who are therefore facing trial, which will help expose, for the first time, links of the politicians with the Jain brothers, who are accused of distributing 64 crores to the different politicians.

In the matter of irregular and illegal allotment of government accommodation in Delhi, the Supreme Court considered evidence identifying illegal occupants, who were leased government housing because of links with political figures. It also looked into cases where politicians had retained houses to which they were not entitled. Furthermore, the Supreme Court has recently acted to close down the factories that are hazardous to the environment. In a move that will be remembered by future generations, the Haryana Government has been ordered by the same Court to supply water to the thirsty people of Delhi and also to remove encroachment and save green belts, which are oxygen lungs of the city. The Supreme Court should also be remembered for making doctors liable, in a Consumer Forum, for their negligence. The matter regarding out of turn allotment of LPG agencies and petrol pumps is also worth noting.

In a nutshell, public interest litigation has been forced upon the Supreme Court, as the Executive and politicians, on account of various pressures, are not able to perform statutory functions. The Supreme Court is the only hope for the common man to get duties enforced from the Legislature and executive.

There are voices in the community that level charges of judicial terrorism. A close scrutiny the cases in question, and an examination of the thorough and often pathbreaking judgements that have been made, indicate that such charges are baseless. The phenomenon of recent interventions by the Supreme Court should be seen as a temporary and passing phase. As soon as the crisis of a derailed Executive and Legislature is over, and as soon as people begin to regain faith in the system, the Court will not interfere.

1950 to 1960

Let us move back a little, and trace the role of the Supreme Court from 1950 to 1960. During this period and early on it its journey, the Court thought it its duty to help the nation solve long-term value questions. The Court was called upon to deal with question on Hindu law, taxes, motor vehicle law and legal problems relating to socio economic value. While deciding the Gopalan case, the Court dealt with issues with judicial dexterity and knowledge. Its role was one of exerting calm and assurance arising out of a sense of authority and power. During this period, there was political stability and the Supreme Court expanded its authority in matters relating to property and in areas on preventive detention. The matter of freedom of the press also came into consideration and it was held that it was a part of freedom of speech (the Ramesh Thapar and Brij Bhushan case). The Supreme Court also happened to deal with the abolition of Zamindari rights, nationalisation of transport and other cases relating to property.

The late Pandit Nehru wrote to the Chief Ministers of all states after Kameshwar Singh's decision by the Supreme Court. It is well known that, for many years, the abolition of the zamindari system had been the principal plank in the Congress programme. Indeed, it may well be said that radical agrarian reform is the basic need of Asia. If this reform is prevented, then our entire social and economic policy fails and hundreds of millions of peasants and agriculturists can well charge us with a grave breach of promise. An intolerable situation will be created. At the same time it is obvious that the interpretation of the Constitution is a function of our superior courts. We have to respect the decisions of the courts, for not to do so is to strike at the very root of our constitutional structure. While our courts have the right to interpret the Constitution and we must respect and honour their decision, the fact remains that the wider social policy of the country must be determined by the Parliament or the State Legislature.

At the time of moving of first Amendment in Indian Constitution in 1951 Pandit Nehru happened to remark that the Courts are not to act third chamber and the amendment was necessitated in view of the striking down the Bihar Land Reforms Act on the question of compensation. So in this era the Supreme Court exercised power of judicial review and Legislature nullified the Supreme Court decision by Constitution Amendment and freedom of press also was established.

1960 to 1970

In this era of 1960, after the death of Pandit Nehru, a vacuum was felt in leadership. The Chinese attack took place, and there was economic deterioration. The government wanted to fulfil its promise of socialism and to uphold the promise contained in the Constitution. Banks were nationalised and privy purses abolished. The Supreme Court nullified both bank nationalisation and Privy Purse abolishment. It was a time of affluent and feudist philosophy, which had clearly permeated the Supreme Court, as described by a jurist. The words of Sir Frederick Pollock are worth mentioning: according to him, the Supreme Court treated Legislature "like an inferior court, which had to give proof of its competence". Justice Holmes of American Supreme Court said: "I suspect that fear of socialism on the part of the comfortable class has influenced judicial action here in England and this was true in India too."

Later on, in the Golakh Nath case later, the Supreme Court held that the Parliament had no power to amend Fundamental Rights. Contrarily, in the Shankari Prasad case, the same Court held that the Parliament had a power to amend the Constitution.

The era of 1960 to 1970 was an era of commercial liberalism, which dominated the philosophy in the Supreme Court's decisions. The same happened in America, when Supreme Court of America struck down the New Deal Recovery Programme. In America, the matter was not taken to the polls; in India, however, Indira Gandhi took the issue to the voters. They argued that the interpretation given by the Supreme Court was not in consonance with socialism, nor was it progressive enough to improve the lot of the people; the Congress Party returned to power with a majority. In 1973, a supersession of Supreme Court Judges took place, to give a push to the Doctrine of Committed Judges. While it was interpreted in different ways, the social aspect of the philosophy was kept in view.

1970 to 1980

The period of 1971 to 1976 was turbulent period. The Supreme Court gave a judgement in the Keshwa Nand Bharti case, after holding that Parliament has a right to amend the Constitution without destroying the basic features of the Constitution. A supersession took place during this period. The philosophy of committed judges was made a predominant feature in the appointment of judges and values were lost. The court as an institution was wounded, as asserted one school of thought. Emergency was declared in 1977 and the Supreme Court then held that people had no right to life and liberty during the emergency. The period was later described as the darkest era in the history of the Supreme Court. After the Emergency was revoked, the Congress lost in the polls, ushering in a period of liberalism. While giving interpretation to the Constitution in the Maneka Gandhi case, a new interpretation was given to Article 21, that nobody can be deprived of his personal life and liberty except in accordance with the procedure established by law. In case the procedure of law is against the principle of natural justice (harsh, arbitrary or oppressive) it would be declared violation of Article 21. As a consequence, the philosophy of liberal rights in favour of prisoners, bonded labourers and daily wage workers saw the light of the day.

1980-1990 -

In later years, the Supreme Court entered into an era of social justice by affirmative action. In 1984, Justice Krishna Iyer spoke of righting the wrongs of "the tongueless, tattered, battered, police-hounded, poverty bitten humans" as the duty of those who have vowed to "uphold the Constitution and laws in the order." He warned that if the Bench and Bar did not play their role to achieve creative mutations in the judicial process, the frustrations of the disillusioned masses hungering for justice would blow up. He gave a different interpretation to the law, saying that judges are governed by a class sub-consciousness, that a judge is a human being with certain inherited biases and attitudes and "as such they often act as agents of the proprietariat against the proletariat." The result, he added, is a strong deterrent even to the cosmetic or peripheral changes that have recently taken place. Very few illegal detenues or bonded labour, he argued, ever reach the courts. "What chill will pass through their spines", he asked, "if social justice, equality in reality and dignity of personality becomes the rule of law.

Justice Hidayatullah, in 1984, remarked that "Justice according to the law has been the motto because I take command from law. When we attempt to decide the cases in teeth of law, it is a perversion of our jurisprudence. We might as well as do away with law altogether and do kazi justice. Social justice varying with the notions and idiosyncrasies of a few might well become a government of men. The present tendency", he warned, "to interfere unduly with the Legislature and Executivemight lead to curtailment of the jurisdictions of the courts." The fear expressed did not prove true because of the complete faith in the dispensation of justice by the judiciary. Rather than think of judicial activism as government by judges, the role of judges in the present era should be seen as one of correction of a derailed system by reminding the Executive and Legislature of their duty. People have responded to the role of the courts and ultimately the opinion of people matters and gives strength to the system.

The Supreme Court has to solve new problems in keeping with daily changes in society. Although it is sometimes said that the Supreme Court is a political court as the American Supreme Court, this is somewhat of a misconception. The Indian Supreme Court is not a political court in the strict sense but deals with political problems of nation when matters are taken to it for adjudication. The same Court also solves human problems; take the case of the Bhopal gas tragedy. Thousands of lives were lost on account of the gas disaster, and even more people became infirm. The Supreme Court performed the role of parent, granted compensation to the victims and framed many schemes for their welfare, trying to solve the problem in a phased manner. Later, the Supreme Court was confronted with another volatile issue: the reaction to the reservation policy arising out of the Mandal Commission. In the Indira Sawhney case, the Supreme Court pointed out that reservations could not exceed the 50% limit. Later on, states tried to bypass this judgement by legislation but the Supreme Court struck down the criteria of the creamy layer laid down by the Bihar and Uttar Pradesh Governments.

The Supreme Court was also involved in the controversy for certain financial illegalities and charges against Ramaswamy, a judge of the Supreme Court; impeachment ultimately took place. This was the first case in the history of Supreme Court that related to itself. It is worthwhile to mention that no work was allocated to Justice Ramaswamy by the late Chief Justice of India, Sabyasachi Mukherjee. The Supreme Court also gave a new turn to the case of the Judges Association, relating to the facility of a subordinate judiciary; their working age was increased to 60 years and the concept was introduced that judicial officers under Indian Constitution could not be equated with civil servants.

In the famous Judges' case, Advocate on Record Association vs. Union of India, the Supreme Court took the appointment of Judges of the High Court, as well as the transfer of judges, into its own hands. Such a step may have been taken to remedy the situation of favouritism. However, it is likely to be a temporary phase, because all Judges are a part of society and are likely to be influenced by various currents and pressures.

The Supreme Court had to face another serious problem: it was to give an interpretation under Article 256 in the Bommai case and, while upholding the scope of Article 256 of the Constitution of India, the Supreme Court held:

"Secularism is a basic feature of the Indian Constitution and the dismissal of the BJP Government was upheld as valid by the President as they followed this principle in the Babri Masjid Case."

Recently, on account of liberalisation policy of the government, policy matters were taken to the Supreme Court. Regarding the telephone policy with respect to tenders to companies, the Supreme Court held that it is in the domain of the government to accept tenders/lay down policy and the courts cannot interfere unless the procedure is found to be arbitrary and discretionary. The Executive was given its own supremacy in the matter of framing policy. Similarly, while interpreting environmental laws and Directive Principles of State, the Government policies were held to be valid, those policies had been framed to protect the environment, regulate or prohibit intoxication and to implement the Chapter of fundamental duties.

The Supreme Court, with the help of the Maneka Gandhi case, gave a liberal interpretation of Article 21 and culled out many rights: the right to education, the right to shelter, the right to livelihood, the right to speedy trial, the right not to die and the right to live life with dignity. The famous jurist Palkiwala expressed his doubt about the role of the judiciary, in an article published in the *Times of India*, December 3, 1995. He expressed the fear that India could not afford government by the judiciary. Judges were not accountable as they were not elected, whereas Members of Parliament were elected and were responsible to the people A debate started on this subject, with those in favour of the Supreme Court actions arguing that the Court was not ruling the country but only issuing directions under Article 32, reminding the Executive to do its duty, as the Executive had failed and had become powerless. According to the then Chief Justice A M Ahmadi, this was a transitory phase; he said that the Courts were only helping society and it is only keeping the balance between the three wings in a plural society. What was required, he stated, was the character and integrity of the person who implement the Constitution, and one should make charges of judicial terrorism.

An American author Ruggero J Aldisert[1] says in one of the article "Role of the Courts in Contemporary Society", published in a book that Ruggero J Aldisert says on page 262 that:

"We expect courts to encompass every reach of the law, and we expect law to encircle us in our earthly sphere and to travel with us to the alien vastness of our outer space. We want courts to sustain personal liberty, to end our racial tensions, to outlaw war, and to sweep the contaminants from the globe. We ask courts to shield us from public wrong and private temptation, to penalise us for our transgressions and to restrain those who would transgress against us, to adjust our private differences, to resuscitate our moribund businesses to protect us prenatally, to marry us, to divorce us, and, if not to bury us, at least to see to it that our funeral expenses are paid. These services, and many more, are supposed to be quickly performed in temples of justice by a small priestly caste with the help of a few devoted retainers and an occasional vestal virgin. We are surprised and dismayed because the system is faltering."

In India also, the people rush to the Courts as the wings of the Government have become weak and the judicial process of the court has to be invoked to address the day-to-day arbitrariness of the Government. To conclude this section, it is worthwhile to mention that the people of India still have an abiding faith in the judiciary. There is a belief in the supremacy of the Constitution, which belief has given rise to this faith. Judicial review is a basic feature of the Indian Constitution and it finds its strength from the sovereignty of the people and the public support behind it.

The Supreme Court is trying to retrieve the pledge given on its inauguration day of "building the nation and establishing itself in the consciousness of Indian people." Only then can the court keep its tryst with India's destiny.

The Government appoints judges but the strength and backbone of the administration of justice is public opinion. The Supreme Court will help the public only if the public is helpless to keep the arbitrary use of power by the other wings of the Government in restraint. Recently, the Supreme Court recently has received applause from foreign countries regarding judicial control. It has interfered more successfully in the arbitrariness of the Executive and the misadministration of the country than any other country in the world, even the United Kingdom and America's highest courts. The people of India and the world will watch its role in the new political scenario, especially with Centre-State relations changing due to the era of coalition Government, where there is no single party in majority at the Centre. All said and done, the Supreme Court has never failed the people, by and large and within the limits of the Indian Constitution. The rulers, on the other hand, have failed in certain situation. Let us remember the famous saying,· "Who will guard the guards?" Ultimately, it is the character of the people that matters and bad workmen should not quarrel with the tools.

References

1. *Judiciary and Constitutional Politics: views from the Bench: A collection of essays edited by Mark W Cannon and David M O'Brien and Forewarded by Warren E.Burger, Chief Justice of United States. Published by Asian Books, New Delhi.*

6
Judges Dilemma

*- Subodh Chandra Verma**

George Bernard Shaw was probably not aware that law sometimes has terrible dilemmas; otherwise he would have used the term "Judges' Dilemma" instead of "Doctors' Dilemma".

Physiologically speaking, the maximum brain cells are used when a man takes a decision. As the theory of evolution goes, man is still in the evolutionary process. Today's human can take better decisions than his or her ancestors took. Millions of years ago, a man called Abraham took a decision. In the "Book of Genesis", it is told that God called Abraham and ordered him to sacrifice his only son Isaac. Abraham, without hesitation, prepared an altar, and was about to slay his son, when an angel of God stayed his hand and said, "Now I know that thou fearest God, seeing thou has not withheld the son, thine only son, from me".

How cruel a test Abraham had to pass to prove his faith in God. The catch in the story is that Abraham had no dilemma. He had no hesitation in obeying a command that was so cruel that it surpassed all the laws of humanity and ethics: to kill an innocent son. In one way, the parable indicates the absolute faith of Abraham in God, in the spirit of Bible. Looked at judicially, this was a man who obeyed blindly in the spirit of 'Yes Minister'. Had God not appeared and stopped Abraham, could he be tried for the murder of his son?

---

* PCS(J), Judge/Dy. Director, Institute of Judicial Training and Research, Lucknow (U.P.)

A similar defense of 'respondent superior' was taken at Nuremberg. Nazi soldiers pleaded that they were simply obeying 'superior orders' in the prosecution and slaughter of the Jews. If they did not obey they were bound to face bullets. Obeying the command of superiors appears to be a social edict that man learns from the cradle. Be it family, school, office, religious places or the like, we are taught to obey. Psychologist S Milgam carried out many experiments and concluded that the human brain easily obeys commands, even if those commands are to inflict pain on others: "A substantial portion of people do what they are told to do...so long as they perceive that the command comes from a legitimate authority".[1] Individual respect for superiors takes its root in the hierarchy of social groups in which we live and in conflicting situations; when the mind is unable to decide the best course, we adopt advice from elders or superiors or commands from religious books or scriptures. This is how humans relieve their conscience from any sense of responsibility.

History shows that during wars, soldiers have unleashed inhuman tyranny and pain on the vanquished people. Soldiers may not be that inhuman individually, but when they know that they have the sanction of superior authority, they do not have any reason to check themselves from criminal acts. A second psychological cause may be that the individual wishes to be part of a crowd that may conceal his identity. Several times in history, the significant question before humans has been whether the 'response' of the law is genuine and true and whether it is a true medicine to guide human conduct effectively.

In annals of legal history on such conflicts, incidents are confined to military actions and wars when soldiers are commanded to commit war crimes. After World War II, the Nazi soldiers were charged with genocide, operating concentration camps, third degree torture, mass rape and so on. According to the structure of the armed forces, a subordinate is not supposed to question an order. If such questioning were permitted, the concept of discipline would collapse and chaos would prevail, particularly in military bureaucratic setups. A subordinate is sometimes in a no-win situation, because if he disobeys, he faces court martial and if he commits the crime under direction, he faces tribunal trial by the enemy after the war. British constitutionalist A V Dicey has said about this awful dilemma:

"The position of a soldier is, in theory and may be in practice, a difficult one. He may, as it has been well said, be liable to be shot by a court martial if he disobeys an order and to be hanged by a judge and jury if he obeys it."[2]

In such situations, what should be the correct approach of the law? In essence, the law is made up of people who have morality as well as practical needs. Earlier history does not have any examples where soldiers were held responsible for any crime they committed under a superior command; the superior Commander was held responsible. The principles of human rights or natural justice were quite unknown. History is full of black spots of torture of the slaves and the vanquished but never is there any example where soldiers or inferior forces were held responsible. The executors were protected and the concept of revolt was unknown and human dignity was never defined until the Magna Carta. The milk of human dignity took centuries to flow into military laws. Until the First World War, the British and American armed forces punished only superior officers who had given criminal orders; subordinates were completely exonerated from any responsibility.

After the Second World War, the Nuremberg Trial was the turning point in the entire concept of 'superior responsible'. The intensity of genocide, mass rape and inhuman torture by German and Italian forces was so high that the victorious countries found it unjust to punish the superior alone. For the first time in history, morality and human dignity saw its lowest form, that too on such a vast scale. The old principle of 'superior responsible' was not considered sufficient. In fact the soldier executor of orders crushed his morality to such an extent that all human values were, for that period of time, extinguished. Such an executor could not protect himself under the garb of obeying a superior order. The judges task at Nuremberg involved the unhappy need to 'invent' a new judicial category, that of 'crimes against humanity'.

Humanity cannot be defined; rather, it need not be defined because whatever is inhuman cannot come under humanity. One is not supposed to forget it even if he is under the stress of obeying a superior order. The tribunal at Nuremberg was able to find excellent logic behind this principle: "Hitler could not make aggressive war by himself. He had to have the co-operation of statesmen, military leaders, diplomats and businessmen. When they, with the knowledge of his aims, gave him their cooperation they made themselves parties to the plan he has initiated. They are not to be deemed innocent because Hitler made use of them if they knew what they were doing. The relation of leader and follower does not preclude responsibility here any more than it does in the comparable tyranny of organised domestic crime."[3]

The judgment of the Nuremberg Tribunal became the backbone of the principles of Human Rights. Earlier, the imperatives of national laws were to be followed by individuals. Even if superior orders were against humanitarian principles, they were to be followed. Rules developed in the Tokyo Tribunal gave new light to international rules to the effect that "When the international rules that protect humanitarian values are in conflict with state laws that contravene those values, every individual must transgress the state laws." This was a veritable resolution both in the field of law and ethics.[4]

The torch of this new principle inflamed further arguments. Some argued that the old principles of state sovereignty could not be discarded by many countries. The UN convention on Genocide (1947) clearly saw the opposition of this principle, particularly in peacetime. "The charter of Military Tribunal of Nuremberg admitted this principle having in mind the crimes of war; but to accept it in times of peace is to invite the armed forces to disobedience." The result was that the Genocide Convention was stillborn. The principle of disobeying a superior order is still an open question, truly reflected in Shakespearian expression of "to be or not to be".

The dilemma of being and not being is not confined to this aspect of international law; the law courts in domestic matters also face such dilemmas. When it comes to what is the correct law, one is bound to recollect what Aristotle said centuries ago: "Law is a formal order, and good law must necessarily mean good order". Peacetime in society generally means good order, which is just opposite during times of war. However, the 80s and 90s have seen a new phenomenon that is neither peacetime nor a time of war in a country. This has been a war by proxy by terrorists.

Terrorism is a concept that is generally suffered within a country. A handful of people tries to enforce their will through the barrel of the gun. The movement generally is not popular and the local people dare not open their mouths, a fact that is sometimes mistaken for silent and apparent support. Killing of innocent people in bomb blasts or making hostages of tourists cannot be justified by any norms of revolution. A state is duty-bound to protect its citizens. However, if its people are being constantly killed, property recklessly destroyed and democratic and secular institutions systematically attacked, an expectation from the State that it should be a messiah of human rights is called into question.

Democracy has been conceived to implement public opinion over individual opinion. In the past, States have frequently been forced to act under pressure of public opinion. In judiciary, which is a part of democracy, one can imagine such pressure; without such public pressure, judicial pronouncements risk becoming arbitrary. The role of the public has grown over the years. In 1931, the eminent English jurist J L Brierly noted that when an individual commits a breach of law, it may go unnoticed by society and even if it is noticed, 'social stigma' is not attached to it. When such a breach of law comes to effect the larger population, however, 'social stigma' is attached to violation of law. Today, the growing power of the press and the mass media has greatly increased the importance of public opinion.

Life and liberty may often be in conflict with social order. Granting all human rights to a terrorist who has eliminated an innocent family will be inhuman itself in the eyes of an ordinary individual. An ordinary man does not understand the refined and delicate legal concepts. Lord Atkin's observation still holds water: "Justice is not a cloistered virtue.

She must be allowed to suffer the scrutiny and respectful, even though outspoken, comments of ordinary men". (Ambard V Attorney General for Trinidad-AIR 1936 PC 136) Lord Danning too had a point to emphasise: "Freedom of the individual must take second place to the security of state". Social security is peace and good order of the community. After much deliberation by sufferer countries, the world conference on Human Rights, in its Vienna Declaration (1993), urged the international community to take steps to combat terrorist activities. In 1994, the UN Human Rights Commission adopted a resolution, unequivocally condemning "all acts methods and practices of terrorism, regardless of their motivation, in all its forms and manifestations, where and by whomsoever they are committed, as acts of aggression aimed at the destruction of human rights, fundamental freedoms and democracy, threatening the territorial integrity and security of states, destabilizing legitimately constituted Governments, undermining pluralistic civil society and having adverse consequences on the economic and social development of the state."

In this context, it will be useful to look in to conceptual aspect of what is law. Institutions are created by society in the consonance of time and space. Gradually, old institutions die, giving place to the new. Kingship is withering away and so is the joint family. In the family, the father was the replica of the king in his dominion; to a wife, her husband was her lord and master. This status was an embodiment of power, power to impose decisions, power to enforce will and power to hold others wrong. Since the beginning, moral codes rule society; social morality has the power of the law and individual morality is based in conscience. Social morality is older than personal morality and is in fact the basis of law and government. Originally, it was tribal law and customs that the law developed. Some primitive societies had elaborate rules as to who may marry whom. They were not just rules but were strictly followed, even without a police force. How these ethical codes manifested themselves into power codes is a matter of deep thinking and sociological research.

The basis of all the institutions is power. As said earlier, this power is indirectly related to authority that imposes decisions, be it the institution of the king, the church, the father or the husband. They were the institutions created by society to give a better life on earth. Kingship was created to counter anarchy, the church for the proper social fabric and the father and husband to create happy family unit.

In modern life also, humans are ruled by state made laws when they are out of home or social codes when they are at home. In his *Origin of Family State and Property*, Lenin attributes the advent of private property to the source or origin of the family. In tribal society there was no question of private property. There was no concept of one's own son because there was no fear of passing the property to another man after death. People had common wives but when the concept of individual morality gradually crept in, it gave birth to the concept of having one's own son so that property may pass to one's progeny after death. Such identification of biological progeny was not possible without a sexual morality code, in which a wife was to observe the sexual morality of having sex with one person only, so that the paternity of the son was confined and so that, after the death of the father, the property may pass to the son.

Thus the family unit was established with a moral code of sexual morality as the basis of this unit. Individual property was the common cake amongst the members. Several such units collected themselves for a better life and the formation of the village was the outcome. Villages, too, had the common interest of protecting their property from neighbouring villages. Bigger villages took the shape of the State. In the family, the father ruled; in the village, the village headman ruled and in the State, it was the will of the king, which gradually took the shape of law. Social morality took the shape of the law, having authority of the State with it, while individual morality remained confined to the conscience of the people.

Essentially, the law is a non-violent expression of force. Force may be of deterrent armies in dictatorial governments or large-scale public condemnation in mature democracies. But if the law is reduced to the mere use of words and force is expressed only by the use of bullets, as argued by Camus, the social fabric will be disturbed. Law should not appear to be mere become words and force behind it should not become bullets. The tug of war between 'force' and 'law' has always been an undercurrent in societies, precisely because, in earlier societies, the law merely endorsed force. Since there has been a general condemnation of force in social administrations, the tug-of-war between these two elements is quite overt.

This struggle between words and bullets can sometimes be frustrating to a sensitive individual, who may feel that people who have the force of the bullet and the power of money are apparently above the law and the law loses its power in such cases, while the meek are forced to follow the law. The dilemma is quite obvious. The law is seen as having tender teeth, as being not strong enough to become a 'force' or 'bullets' against real criminals. Such a benign law, if it really is so, should be seen as a happy state of affairs. If the law were made a 'bullet', we would revert back to the middle ages, where a tooth for a tooth and an eye for an eye was the uncomplicated law reflecting a true uncivilized society.

Camus's term of 'bullets' and 'words' is a 'twilight' area, where our present judicial scale is trembling between judicial activism and judicial restraint. A fine balance between the two is required, which people are looking for. A person in the street sometimes adopts contradictory theories on the subject; when suitable, the person pleads for judicial activism, otherwise demands for judicial restraint are made. An act either of the government or of the judiciary, having the support of the 'general will', to use Hobbes's term, is truly democratic. But the question remains if it has no support of `gereral will' will it be arbitrary or not.

People generally hold the key for all problems in common sense and the fundamental principle of logic and justice. But sometimes solutions to problems are locked away in legal rules and edifices. When the courts are confined within their locks, it is judicial restraint but when they break those locks, it is judicial activism. Judicial activism and judicial restraint are the devil and the deep sea between which the judge has to survive.

Bertrand Russell, though pragmatic, appears to be orthodox when he says "Law is too static, too much in the side of what is decaying and too little on the side of what is growing. So long as law is in theory supreme, it will have to be tempered, from time to time, by internal revolution". Russell probably dreamed about the present conceptual revolution taking shape in judicial corridors in the form of judicial activism.

The tilt in favour of judicial activism is a development of which no amount of crystal gazing fifty years ago could have given any glimpses. Judges and advocates were considered a hundred years old. Justice V K Krishna Iyer's words reflect the attitude of the earlier judiciary: "Judicial engineering assumes credibility only if therein jurisdiction simplicity procedure fairness and naturalness is the rule of evidence. Unfortunately our system is more of less negatives both".

The 42nd Constitutional Amendment gave a toothless provision in the form of fundamental duties, which the courts took as grounds for judicial activism. Courts took a liberal interpretation of the Directive Principles of State Policy and Fundamental Duties, though they were only conceptual provision without any force of law, like a million-dollar cheque that the State was not bound to honour. During the deliberations of the Swarn Singh Committee, the empowering of Parliament to impose punishment for breach of such duties; however, this was ignored in the final draft. Similarly, the State cannot be compelled to follow the Directive Principles. But the provision of Directive Principles are stronger, because if the State wants to enact the law giving effect to the Directive Principles of State Policy, it can make effective law even if the law is inconsistent with the Fundamental Rights confined by Article 14 and Article 19. Earlier, this protection was limited only to directives given in Art.39 (b) & (c). Since the law is dynamic and legal pronouncements are reflections of changing society, the lawmakers felt that social progress is primary and that the law should be in time with it.

Similarly, the fundamental duties were inserted in the year 1976. Due recognition has been given to this concept in Sachitanand Pandey vs. State of West Bengal, AIR 1988 SC 1109: "When the court is called upon to give effect to the Directive Principles and Fundamental Duties, the court is not to shrug its shoulders and say the priorities are matter of policy and so it is a matter for policy making authority. The least the court may do is to examine whether appropriate considerations are born in mind and irrelevancies excluded." As society progresses, judicial fundamentalism is breaking, and the judicial dilemma is gradually withering away. Courts are liberally interpreting the constitutional provisions in favour of the people and progress. In Mumbai Kamgar Sabha v. Abdul Bhai, AIR 1976 SC 1455, it was held that the courts may also look at fundamental duties while interpreting equivocal statutes that admit of two Constitution. The Supreme Court, in Mohan vs. Union of India (1972) Supp(1) SCC 594, went to the extent of saying that courts should uphold the constitutionality of a statute the object of which is in consonance with the provision in Art.51 (A).

Now, it is not surprising that one Sheela Barse or one M C Mehta comes forward with a Public Interest Litigation espousing the rights of women prisoners on grounds of 'humanism', or agitating for peoples' rights against polluting hazardous industries in the name of environmentalism. In a way, Public Interest Litigation is the direct result of the Apex Court's recognition of the rights of the citizen. Age-old technicalities and procedures were disregarded just to uphold the rights of people. It is true that there are rules made by the Supreme Court prescribing procedure under Art. 32 and in the High Court under Article 226 and they require procedural formalities to be gone through by a person wishing to approach the court. But the present humanist atmosphere prevailing in the judicial corridors indicates that the clouds of dilemma are evaporating and the public interest is becoming all superior.

The public interest is not always in consonance with individual interest. In fact two groups of public have conflicting interest.

The law never offers clear-cut solutions to problems and never gives one and only one answer to questions posed by humans. It is not desirable to expect lawmakers to deal with every contingency attached to human activity. Some contingencies, however, may be dealt with by judicial discretion, which may function either in the form of restraint or activism, both of which ought to be in tune with impartiality. Impartiality, as envisaged, is not only between litigating parties but also conceptual; and this conceptual impartiality is the essence of the judiciary. The rule of life and the rule of law are not conflicting and must be allowed to interact, since both the law and humans are made for each other. It is only when the law and the human are inseparable that we think of human beings as the choicest creation of the Almighty. They are seen as being showered with fine virtues, one of which is the capacity of being able to maintain and regulate themselves. Of course, an ideal society is imagined as one that has no laws, where humans in a community are regulated by high words and ideals. It was probably with this ideal in mind that Plato believed that the law was an evil and mankind had to get rid of all laws. Then, he argued, there will be morals only.

Morals have no definite formats; they are fluids, the law makes them solid. Ultimately, the law must be vested in those hands that have morals behind them. For truly free and fair interaction, we have to surrender to the law from time to time. Cicero puts it in an interesting way: "We are slaves of law in order to be free". This surrender is shaded with logic and is therefore rational. Logic and rationality is the essential fabric that covers every judicial pronouncement. "I feel so" in a judgment is not acceptable, unless it is coupled with "why I feel so". This logic cannot be that of the individual but that of the public at large. After all, no game is possible without an umpire.

Conflict between the individual and society is an age-old phenomenon. A judge may be faced with a dilemma when a proclaimed terrorist, who has eliminated an entire family, comes to court pleading for human rights. All the constitutions of the world have included these rights within them. The Indian Constitution guarantees the right of life and liberty to all people in India and this right is not confined to citizens alone. A proclaimed offender, a hardened terrorist or even a jail inmate can claim human rights or protection of his right to life and liberty. The Hippocratic oath protects doctors from such dilemmas, since they have to treat a patient even if the patient is a criminal. There is no such oath for judges, so they have to face a human dilemma.

A judge has to strike a balance between social and individual interest. American Justice Cardozo had to wrestle with similar conflicts with individual rights and wisely held that society comes first. "That question is whether protection for the individual would not be gained at a disproportional loss of protection for society. On the one side is the social need that crime shall be repressed, on the other the social need that law shall not be flouted by insolence of office. There is danger in any choice".

Striking a balance is a difficult task. "Perfection is impossible, like other human institutions criminal proceedings must be compromise". The law too is relative and changing; therefore, it cannot afford to be absolutist. Like all human institutions which change face over time and space, so is the law ever shifting in search of the absolute, which is difficult to find; it is definite, however, that such an absolute is not different from the ethics of humanity.

References

1. *S Milgram, "Some conditions of obedience and disobedience to authority", Human Relations 8(1965) page 75.*
2. *A V Dicey, Introduction to the Study of Law and the Constitution, page 303.*
3. *Trials of Major War Criminals Vol. I. page 226.*
4. *Antonio Cassese, Violence and Law in the Modern Age, page 132.*

7

Supreme Court as Political Jurist

*- Nilay V. Anjaria**

It was an assiduously opposed idea, at the time of the establishment of the Supreme Court after Independence, that the institution of the judiciary should have any place in the political life of the country. The dominant political class led by Pandit Nehru and riding high on the spirit of Independence, which had been a product of a painstaking political struggle, was visualising an unflinching commitment to the notion of political sovereignty. Its conditioned vision could not perceive the Supreme Court in the robes other than of iron-jacket ones of traditional legalism. How could they have foreseen that one day the Court would assume the role of political jurist, political arbiter, political umpire and political philosopher in the country's democracy?

On Nursery Slopes

Enthused by political independence, Jawaharlal Nehru then said:

"No Supreme Court, no Judiciary, can stand in judgment over the sovereign will of Parliament, representing the will of the entire community...in the ultimate analysis, where the future of the community is concerned, no Judiciary can come in the way.... Ultimately, the fact remains that the Legislature

* Advocate, High Court of Gujarat, E/203, Gangotri Apartments, Lad Society Road, Nehru Place, Vastrapur, Ahmedabad- 380 015, Gujarat.

must be supreme and must not be interfered with by the Courts of Law in such measures as social reform."

The Apex Court was thus born, and was intended to be brought up as an orthodox legal body. It is a picture of contrast that at present, after four decades of independence, the Apex Court is witnessed as an institution setting up political agendas for the government and controlling a wide range of political activities in the country, overseeing with a commanding authority the conduct, commissions and omissions of politicians. It can even be said to have become the initiative-producing agency for the government.

The outlook of the founding fathers was naive, both in its wisdom and vision, as also in discordance with the system of country's governance, which they themselves had designed. With their deft hand, they had achieved, in enacting the provisions of the Constitution, a wonderful harmony between Parliamentary sovereignty and a written Constitution, a unique democratic system striking midway between the American system of judicial supremacy and the English doctrine of parliamentary supremacy. The judiciary was vested with the power to declare a law enacted by the Legislature as invalid when it travels beyond permissible boundaries drawn by the Constitution. These boundaries were to be the Fundamental Rights, the distribution of power, other mandatory provisions and the ultimate letter and spirit of the Constitution.

Their Own Creation

The role of the Supreme Court was slated to be the ultimate arbiter to the Constitution. In this way, the Supreme Court, by its very nature, was destined to be a significant actor against the political executive and was inevitably to interplay with political concerns crucial in the democratic advancement of the nation. The Constitution envisaged the rights and liabilities of the State, defined the functional role of State authorities, provided instructions of governance and conferred Fundamental Rights upon the citizens and individuals against the State. In the adjudicatory process, therefore, the Court was sure to pose against the government, its policies, its programmes, its political ideologies and also against the power centres in the Constitutional and governmental setup.

Yet astonishingly, Dr. B R Ambedkar, in spite of being a legal luminary, was holding a misconceived view about the judiciary. He said: "The judiciary decides cases in which government has, if at all remotest interest, infact no interest at all. The judiciary is engaged in deciding the issues between the citizens and very rarely between citizens and government." One wonders whether Babasaheb was blinkered or biased in his view when he said: "I do not see how five or six gentlemen sitting the federal or Supreme Court examining laws made by the Legislature and by dint of their conscience to their powers or their prejudice be trusted to determine which law is good and which law is bad."

Charting the Future Course

Notwithstanding the staunch views of the political fathers, the reality was that the system adopted under the Constitution was a system of 'limited government'. The Indian Parliament was not made the ultimate sovereign. The Supreme Court was to authoritatively scrutinise the laws made by the legislative wing of political government. Having provided a system of checks and balances, whereunder the Supreme Court could pronounce upon the legislation of Parliament, set them aside as invalid or quash the Executive actions, it was evident that the Court was endowed with a kind of political authority extending beyond the mere interpretation of law. Vis-à-vis Parliament, the Supreme Court wielded power with consequences of infinite importance.

In the inaugural function of the country's highest court, the first Chief Justice of India, said in his address that the Supreme Court would not work in the spirit of barren legalism, but would make a substantial contribution towards the formation of India into a great unit, retaining its civilisation, traditions and customs. The first Attorney General also spoke to say that the task before the judiciary was to build a nation alive to its national and international duties, consisting of a strong centre and federal units. Thus, if the political class had wanted only political institutions to take up the task of shaping independent India's destiny, the judicial fraternity appeared clear in its vision that the Supreme Court would play a salient role in the socio-political affairs of the country.

It is interesting to examine how the theoretical role-model of the Court was converted into political role-behaviour in actual practice.

Power and Authority

While examining the political role-model of the Supreme Court and its actual political role-behaviour, certain theoretical foundations have to be set down and understood. They are the concepts of power and authority, the relationship between law and politics, the principles of political science and of law, the theory of separation of powers, 'wisdom' of political legislature and judicial prudence.

In political science, a distinction is drawn between power and authority. The concept of power has a wider import, while authority is one of the forms of power. Since the Constitution is a political document, its functioning implies democratic politics set into motion. Like the functioning of politics, the functioning of the Constitution is a source of power. The authority to control such a power vests in the Supreme Court, which is the controller and supervisor. Power emanates from the supreme document; politics is the ground where power is played and the Apex Court performs as would an umpire.

Since the Supreme Court has the authority to interpret, upset and propound statements of law, it controls the power of the political process, to keep it within Constitutional parameters. The norms and limits for the exercise of political power are demarcated by the Constitution. In the process, the Court spells out, preaches and pronounces political philosophy. This political philosophy, emanating from judicial wisdom, has democratic content and Constitutional sanction.

Law and Politics

One must steer clear of the misconception that the law and politics belong to different creeds and should be kept away from each other. The school that believes that the Supreme Court is supposed to be a non-political institution and politics is alien to the process of law forgets Lord Scarman, who said that the "fundamental truth is that law and politics cannot and, at a higher level, must not be kept separate". While it is true that the Court should dissociate itself from politics, what is suggested thereby is that the Court in its functioning should not become political in the adjudicatory process. However, under its Constitutional jurisdiction, the Supreme Court will be invariably pitted against matters with political overtones and will consequently interact with the political process. The issues that come up for consideration before the Court are, by nature, bound to be politico-Constitutional, politico-legal and socio-political. In fact, at the higher echelons of the Constitutional process, it is always desirable that the law and politics inform each other. The higher the level of the Constitutional process, the greater in degree the intermix of law and politics.

Political Question Doctrine

The political question doctrine represents the prudential attitude of the courts, where judges voluntarily abstain from embarking upon an issue of a political nature, once it is noticed that it falls within the domain of other branches. In the United States of America, such abstainance is described as a way of avoiding a principled decision damaging to the Court or an expedient decision damaging to the principle. This doctrine owes its emergence to the theory of the separation of powers.

Our system also adopts the theory of separation of powers. The functions of the state are classified as legislative, judicial and executive; each branch is required to confine itself to its respective functional sphere. However, the idea of separation is not as rigid as it is in the United States of America. The democratic scheme of governance provides for practical flexibility. The Court need not be so handcuffed by this doctrine so as to always dissuade itself from considering political questions during its Constitutional adjudicatory process. In H H Maharajadhiraja Madhav Rao Jivanji Rao Scindia Bahadur vs. Union of India, AIR 1971, Supreme Court 530, the Supreme Court said that the Constitutional mechanism in a democratic polity does not contemplate the existence of any function that may, *qua* citizens, be designated as political. Orders made in exercise whereof are not liable to be tested for their validity before lawfully constituted courts. The suggestion is that, once the question involves the Constitutional rights of citizen or the duty of the State, political colour is obliterated.

In Indira Nehru Gandhi vs. Raj Narain, AIR 1975 SC 2299, the Court indicated that examining the political question is itself an exercise in Constitutional interpretation. The Court supported its point by quoting observations from the American Supreme Court decision in Baker vs. Carr (1962) 369US 186: Deciding whether the matter has in any measure will be committed by the Constitution to another branch of government or whether the action of that branch exceeds whatever authority has been committed, is itself delicate exercise in Constitutional interpretation and is a responsible of this court as ultimate interpreter of the Constitution.

Politico-Constitutional Issues

Thirty years after Independence, a time span which is not very long in terms of the evolution of a Constitutional process, the Supreme Court pronounced unequivocally that it has justification to inquire into political questions, once a legal or Constitutional right was traceable therefrom. In the case of Rajasthan vs. Union of India, AIR 1977 SC p. 1359, it was the contention of the Additional Solicitor General that the question of whether, in a particular state, a situation had arisen where the Government of State could not be carried on in accordance with the provisions of the Constitution and therefore action should be taken under Article 356(1), was essentially a political question and, having regard to its political nature, the Court must abstain from inquiring into it. The Court reacted with these words:

> "...merely because a question has a political complexion, that by itself is no ground why the Court should shrink from performing its duty under the Constitution if it raises an issue of Constitutional determination. Every Constitutional question concerns the allocation and exercise of governmental power and no Constitutional question therefore fails to be political. A Constitution is a matter of purest politics, a structure of power....It will, therefore, be seen that merely because a question has a political colour, the Court cannot fold its hands in despair and declare 'Judicial hands off'....We cannot therefore decline to examine whether there is any Constitutional violation involved in the President doing what he threatens to do, merely on the facile ground that the question is political in tone, colour and complexion."

The Court further stated that there are numerous decisions where Constitutional issues have been adjudicated upon, though they have been enmeshed in religious tenets, social practices, economic doctrines or educational policies. Constitutional issues may have other overtones and facets, including political; yet, that is no dissuasion for the Court to extend its jurisdiction.

Adjudicating Political Questions

The case of Indira Nehru Gandhi was yet another instance where the Supreme Court categorically stated that it would not desist from its Constitutional duty simply because the question posed before it was of a political nature. The

Supreme Court was examining the validity of the Constitution (39th Amendment Act, 1975), in which Article 329A was amended by the then Indira Gandhi government, whereby the election of the Prime Minister and matters connected therewith were not to be decided in the courts but by a special body named by Parliament. The amendment also provided that election laws would not be applicable to the Prime Minister and would not be deemed to be ever applicable and, notwithstanding any order of the Court, the Prime Minister's election would not be deemed to be invalid. A swirling political situation had provided the impetus for this amendment; the High Court of Allahabad had set aside the election of the then Prime Minister, Indira Gandhi and had disqualified her as a member of the Lok Sabha. The 39th Amendment in Article 329 was a counter-attack from her.

It was argued that the amendment was in relation to the special position occupied by the Prime Minister and was in the context of a peculiar political consideration with a political object, that it was an exercise of a very special constituent power. Since the whole issue was a political one, the argument concluded, it was out of reach of examination by the Court. The Court, however, said,"Undoubtedly Clause 4 of Article 329A would be said to have a political object in the context in which it was introduced and we could perhaps take judicial notice of this context even if it was possible beyond the statement of objective reasons and to hold that clause 4 Article 329A is that essentially for demonstrating the strong position of the governments and of the Prime Minister of this country to all inside and outside country so as to expire the necessary convenience in and give the necessary political legal strength to the government."

The judge said he failed to see why this should make it necessary to exclude the jurisdiction of the Court, so as to prevent it from considering the case, which would have been very much sooner, if we had not been confronted with difficulties, at the very outset, in examining the merits of the case, when the context and the political consideration placed before us could be relevant in understanding the real meaning of clause 4, Article 329A of the Constitution.

Centrepoint of Authority

The Supreme Court was justified in expressing its willingness to go into political questions that had Constitutional dimensions. This role-behavior is necessary in order for the Court to effectively discharge its own Constitutional duty and to assert the wide authority the Constitution invests in it. A refusal to go into questions of a political nature would mean truncated exercise of its authority and an inchoate Constitutional adjudication.

The Supreme Court enjoys superior authority over all governments, Union and State legislatures, Constitutional and administrative authorities. Derived from the Constitution, the Apex Court has the power of judicially reviewing all laws enacted by the Legislature, actions, inactions and omissions of governmental authorities and the conduct and exercise of powers even by the highest Constitutional functionaries and political occupants; it is empowered to scrutinise each and every decision by the political and administrative wings, whether based on the Constitution or statute, whether taken on considerations of political policy or administrative grounds, whether in nature economic, commercial or even educational. Since the whole range of activities of the other two wings are subject to verification and approval of the Court through the medium of judicial review, it is inevitable that the Supreme Court takes the position of a center-point authority, which exercises its dominance and thereby plays a major role in guiding and shaping the political process in the country.

Constitutional Jurisdiction

For the purpose of exercising its pervading authority, the sweep of the jurisdiction of the Supreme Court is threefold: plenary or writ jurisdiction, original jurisdiction and appellate jurisdiction. In its writ jurisdiction, the Court gets umpteen occasions to determine scope and content of the enjoyment of Fundamental Rights, which are civil and political in nature. Of these rights available against state authorities, the Supreme Court acts as a sentinel. Activist expansion, innovative interpretation and prescription of limits in the nature of reasonable restriction on these rights are, in other words, a politico-democratic jurisprudence. The original jurisdiction of the Supreme Court covers disputes of a federal nature. As the highest federal court, it has the exclusive jurisdiction to settle disputes between Union and states and among the states. Under this jurisdiction, the issues that come up for adjudication before the Court will necessarily have political overtones and ramification and are often themselves political. They touch upon areas of federal governance, relate to political and legal obligations stemming from centre-state relations under the Constitution. Under its appellate jurisdiction, the Supreme Court entertains appeals for the decisions of the High Court. Moreover, Article 143 provides for advisory jurisdiction of the Supreme Court, where it may be consulted by the President on any question of law or fact of national importance. Vexed questions have come to be referred to the Supreme Court, which are political in their origin and which may be complex, prolonged and aggravated. The dispute of Ayodhya is an instance.

Judicial Review: a Political Power

The entire width and breath of the Supreme Court's authority and jurisdiction is condensed in its one power: that of judicial review. The power of judicial review extends even to those issues and actions that are not justiciable. The magnitude of the authority of the Supreme Court is discernible from its power of judicial review, which is, in nature and effect, virtually a political power. Exercised by an unelected body of persons, the power of review and the judicial hegemony of the Supreme Court are considered by some to be undemocratic. However, the Supreme Court by its vision, wisdom and commitment to Constitutional causes, notwithstanding having projected itself as an overwhelming force even politically, has justified its role model. The country's highest court, by creative utilisation of the power of judicial review, has performed the role of the Third House of correction. It is natural that, in this process, the mood of the Court finds tune with public opinion, as political activities so in a climate of favourable public opinion. Justice Jackson appears to justify judicial review by the Supreme Court as an alternative to political institutions: "Legislation, whose basis is economic wisdom, can be redressed by the process of the ballot-box or the pressure of opinion. But when the channels of opinion and of reasonable persuasion are corrupted or chugged, these political corrections can no longer be relied upon and the democratic system is threatened at its most vital point. In the event, the Court, by intervening, restores the processes of democratic government, it does not disrupt them.

Judges as Statesmen

In the recent decision of S S Bola vs. B D Sardana, AIR 1997 SC P. 3127, the Supreme Court highlighted the doctrine of judicial review as an instrument for the welfare of people, social progress, peace and order, as a breath of Constitutionalism meant for moulding the governmental process and to help regulate the social and economic structure of society. It also indicated that this process of judicial scrutiny had the role of harmonising political activities in the country.

> "[Judicial review's] historical and philosophical approach leads to test the enactment of only legal laws based on ethical and rational thinking, which protects and maintains individual liberty and fundamental freedoms, creates social and economic harmony and has the glorious role of reconciling political imbalance and denying democratic despotism

by establishing Constitutional balance and justice in society....Judicial review has become the linking force between the individual and the social interest and political stability and ethical considerations have often been counter balanced the ultra vires acts by judicial decisions."

With the help of judicial review, the Court has protected the basic human rights of individuals. It has guided, by the process of interpretation, the legislative acts and the actions of the political class towards social advancement, economic progress and political health and has evolved a socio-economic philosophy for the reconstruction of our democratic society. Judges are, per force, judicial statesmen.

In the early days of its history, the Court laid the foundation for future, by asserting, in State of Madras vs. V G Row, AIR 1952 SC 196, that, though not out of any desire to tilt at legislative authority with a crusader's spirit, but in discharge of its duty, it would not shun its power. While the Court naturally attaches great weight to legislative judgement, it cannot desert its own duty to determine finally the Constitutionality of an impugned statute. This power of judicial review is a basic unamendable feature of the Constitution. Starting with Keshavananda Brarati's case, this principle has been repeatedly reiterated and recently again, in L Chandra Kumar vs. Union of India, AIR 1997 SC 1125. The range of judicial review in the superior judiciary in India is perhaps the widest and most extensive known to the world of law.

Assistant to the Government

In the recent years of the country's political independence, when the political class and the Executive had only recently begun to run the democratic self-government, the institution of the Supreme Court performed a twofold task. Its Constitutional authority and independent status helped to check and prevent possible abuse of power by the Executive; and, at the same time, it acted to legitimise the acts of the government by upholding the legislations and approving the acts of the Executive in important spheres of national activities. The executive was under the Legislature and was liable to it for its deeds. But it was only the Supreme Court that could rectify the faults of both bodies in their Constitutional performance. The Apex Court had taken the clue and realised its authority and responsibility.

In the process, the Court was, knowingly or unknowingly, moulding a political outfit for Indian democracy and was automatically widening its own field. The political quarters had undertaken the gigantic task of ushering in independent India into the arena of socio-economic reform and politico-cultural renovation, in tune with the goals and ideals embodied in the Constitution. The Parliament and State legislatures, therefore, enacted statutes on these crucial areas of social, economic cultural or political rights of citizens, which laws were taken to the Court for scrutiny. Even during these early stages, the Apex Court sensed that its role was not to be limited to that of mere Constitutional interpreter, but in reality was to be that of political preceptor, political approver and political jurist.

The Supreme Court readily and happily embraced this role for itself, while dealing with cases involving vital concerns of individual liberty, like preventive detention laws, public peace, and law and order, private property rights, acquisition of property and legislative acts on land reforms and agrarian reforms. By judgments on these subjects, the Court enunciated the socio-economic philosophy of the State, the goals of the welfare state, the norms of Constitutional ideals like social justice or secularism, the guidelines for social control and economic development and the parameters of religious activities.

Monitor of Political Values

In respect of that which the political government and its executive had Constitutional responsibility, no area remained out of the purview of the Court.

The Court pronounced upon crucial concepts under the Constitution, like equality and equity, socialism, secularism, what is just, fair and reasonable in law, the idea of compensation, the extent of natural justice to be observed by both quasi-judicial and administrative authorities while exercising their statutory powers and a variety of other socio-economic and Constitutional ideals. The interpretation by the Court of these issues was to have far-reaching consequences in the political future of the country. In its function of such a vital adjudication, the Court had also silently entered into the policy-making domain. Wittingly or unwittingly, the political ruling class had to submit themselves to the decisions of the Apex Court, which charted even the socio-economic policy for the nation. Among the caravan of cases that came to be handled by Apex Court, those that rank first are R C Kooper vs. Union of India AIR 1970 S.C. 584, known as the Bank Nationalisation case and H H Maharajadhiraja Madhav Rao Jivaji Rao vs. Union of India AIR 1971 SC 530, known as the Privy Purses case.

While the Court had dealt with statutes on the subjects of almost all corners of the major activities of the government, it had also said that the wisdom of the Legislature was to be presumed. The Court laid down strict criteria, holding that it would be slow to upset the intentions of the Legislature and invalidate the laws made by it under the competent exercise of legislative powers. Nevertheless, the Apex Court had learned how to govern the political affairs of the country through the process of the examination of the laws of the Legislature. Let us now discuss some of the major areas where the Supreme Court has played the role of political jurist.

Manner of Enacting Laws

The Court has also spoken and reacted not only on the kind and nature of laws, but also over the manner of legislating. Ordinarily, the function of making law is assumed to be that of a competent legislature, but the President and Governor of State enjoy, under Articles 123 and 213 respectively, power to issue ordinances. In the exercise of this power, the President or Governor cannot act except in accordance with the aid and advice of the Council of Ministers. It is unusual for the Executive to enact the law, noted the Court in R K Garg vs. Union of India 1991(4 SCC) 675:

> "...because according to the traditional outfit of a democratic political structure, the legislative power must belong exclusively to the elected representative of the people, and vesting it in the Executive, though responsible to the Legislature, would be undemocratic, as it might enable the Executive to abuse this power by securing the passage of an ordinary bill without risking a debate in the Legislature."

The life of an ordinance has to be strictly of a limited duration. It ceases to operate at the expiration of six weeks from the reassembling of Parliament, unless it is tabled before the Parliament; the maximum life of an ordnance can be seven and half months. In the case of Dr. D C Wadhva vs. State of Bihar, AIR 1987 SC 579, the Apex Court found that the Governor of Bihar had promulgated, between 1967 and 1981, as many as 256 ordinances and all those ordinances were kept alive for periods ranging between 1 to 14 years by re-promulgation from time to time. Without hesitation, the Court frowned upon such a practice. It stated:

> "The power to promulgate an Ordinance is essentially a power to be used to meet an extraordinary situation and it cannot be allowed to be perverted to serve political ends....Such a stratagem would be repugnant to the Constitutional scheme as it would enable the Executive to transgress its Constitutional limitation in the matter of law making in an emergent situation and to covertly and indirectly arrogate to itself the law making function of the Legislature."

There must not be an Ordinance Raj in the country, the Court warned:

"The startling facts which we have narrated above merely show that the Executive in Bihar has almost taken over the role of the Legislature in making laws, not for a limited period but for years together in disregard of the Constitutional limitations. This is clearly contrary to the Constitutional scheme and it must be held to be improper and invalid. We hope and trust that such practice shall not be continued in future and that whenever an Ordinance is made and the government wishes to continue the provisions of Ordinance in force after assembling of the Legislature, the Bill will be brought before the legislation for enacting those provisions into an Act. There must not be Ordinance Raj in the country."

On Ordinance Raj

The hope expressed by the Supreme Court was not to come true; rather, the practice of 'Ordinance Raj' continued with more audacity. The State of Bihar went ahead and issued a series of ordinances. The issued was again brought to the notice of the Supreme Court. In the recent case of Krishnakumar Singh vs. State of Bihar 1998 (5) SCC 643, the State of Bihar had, for the purposes of taking over the Private Sanskrit Schools, undertaken the exercise of promulgating, replacing, correcting, extending and repromulgating a series of ordinances. The Court reprimanded the state of Bihar in these words:

"The State of Bihar has a grievance that the High Court, in its impugned judgment, has stated that there was Ordinance Raj in the State. I think this criticism is rather mild, particularly when this Court did not approve the action of the State Government in promulgating successive Ordinance in the case of D C Wadhwa vs. State of Bihar. It is rather unfortunate that after the decision of this Court in D C Wadhwa case, which was delivered on 20.12.1986, the State of Bihar continued to indulge in its illegal practice of repromulgating the

Ordinances successively without having to face the Legislature and acted in an unConstitutional manner."

The Court also observed that notifications of successive ordinances may amount to breach of privilege of legislature.

First among Equals

In a system where the written Constitution is supreme and the ultimate source of power, the democratic organ that would draw maximum power for itself would naturally enjoy dominance in the affairs of the country. Though it was wished otherwise, on one hand dominating political leadership, supported by the civil services, asserted itself and on the other, the Court, claiming to be watch-dog of Constitutional values and spirit, posed as the final authority. This was reflected most with respect to Article 368, which provides for procedure for amending the Constitution.

The race to control the Constitution can be discerned from the fluctuating fortunes of Article 368. The framers had tried to achieve the sovereignty of Parliament, by prescribing a relatively easier mode for changing the Constitution. There was indeed a political significance in adopting a facile procedure for amendment. The power of amending the Constitution was vested with the Parliament, to the exclusion of the State legislature. According to the prescription of the framers, any amendment of the Constitution would need to be initiated according to the procedure of amendment, by introducing a bill, which would then have to be passed in each House by a majority of not less than 2/3rd of the members of a House present and voting. In initiating the amendment, no previous sanction of the President was required, nor could the President, unlike in ordinary bills, could withhold assent to the Bill for amendment of the Constitution passed in both the Houses of Parliament. The very first amendment, enacted in 1951 by Nehru, placed beyond judicial review State enactments which were violative of Fundamental Rights.

Politics of Amendatory Power

Perhaps because, in the early years of Independence, it was either unable or unwilling to rub shoulders with strong political leadership, the Supreme Court had been holding that no part of the Constitution was unamendable and Parliament, by passing an Act in compliance with the requirements of Article 368, could amend any provision. The cases of Shankari Prasad vs. Union of India, AIR 1951 SC p. 458, Sajjansingh vs. State of Rajasthan, AIR 1965 SC p. 845 spoke on these lines. Until then, conflict was dormant. It surfaced for the first time in 1967, when, in the case of Golaknath, the Supreme Court held that a Constitutional amendment Act passed according to Article 368 is a 'law' within the meaning of Article 13 and is subjected to the same restrains as any other ordinary law. The effect of this pronouncement was obvious: even the exercise of constituent power by the Parliament and the Constitutional Amendment Act passed by it would have to be subjected to the scrutiny of the Court. The Supreme Court had acquired a source to control even the constituent power of the Parliament by extending the power of judicial review from Constitutional amendment, as in respect of an ordinary law. It is said that, with the delivery of the Golaknath judgement, the Supreme Court, for the first time, became law-maker rather than law-giver.

Parliament immediately asserted itself by passing the Constitution (24th Amendment) Act, 1971 and inserted sub-article (4) to Article 13, providing that "nothing in this article shall apply to any amendment made under Article 368", with a corresponding change in the provision of Article 368. It was an answer from the political wing of the government to the judiciary that the constituent power of the Parliament was supreme and not amenable to the jurisdiction of the Court.

Jurisprudence of Keshavananda

The 24th Constitutional amendment came to be challenged in the historical case of Keshavananda vs. State of

Kerala -AIR, 1973 SC 1461, which was heard by a full bench of 13 judges, the decision in which became a prominent milestone in Constitutional history. A wafer-thin majority of the full Bench upheld the validity of the 24th Amendment, overruling the case of Golaknath. It is said about the judgment, however, that it decided nothing, for almost every judge propounded his own Constitutional philosophy, with the least degree of agreement in the reasoning.

The judgment in the Keshavananda case can better be described as political jurisprudence propounded by the highest Constitutional court of the country, wherein the judges elaborately discussed almost every provision of the Constitution, closely examining its entire scheme and framework. While taking a view contrary to Golaknath, which had said that the amendment to the Constitution, Article 368 is not 'law' within the meaning of Article 13 and even the Fundamental Rights can be amended by an Act passed under Article 368, the Bench approved another proposition than that asserted in the Golaknath case, saying that there are certain basic features of the Constitution that are unamendable.

The basic structure theory discovered by the Supreme Court in this case lent finality to the kind and nature of system of political governance of the country. Any amendment in the Constitution has to be tested for its validity on the grounds of whether it offends the basic features drawn up by the Supreme Court. Without being exhaustive, the sovereignty and territorial integrity of India, the federal system, judicial review, the democratic form of government, were some of the basic features mentioned by the Court in the Keshavananda case. From the various subsequent decisions that have carried further the basic structure theory, the features that are held to be basic are: the supremacy of the Constitution; the rule of law; judicial review; power under Articles 32, 226 and 227; the federal system of government; the sovereign, democratic and republic nature of the system; the objectives in the Preamble; the unity and integrity of the nation; the dignity of the individual; the principle of equality as the quintessence of equal justice; the essence of other Fundamental Rights; the harmonisation between Fundamental Rights and Directive Principles; the parliamentary form of the government; the independence of the judiciary; the secular character of polity; the principle of separation of power rule of law, etc.. In the judgment, each of the thirteen judges had become jurists, to produce a collective political jurisprudence for the democracy of the country. In reading implied limitations on constituent power, the Court made a new law of its own kind. It had assumed a political power, whereby it was to control the other two organs. The experts said the Constitutional adjudicators had assumed the role of Constitutional governors.

Limits of Constituents Power

In the immediate post-Keshavananda period, the politics in the amendatory process was at its peak, especially in the 42nd, 43rd and 44th Constitutional Amendments. Enacted during the Emergency, the 42nd Amendment had virtually brought about a revision of the Constitution by amending, inserting and altering several Articles. But the mischief was undone by the Janata Government, as soon as it assumed power after ousting Indira Gandhi.

The Supreme Court was not to tolerate the attempt made to arrest the implications of the Keshavananda Bharati and to trample upon its judicial review power. Clauses (4) and (5) in Article 368, inserted by the 42nd Amendment, to provide that no Constitutional Amendment Act shall be called in question in any court on any grounds and that there shall be no limitation on the constituent power of Parliament, were struck down by the Supreme Court in Minerva Mills vs. Union of India, AIR 1980 SC 1789. The grounds were twofold: that the judicial review was a basic feature and could not be taken away in the exercise of Constituent power; and that the power acquired by the Parliament was the power to destroy, not the power to amend.

"The newly introduced clause (5) of Article 368 demolishes the very pillars on which the Preamble rests by empowering the Parliament to exercise its constituent power without any "limitation whatsoever". No constituent power can conceivably go higher than the sky-high power conferred by clause (5), for it even empowers the Parliament to "repeal the provisions of the Constitution"...to abrogate the democracy and substitute for a totally antithetic form of Government."

Court: A Political Scientist

The Parliament would not be allowed to expand its constituent power to abrogate the Constitution or to destroy its essential features, declared the Court and warned:

"That can most effectively be achieved, without calling a democracy by any other name, by a total denial of social, economic and political justice to the people, by emasculating liberty of thought, expression, belief, faith and worship and by adjuring commitment to the significant deal of society, of equals".

In the language of the political scientist, the Court said the Parliament enjoys only a limited power:

"Since the Constitution had conferred a limited amending power on the Parliament, the Parliament cannot under the exercise of that limited power enlarge that very power into an absolute power. Indeed, a limited amendatory power is one of the basic features of our Constitution ....The donee of a limited power cannot by exercise of that power convert the limited power into an unlimited one."

About Article 368(4), which deprived the Court of the power to call in question any amendment of the Constitution, the Apex Court said, without mincing words, that it should suffer the same fate:

"A controlled Constitution will then become uncontrolled....The conferment of the right to destroy the identity of the Constitution coupled with the pronouncment upon the validity of such destruction seems to us a transparent case of transgression of the limitations on the amending power."

Question of Priority

The justiciable Fundamental Rights and the non-justiciable rights known as the Directive principles of State Policy are the two crucial areas in respect of which the Supreme Court fondly exercises its jurisdiction and determines the validity or otherwise of laws. While Fundamental Rights enforceable as law, have legal sanction and thus constitute limitations upon state actions, the Directives have political sanction and are the fundamental principles specifying goals for the government. However, the Court cannot enforce them. These norms with political sanction enjoy primacy over the rights with legal sanction, in the sense that the Directives can delimit the enjoyment of Fundamental Rights. The latter have to submit to the former in their expansion. The interworkings of Fundamental Rights with the Directives is not just a Constitutional process; it throws open the question of priority between the political and the judicial branches of democracy. And when the Supreme Court deals with the issues arising out of the interaction and conflict between the two, it again becomes a political jurist in its adjudicatory function.

In State of Madras vs. Champakam (1951), S.C.R. 523, the Supreme Court laid down a general preposition that, in the event of conflict between the Fundamental Rights and Directives, the former should prevail and the Court could not declare any law as void, if it was otherwise valid, on the grounds that it contravened any of the Directives. Unhappy with this overriding fiat, the ruling political quarter introduced Article 31C to the Constitution Act in 1971(24th Amendment), which was expanded in 1976 by the 42nd Amendment to the Constitution Act, providing that any law enacted to implement any of the Derivatives contained in part IV of the Constitution would be totally immune from unconstitutionality on the grounds of contravention of Fundamental Rights under Articles 14 and 19. The pre-1976 position was that the law would be protected by Article 31C, if it was made to implement the Directives in Article 39(b) and (c) only.

However, the Supreme Court undid this widening, in the case of Minerva Mills, when by majority it was held that such total exclusion of judicial review offended the basic structure of the Constitution. The Court observed that Articles 14 and 19 confer rights which are the essence of democracy and the withdrawal of the availability of these elementary rights to citizens would be a subversion of the functioning of democratic polity. The object and purpose of the amendment of Article of 31 was to save laws that could not be saved under Article 19(2) to (6), the Court pointed out.

No Overriding Place

In invalidating the widened Article 31C, the Supreme Court was perhaps proclaiming dominance of its own position over the political branch, stating that if Article 14 and 19 were put out-of operation in regard to the bulk of laws that the Legislatures are empowered to pass, Article 32 would be drained of its life blood. The Court observed:

> "If the discipline of Article 14 is withdrawn and if immunity from the operation of that Article is conferred, not only on laws passed by the Parliament but on laws passed by the State legislatures also, the political pressures exercised by numerically large groups can tear the country asunder by leaving it to the Legislature to pick and choose favoured areas and favourite classes for preferential treatment."

According to the Court, the group of freedoms in Article 19(1) are the basic political rights conferred upon the citizens and could not have been withdrawn under the cloak of implementing the Directives Principles. With reference to the example of Article 19(1) (d), it observed:

> "Then again, regional chanvinism will have a field day if Article 19(1) (d) is not available to the citizens. Already, there are disturbing trends on a part of the Indian

horizon. Those trends will receive strength and encouragement if laws can be passed with immunity, preventing the citizens from exercising their rights to move freely throughout the territory of India. The nature and quality of the amendment introduced by section 4 of the 42nd Amendment is therefore such that it virtually tears away the heart of basic fundamental freedoms."

Arbitration between Rights and Principles

The Apex Court ruled to restore the pre-1976 position, giving the upper hand to Fundamental Rights over Directives Principles, except in respect of Article 39 (b) and (c), reasoning that the two categories of provisions should be harmonised without giving any general preference to the Directive Principles. The Court was thereby suggesting that it would not allow political intendments to score over Constitutional imperatives, and that the Fundamental Rights would not be eclipsed by the Directives but would be enriched by them:

"...it is only in the framework of the socio-economic structure envisaged in the Directive Principles that the Fundamental Rights are intended to operate, for it is only then that they can become meaningful and significant for the millions of our poor and deprived people who do not have even the bare necessities of life and who are living below the poverty level".

While advocating reconciliation of Fundamental Rights and Directive Principles, the Court emphasised that the dynamic provisions of the Directives Principles fertilise the static provisions of Fundamental Rights. It traced the genesis of this inter-relationship back to the freedom struggle, in which the leaders had realised the supreme importance of the political and civil rights of the individuals and the necessity to create socio-economic conditions for the enjoyment of those rights.

"The Directive Principles, therefore, impose an obligation on the State to take positive action for creating socio-economic conditions in which there will be an egalitarian social order with social and economic justice to all, so that individual liberty will become a cherished value and the dignity of the individual a living reality, not only for a few privileged persons but for the entire people of the country...."

Review of Political 'Satisfaction'

Article 352 and 356 empowers the President to issue a proclamation of Emergency and of imposing President's rule in a state on being 'satisfied' that the situation contemplated in these provisions exists. The term 'satisfaction' indicates purely a political satisfaction, as the deriving source of such satisfaction is the advice tendered by the Council of Ministers headed by the Prime Minister. The satisfaction contemplated under both Article 352(1) and 356 (1) are at an equal footing in their nature and for interpretation. The Supreme Court has wanted this satisfaction to fall within the purview of judicial review. In the case of Minierva Mills, the Court dealt with the challenge to clause (5) of Article 352 inserted by the 42nd Amendment. The Amendment provides that the satisfaction of the President shall be final and conclusive and shall not be questioned in any court on any ground and that neither the Supreme Court nor any other court shall have jurisdiction to entertain any question regarding the validity of or the continuation of the proclamation under Article 352 (1),

> "Let it not be forgotten", asserted the Court, "that to this court as much as to other branches of government, is committed the conservation and furtherance of Constitutional values.... Tact and wise restraint ought to tamper any power but courage and acceptance of responsibility have their place too."

The Court went on to say:

> "A proclamation of emergency is undoubtedly amenable to judicial review though on the limited ground that no satisfaction, as required by Article 352, was arrived at by the President in law or that the satisfaction was absurd

or perverse or malafide or based on an extraneous or irrelevant ground."

In order to supply cogency to its conclusion for judicial reviewability, the Court reasserted that judicial review was part of a basic structure and it would not shirk its responsibility. The Court also discussed how drastic and anti-democratic the consequences of Emergency were:

"The issue of the proclamation of emergency makes serious inroads into the principle of federalism and emasculates the operation and efficacy of Fundamental Rights. The power of declaring an emergency is power fraught with grave consequences and it has the effect of disturbing the entire power structure under the Constitution.... But it is a necessary power given the Central government with a view to arriving at it adequately to meet an exceptional situation arising out of threat to the security of the country. It is therefore a power to be exercised with the greatest care and caution and utmost responsibility".

The Court and Political Mood

Though the exercise of such power, *de jure*, is that of the President, it is exercised *de facto* by the Council of Ministers headed by the Prime Minister, at whose advice the President is bound to act. Such advice cannot be but based upon a bundle of political considerations. Then, to what extent and in what fashion the Court should enter this political thicket has been a question, perhaps perennially moot.

In State of Rajasthan vs. Union of India, AIR 1997, SC 1361, the Supreme Court dealt with the presidential proclamation to impose central rule under Article 356(1) in the States of Bihar, Madhya Pradesh, Punjab and Rajasthan. The Janata Dal government, which had taken over the reins of power, sought to justify its action on the grounds that, in view of the results of the Lok Sabha elections, the State government in the four states ruled by the Congress had lost the political legitimacy to govern. The Court said invoking Article 356 was a matter of political judgement that could well fall within the subjective satisfaction of the President at the instance of the Council of Ministers headed by the Prime Minister, as a consideration germane to Article 356. This is how it was put:

> "...Attempts to secure political victories, by appeals to the electorate, are part of the recognised rules of the democratic system of government, permitting contests between rival parties so as to achieve certain other objectives. Such a contest, with a desire of achieving a political victory in order to enforce certain programmes believed by the members of a party to be beneficial for the people in a state, as a method of achieving the objects set out in the Preamble, is not only legal and permissible under the Constitution, but obviously constitutes the only possible legitimate and legal means of attaining the power to enforce the policies believed to be correct by various parties according to their own rights. It could not possibly be asserted that procuring the dissolution of a State Legislative Assembly, with the object of gaining a political victory, is in itself an extraneous object, which could not fall at all under Article 356 of the Constitution."

A Political Response

The Court opined that the choice between a dissolution and re-election of the same membership of the Legislature or the government for a certain period could be a matter of political expediency and strategy, that under our system the quest of political power was legal when asserted by various political portions with difference socio-economic ideologies. It remains a question whether the Court wanted to identify itself with the political mood of the country and wanted to support the new party in power, installed by decisive popular mandate and a thumping political victory. Historically, it has always been the case that significant judgments by the Supreme Court often come as a response to political waves, rather than a deliberate independence or a strict judicial exercise by a judge.

Notably, Article 356 speaks of the breakdown of the constitutional machinery in the state as being a condition for an invocation of the provision; this can hardly be said to arise on consideration of political expediency. Nevertheless, the judges stated that the political judgment of the rulers should prevail. If the Union Government thinks that the circumstances of the situation demand that the state governments must seek a fresh mandate, resort to Article 356 cannot be unjustified.

> "In so far as Article 356(1) may embrace matters of political and executive policy and expediency, the Court cannot interfere unless and until it is shown what constitutional provision the President is going to contravene or has contravened on admitted grounds of action...."

Regarding the extent of permissible inroads by the Court in such subjective satisfaction, it appears that the judges were milder in the Rajasthan case than they were in their observations in the Minerva Mills case, when they stated that what was enough was that no 'extraneous' considerations were disclosed in petitions and that the Court would not concern itself with the sufficiency or adequacy of the grounds. In other worlds, the Court's view was that political expediency was not an extraneous consideration.

Swing of the Pendulum

The prudence of the Court with regard to the scope of subjective satisfaction under Article 356, expressed in the State of Rajasthan vs. Union of India, became increasingly obsolete with the occurrence of repeated instances of the political use of the provision. It was ultimately in the case of SR Bommai vs. Union of India, AIR 1994, SC 1918 that the Supreme Court completely reversed its opinion rendering the law in the state of Rajasthan to be bad. There was a sea-change in the thinking of the Court as to what criteria govern the satisfaction of the President, which were possibly effected because of the atmosphere of demeaned politics in resorting to the provisions of Article 356.

"The mere defect of the ruling authority at the centre cannot by that without nothing more entitled to a new elected party which comes to power at the Centre to advise the President to dissolve the Assemblies of those states where the party in power is other than the one in power at the centre. Merely because the different political party is elected to power at the centre, even if with a thumping majority, is not ground to hold that "a situation has arisen in which the government of the State cannot be carried on in accordance with the provisions of this Constitution", which is the requirement for the exercise of power under Article 356(1)."

The Court said it is a matter of common knowledge that people vote for different political parties at the Centre and in the States, and therefore, if a political party with an ideology different from the ideology of a political party in power in any state comes to power in the Centre, the Central Government would not be justified in exercising power under Article 356(1) unless it is shown that the ideology of the political party in power in the state is inconsistent with the Constitutional philosophy. The Judges looked upon the provision of Article 356 in the conspectus of the basic features of the Constitution, and stated,

"It will be an inexcusable error to examine the provisions of Article 356 from a pure legalistic angle and interpret their meaning only through jurisdictional technicalities. The Constitution is essentially a political document and provisions such as Article 356 have the potentiality to unsettle and subvert the entire Constitutional scheme. The exercise of power vested under such provision needs, therefore, to the circumscribed to maintain fundamental Constitutional balance."

"Political Satisfaction" Defined

In the Bommai judgment, the Court interpreted the phrase "the government of the state cannot be carried on in accordance with the provisions of this Constitution" to contain a situation of impasse. By laying down various criteria in the proper exercise of power under Article 356, the Supreme Court defend the scope and of political subjective satisfaction to be arrived at by the President on the basis of advice tendered by the Council of Ministers headed by the Prime Minister. Enlisting the situations which, according to the Court, would not amount to the failure of the constitutional machinery, it specified that the use of Article 356 will be improper where the situation obtained is only that of maladministration in the State; where the situation is of internal disturbances not amounting to or verging on abdication of its governmental powers by the State government; where the situation is of stringent financial exigencies of the State or a situation where serious allegations of corruption are made against the State Ministry; where the Governor fails to explore the possibility of installing an alternative government; where the Government dissolves the Assembly without giving the ministry an opportunity to demonstrate its majority support through the "floor test"; where the dissolution is accommodated upon on the sole ground that in the general elections to the Lok Sabha the ruling party in the State has suffered a massive defeat; where the President gives no prior warning or opportunity to the State Government to correct itself; and where the State government has either applied the corrective steps or has satisfied the Union executive that the warning or direction was based on incorrect facts.

The Supreme Court, while pronouncing upon the ideal use of the provision to impose President's rule and laying down the guidelines therefore, extended its jurisprudence on the various attendant aspects of the Constitution and the basic constitutional concepts like federalism, secularism, and the mixing up of religion and politics. This had arisen in the context of the Assembly of Uttar Pradesh being dismissed as a fallout of the incident at Ayodhya.

Into the Political Thicket

The Court went a step further in laying down the scope of its powers of judicial review over the Constitutional proclamation. The Court entered, and entered consciously, into the political arena, when it commanded that material on the basis of which the actual advise was tendered to the President was liable to be produced before the Court.

If said that, since reasons would form part of the advice tendered to the President, the Court would be precluded from calling for their disclosure but Article 74(2) was no bar to the production of all the materials on which the ministerial advance was based. Though the proposition in the Rajasthan case was maintained, that the Court would not be examining the sufficiency of material, the Court extended its arm enough to examine everything about the exercise of political power under this Article.

In RK Jain vs. Union of India, AIR 1993, SC 1769, the Court observed along similar lines:

> "We hold that the communication of a cabinet decision or policy to the President under Article 74(1) gives limited protection by Article 74(2) of judicial review of the actual advice tendered to the President of India. The rest of the file and all records forming a part thereof are open to in-camera inspection by this Court."

The Court ruled that in a petition challenging the President's proclamation under Article 356, it can grant interim relief to restrain the Executive from holding fresh elections, can restore the dissolved Council of ministers and, concerned with the merits, can examine "the manner in which the decision was made" to impose Article 356.

Stablising Force

In its exercise of authority over Constitutional functionaries, high executive positions and governmental offices, the Supreme Court has proved itself to be a politically stabilising force. This point may be explained with reference to decisions in respect of the functioning of the Election Commission.

In SS Dhanoa vs. Union of India, AIR 1991, SC 1745, the Supreme Court dealt with a case where the President of India, by two notifications in the exercise of his power under Article 324(2) of the Constitution, had appointed two Election Commissioners, including the petitioner SS Dhanoa, to the Election Commission, in addition to the chief Election Commissioner, which notifications were however rescinded by subsequent notifications within four months, resulting in the termination of the services of the newly-appointed Election Commissioners. The subsequent notifications abolishing the posts were assailed on the grounds, inter alia, that the ECs were appointed for a full tenure of five years, determined under the rules, and that their premature termination amounted to interference in the independence of the Commission.

Besides holding that the abolition of the posts was the prerogative of the Executive and the exigency of service and that the President was justified in acting on his subjective satisfaction on the basis of advice tendered by the Council of Ministers headed by the Prime Minister, the Supreme Court noted, with strong disapproval, the differences, disputes and disharmony in the functioning of the Election Commission generated by the new appointees vis-a-vis the chief Election Commissioner.

"The experience of the short period during which the petitioner and other Election Commissioners were in the Commission...shows that were it not for the restraint and sagacity shown by the Chief Election Commissioner, the work of the Commission would have come to a standstill and the Commission would have been rendered inactive.'

Lack of Co-ordination Deprecated

Referring to the two instances where the Election Commissioners, by their conduct, were at loggerheads with the Chief Election Commissioner, thereby creating hurdles in the smooth functioning of the Commission, the Court expressed unhappiness:

> "We do not propose to refer to all the other disputes which arose between the Chief Election Commissioner and the others. But it appears...that the petitioner and others probably misunderstood their role and thought that they were appointed to control the Chief Election Commissioner at every stage.... The attitude adopted by them in the discharge of their functions was hardly calculated to ensure free and independent functioning of the Commission, much less its smooth working....No one need shed tears that the posts were abolished."

One may say that the Court implicitly endorsed the decision to terminate the non-co-operative Election Commissioners for reasons of lack of co-ordination. The Court also had a jurisprudential message for the Government. It opined that the facts on record showed that there had been no need to make two new appointments and that the Union of India would do better to show candidness and admit the initial mistake rather than defend it on non-existent grounds:

> 'It appears that there is an impression in some quarters that, if the government admits its mistake, whether it is committed by the same government or the earlier government, it loses its face. Nothing can be farther from reality. In a democratic regime, the government represents the people. It adds to its respectability and credibility if the government also owns its mistake frankly.'

No Seshanisation

Interestingly, later on the Supreme Court came across with exactly a converse set of circumstances, where the President had appointed two Election Commissioners by an ordinance which was challenged as ultra virus and arbitrary by none other than the Chief Election Commissioner. It was during the time when the Election Commission of India was under the hegemony of TN Seshan, who had by his own style of functioning brought alive the independence of the Commission, but at the same time his single handed control raised the eye-brows of many, and the allegation that the Election Commission was behaving like a parallel government.

The Presidential ordinance appointing two other Election Commissioners, for the alleged purpose of cutting the wings of the Chief Election Commissioner, was challenged before the Supreme Court in TN Seshan vs. Union of India and others-JT 1995 (5) SC 307. Seshan pleaded that the party in power was irked with him because he insisted on strict compliance of the model code of conduct by political parties, because he had declined to postpone elections for four State Assemblies and because he had filed a writ petition to enforce the right of the Election Commission for staff. It was urged by Seshan that the ordinance was mala fide, as it was on the above stated motivation that the President was advised to issue the ordinance to sideline Chief Election Commissioner, to erode his authority by making the Commission a multi-membered body. The Supreme Court dismissed the petition, observing:

> "It would be wrong to project the individual and eclipse the Election Commission. Nobody can be above the institution which he is placed to serve. He is merely the creature of the institution, he can exist only if the institution exists. To project the individual as mightier than the institution would be a great mistake; therefore, even if the Election Commission is a single member body, the CEC is merely a functionary of that-body".

The constitutionality of the ordinance was not only upheld, but the Court said that in a multi-membered body, the CEC is obliged to act as its Chairman and other Election Commissioners are part of the Commission, who would have a say in the decision making process, with a voice of advice of equal importance.

Supplier to the Needs of the Time

In the SS Dhanoa case, the Court had observed that the independence of the institution depends upon the individual who mans it and even a single individual could withstand the pulls and pressures which many may not be able to; that view was clearly not found workable in the later case of TN Seshan.

The Supreme Court itself is a democratic institution. The method and process of appointments of judges in the higher judiciary has always been a matter of controversy. The view in SP Gupta vs. Union of India, AIR 1982, SC 149 identified as "the judge's case", the position as settled by the Supreme Court that was that, in the appointment of judges, the Executive should have privacy. The judgement came to be overruled in SC Advocates-on-record Association vs. Union of India, AIR 1994, SC 268, where the Court said that the consultation of the Chief Justice of India contemplated under the Constitution in the appointment of judges has to be meaningful and not illusory, and that the CJI's opinion must enjoy primacy. Giving the example of the Pope, who enjoys supremacy in ecclesiastical and temporal affairs, the Court said that the CJI, being the highest judicial authority, has a right of primacy, if not supremacy, to be accorded in affairs concerning the "Temple of Justice". The Court observed:

> "The judiciary may be the weakest among the Constitutional functionaries, for the simple reason that it is not possessed of the long sword (that is the power of enforceability of its decisions) or the large purse (that is the financial resources), but if the opinion of the Executive is to prevail over the opinion of the CJI in matters concerning the judiciary on account of that reason, then the independence of the judiciary which is a power of strength for all, particularly for the poor, the downtrodden and the average person confronting the wrath of the Government, will be a misnomer".

Notion of Accountability

Judges have to be accountable in their functioning, like the politicians in their conduct. About the notion of accountability, the Court spoke in the case of SC Advocates-on-record. Prior to this judgment, it was a cherished convention that the view of the Chief Justice was respected above the say of executive; gradually, the convention began to be observed in the breach only, and executive supremacy was sought to be justified on the grounds that Parliament is accountable to the people and the CJI or the judges are not so. Justice JS Verma, then the CJI, spoke for the Constitutional bench in the above SC Advocates Association case, to counter this:

> "The majority view in AIR 1982, SC 149 (the Judges Case) to the effect that the Executive should have primacy, since it is accountable to the people, while the judiciary has no such accountability, is an easily exploded myth, a bubble which vanishes on a mere touch....In actual practice, the Chief Justice of India and the Chief Justice of the High Court, being responsible for the functioning of the Courts have to face the consequences of any unsuitable appointment which gives rise to criticism by the ever vigilant Bar...[they] in the selection process bear the consequences and become accountable."

It may be observed that the aforesaid interpretation as regards the primacy of CJI's opinion is an activist interpretation, to the extent that it supplies to the need of times. The spirit of the Constitution is ultimately the spirit of times. If one reads between the lines of the reasoning behind the view that the Executive should not dominate, it can be seen that a political justification has been sought to be supplied by the Court.

Would it not be disastrous to give a carte blanche to the Parliament represented by the elected members to select the appointees to the higher judiciary? The statistical graph of the composition of each successive Parliament would suggest that there is a steady decline in the educational and intellectual standards of the MPs and MLAs who get elected, and many of them, including those who become ministers, happen to be the criminals and 'history-sheeters'. The political clan in our country has become morally and ethically bankrupt. Further, politicians are being tried in the Courts for their involvements in scams and anti-national activities. If one cannot become the judge of ones own cause, can one say in the appointment of a judge who may try one's cause? The process of selection of judges should be such that it is protected from the vagaries of political thinking and the self-serving nature of political rulers.

Controller of Constitutional Functionaries

In Election Commission of India vs. SBI Staff Association, JT 1995 (2) SC 61, the Supreme Court considered the claim of the Election Commission that, in view of clause (vi) of Article 324 of the Constitution and section 159 of the Representation of the People Act, 1951, the President or Governor must make available to it such staff as may be necessary for the discharge of functions conferred upon it under Article 324. Granting such a request would mean allowing the Election Commission to override the Executive authority of the President or the Governor. Rejecting the plea of the Election Commissioner, the Court ruled that the Election Commission can get only such staff that is under the control of the President or the concerned Governor, on whom they are in a position to exercise disciplinary powers.

Another area where the Supreme Court indirectly controls political activities is while it examines the legality of the decisions of the Speaker of the House, under the Anti Defection Laws. In Manilal Singh vs. Boro Babu Singh, AIR 1994, SC 505, the Court held that, when the Speaker decides on the disqualification or continuance of a member, he becomes a statutory authority and his decision is subject to judicial review. The Supreme Court has oriented Constitutional functionaries in its duties, has taught lessons of the limits to be observed in the discharge of their power, has restrained them from crossing the limits of their jurisdiction and has taken them to task when deemed proper.

Policy Agendas

With reference to the Directive Principles of State Policy, the Supreme Court has, in several cases, passed directions to perform something which otherwise would fall within the realm of policy of the Executive. In Himachal Pradesh vs. HP State Recognised and Aided School Managing Committees, JT 1995 (8), SC 406, the Court ruled that the government was under obligation to provide grant-in-aid and for that purpose the state should earmark the amount in its budget.

> "The Constitutional mandate to the State, as upheld by this Court in the Unni Krishan case, to provide free education to children up to the age of fourteen, cannot be permitted to be circumvented on the grounds of lack of economic capacity or financial incapacity. The right to education is equally guaranteed to children who are above the age of fourteen, but they cannot enforce the same unless the economic capacity and development of the State permits the enforcement of the same. The State must endeavour to review and increase the budget allocation under the head 'Education'."

In Maharashtra vs. Manubhai Pragati Vashi, JT 1995 (6), SC 119, the Supreme Court judges directed the state government to extend the grant-in-aid scheme to the private law colleges, virtually setting policy guidelines in the field by observing that was the mandate of Article 39A.

> "The principles contained in Article 39A are fundamental and cast a duty on the State to secure that the operation of the legal system promotes justice."

> "In order to enable the State to afford free legal aid and guarantee speedy trial, a vast number of persons trained in law are essential."

> "If the State is unable to start colleges of its own, it is only appropriate that private law colleges, which are duly recognised by the concerned University, should be

afforded reasonable facilities to function effectively and in a meaningful manner. That requires substantial funds. Under the label of self-financing institutions, the colleges should not be permitted to hike the fees to any extent in order to meet the expenses to provide the infrastructure and for appointing competent teachers and staff."

The Apex Court in the case of Municipal Council, Ratlam vs. Vridhichand, AIR 1980, S.C. 1622, directed the state government to make available sufficient financial aid to Ratlam Municipality, observing as under:

"State will realise that Article 47 makes it a paramount principle of governance that steps are taken for the improvement of public health as amongst its primary duties. The Municipality will also slim its budget on low priority items and elitist projects to use the savings on sanitation and public health."

In the case of Shah Bano 1985 (3), SCC 643, the Supreme Court stressed the need to enact a common civil code, an issue which was brought up again in Sarla Mudgal vs Union of India,AIR 1995, SC 1531:

"One wonders how long will it take for the Government to implement the mandate of the framers of the Constitution under Article 44 of the Constitution of India. The traditional Hindu law, personal law of Hindus governing inheritance, succession and marriage was given the go-by as far back as 1955-56 by codifying the same. There is no justification whatsoever in delaying indefinitely the introduction of a uniform personal law in the country....We request the Government of India through the Prime Minister of the country to have a fresh look at Article 44 of the Constitution of India and endeavour to secure for the citizens a uniform civil code throughout the territory of India."

Many judgements are political in their reasonings and ratio. For instance, in Indira Sahani vs. Union of India, AIR 1993, SC 477, known as the Mandal judgment, the Court dealt with the issue of reservation under Article 16(4) of the

Constitution and declared that the reservations be confined to initial appointments only and not be extended in the matter of promotion. In that case, the Court permitted the convenience of the policy of reservation for promotion till 16 November, 1997. The decision of the Court, however, was set at naught by 77th Constitutional Amendment Act. Looking to the range of decisions of the Supreme Court, it is evident that the Court has become more and more outward in its political role behaviour.

Activist Backlash

It has been well said that judicial power emerges as an instrument of history when the Executive and Legislative powers emerge as momentary adventurists, forgetting India's mission. Observers rightly point out that the Supreme Court began to assert itself after the period of Emergency, during which, by the 42nd Constitutional Amendment and by all other means, its authority was attempted to be smothered and its power to be scuttled. The judiciary then raised its head emphatically, seizing every opportunity and discovering new areas of the exercise of its jurisdiction. It widened its net from treating a postcard as a writ petition for the purpose of enforcing the Fundamental Rights of citizens to orienting the government and its authorities to steadfastly perform their duties under the Constitution and as a welfare state, to initiating suo motu proceedings against politicians occupying high power-seats.

One wonders how the Court inserted itself into the innovative areas of politico-Constitutional adjudication, introduced itself into a phase which is more independent, assertive and authoritative than ever before, learning lessons from the lethal times of political autocracy that had demeaned its status. The 44th Amendment had, to a great extent, given the judiciary the opportunity to recover its lost dignity, a chance that the judiciary did not miss and, with the assistance of some epochmaking contemporaneous judgments, it reached a stage that later came to be known as judicial activism. From the assertion of its authority to its display of the activist mood is an exercise in backlash where the Apex Court has become more overt in its political role-behavior.

Assertiveness via PIL

With the advent of public interest litigation and with its innovative expansion, the judicial process has resurged with its pervading assertiveness. The Supreme Court, through the medium of public interest litigation, which has acquired a prominent place in public law jurisprudence, has been able to enlarge its role in the political life of our nation. While the ultimate idea of public interest litigation may be to achieve the objectives of the Constitution and enforce the rule of law, the trends of recent years have shown that this kind of litigation has taught lessons of accountability and ethico-morality to civil servants politicians. A stock grievances against the use of public interest litigation is that the Courts intrude into the policy domain of the Executive and overstep their jurisdiction; however, PIL has served the purpose of making the entire political class feel uncomfortable about the possible uncovering of skeletons in their cupboards. The Supreme Court, by entertaining a number of PILs that raise the stink of corruption among highly placed political leaders, placed itself in a position of the most efficacious institution to oversee the quality of public life and uplift the democratic standards of governance. The storm created by PIL in political areas has had been so intense that the Gujral government had contemplated introducing a controversial legislation to scuttle the scope of PIL and to restrict repeated resort to it.

Spadework for Political Justice

In the process of entertaining, effectuating and enlarging the field of public interest litigation, the courts, in addition to espousing social causes and facilitating their redressal, have contributed much to secure political justice, a very important facet of democracy and an avowed object enshrined in the Constitution, which has so far somehow stood inconspicuous, perhaps because in the early years of our independence, and until recently, it was social justice that was considered as the benchmark of real democracy.

The Court, sitting as public interest jurist, has sent a message that democracy will be distorted unless the idea of political justice is seriously attended to and effectively secured. That real democracy can be achieved only by securing social and economic justice was the view propounded by Jawarharlal Nehru, which was more a romanticist view than a realistic. The mismanaged ideal of social justice by political rulers has led to perilous consequences to the fabric of society and in the nature and kind of politics in the country, demystifying the Nehruvian blind endearment to social justice.

The Apex Court has tacitly suggested that overlooking the ideal of political justice and emphasizing social and economic justice would be like putting the cart before the horse. The experience gained has shown that unless political justice is ensured, expectations of socio economic justice can hardly materialise. The quality of polity and the purity of political culture is essential to erect the edifice of social and economic justice. The Courts have done this spadework splendidly through the medium of public interest litigation.

Political justice is a bundle of rights: Fundamental Rights, other constitutional rights and as such all kinds of rights democratic in nature and emanating from the system itself. They are a group of rights to be made available to the people from the political state performing as welfare state. Broadly stated, these are the rights to be governed by a responsive and accountable government and are the entitlement of the electorate to subject elected leaders to the dictates of the law of the land for their omissions and commissions. Citizens also have the right to be informed of the conduct of governmental affairs in all spheres, to obtain a congenial socio politico-democratic climate, to enjoy fundamental and Constitutional rights fully and freely etc. The political justice brought alive through public interest litigation is the ideal that democracy is for the people, of the people and by the people. It is these rights enforced by the Court.

Dispensation of Political Justice

In a public interest proceedings, when an activist judiciary exposes a political scandal, it accords political justice. When it refuses to give relief to high-standing politicians charged with serious economic and moral offences and submits them to the process of the law, political justice is sensed by the people of the country. When it directs the disclosure of information kept back by the government under the guise of secrecy, public good is achieved, resulting in political justice. When it subjects the deals and policy decisions of the politically motivated government to judicial scrutiny, political justice is brought to the doorsteps of common citizens. The charge that, by public interest litigation, the judiciary trespasses upon the policy field of government, is misconceived. What the Courts basically do is to frown upon the unconstitutional steps taken by political rulers under the guise of policy. In the wake of plummeting standards of ethico-moral conduct of the political class and the fast-vanishing probity of public life, the PIL is innovatively instrumentalised by the judiciary and has catered to the need of the time. It has also given a face to judicial activism and justified the political role-behaviour of the Apex Court. In its crusade to cleanse the polity of the country of political sleaze, the Court has promoted the health of the body politic, strengthening the conditions in which people can enjoy real democracy. But for this salutary role, politics would have always remained a betrayal of Constitutional ideals and values.

From Sentinel to Saviour

The political jurisprudential role of the Supreme Court can be defended by the argument that the expansion of judicial activism is the effect of the decline of the role and responsibility of the other two organs of democracy, namely the Legislature and executive. Judicial activism is not a recent invention, for, in its higher form, it is hidden in the

Constitution itself, a fact which the Supreme Court merely discovered in the course of its politically reactionary mood. The Court them became the political jurist of the constitutional functioning of the values, ideals and basic democratic rights enshrined in the Constitution. Notwithstanding the criticism of overstepping that the Court is often subjected to, it has actually performed as a sentinel on qui vine; it has taken up the role of a saviour when these values are endangered during the fall of democratic institutions, constitutional functionaries and political standards,.

Extended Arm

A century ago, French observer Alexis de Tacqueville said: "Scarcely any political question arises in the United States that is not resolved, sooner or later, into a judicial question." For the Indian Supreme Court, this has been proved vividly true.

As recent cases suggest, the Apex Court has became more and more courageous in its political role behaviour. In times when political standards in the country have plummeted, the politicians and their parties have degenerated from Constitutional politics into demeaning power-politics. Political activities at all levels need to be vigorously informed by Constitutional commands and values; the Court has extended its arms with a purpose of reclaiming democratic values and probity in public life.

The writ jurisdiction of the courts, especially the writ of *mandamus,* which essentially belongs to public law as observed by Professor Wade, has been employed by the Court ingeniously to make the political and executive class ethical and accountable. Justification is provided by the Court itself that the Executive authorities have fallen short of expectations, as observed in the case of the Indian Council for Environmental Legal Action 1996 (5), SCC 281.

> "The primary effort of the Court...is to see that the enforcement agencies, whether it be the State or any other authority, take effective steps for enforcement of

law....Even though it is not the function of the Court to see the day-to-day enforcement of the law, that being the function of the Executive, because of the non-functioning of the enforcement agencies, the Courts, as of necessity, have had to pass orders directing the enforcement agencies to implement the law."

Judges the Rulers

In a number of other cases, the directions issued by the Apex Court are of such a nature as to have taken upon itself the task of administration. It has issued directions for the protection of national monuments, has required authorities to take safety precautions when the Army conducts test firing in any area, has shown anxiety about the jeopardising of interest of small depositors by big companies, has issued directions in respect of the rehabilitation of Chakma refugees and, in several cases with regard to pollution, has directed to take measures for protecting the environment. It has propounded a public trust doctrine, which requires the government to conserve and optimally use the national resources available in the country. The Supreme Court has, in the most assertive posture, dealt with cases of misuse and corruption among high-ranking politicians.

The Court, perhaps, has began to realise that, by not acting on matters of public concern and by allowing the public good to be sacrificed at the hands of unethical and corrupt leaders, the country will reach a stage of political anarchy. In contemporary times, the Court has issued directions even over-looking the lesson from Patric Dilvin, that enthusiasm is not and cannot be a judicial trait. The cases where the Court set aside the allotment by the Petroleum Minister of petrol pump dealership out of his special quota, the case with regard to out-of-turn allotment of quarters, the fodder scam case or the havala case are examples of the zeal of the Court to act in a politically corrective role. The Court has sought to monitor executive agencies dealing with cases of corrupt politicians, assuming its own control on the investigations carried on by such agencies. Whether it is the transfer of the Enforcement Directorate or the ordinance on the Central Vigilance Commission, it is the Supreme Court that will have the final say. Its omnipresence is in every nook and corner.

Responsive to Politics

Chief Justice Marshall of the United States once said: "Never seek to enlarge judicial power beyond its proper boundary, nor fear to carry it to the fullest extent when duty requires." The Supreme Court has clearly indicated that the latter part of Chief Justice Marshal's advice is more relevant to the political conditions of the country. The Supreme Court's role as political jurist is inherent in the Constitution itself, a fact that the Apex Court has highlighted by extending its jurisdiction into the area traditionally known to political and executive fields. Thereby the Supreme Court has shaped, streamlined, sustained, and even superimposed itself, when necessary, over the political process and activities in the country. There is little to be concerned about if the Court develops a responsive attitude to political affairs in its Constitutional role and examines the wisdom of politics with judicial prudence.

Given the context of the Indian Constitution, the position of the Supreme Court thereunder and its role-behaviour, how befitting it is when it is said that the Constitution is a political document, the Supreme Court is a political institution, the judge a policy-maker guided by internal and external influences, and a case under the Constitution a political event. Is not every judgment by the Apex Court a separate chapter in the book of the Supreme Court's political jurisprudence ?

8

The Independence of Judiciary

*- V.P. Srivastav**

Judicial independence is not a matter of compromise. It is the soul and inner strength of the judiciary, which helps it in safeguarding the Fundamental Rights and civil liberties of people against executive actions and encroachment by other powerful groups. Only an impartial and independent judiciary can protect the rights of the individual and provide equal justice without fear or favour.

There are no two opinions that the judiciary has served the country well even in difficult times. It has produced judges of outstanding integrity and ability. The people of India have confidence in the judiciary because it has functioned independently and impartially. Judicial independence is the foundation on which the whole concept of justice is based. If judges are not independent and impartial, who will have faith in the administration of justice?

Independence of the judiciary: How it is maintained under the Constitution

It is true that the quality of justice depends upon the independence enjoyed by the judiciary. It is, therefore, very necessary that the Court should be allowed to perform its functions in an atmosphere of independence and that it should be free from all kinds of political pressures. The

* Ex. Public Prosecutor, presently posted as Copyright Information Officer Ministry of Human Resource Developments, Deptt. of Education, Shastri Bhawan, New Delhi - 110 001.

Constitution has made several provisions to ensure independence of the judiciary. They are:

(1) Security of tenure

The judges of the Supreme Court have security of tenure. They cannot be removed from office except by an order of the President and that also only on the ground of proved misbehaviour or incapacity, supported by a resolution adopted by a majority of total membership of each House and also by a majority of not less than 2/3 of the members of the House present and voting. Parliament may, however, regulate the procedure for the presentation of the address and for investigation and proof of the misbehaviour or incapacity of a judge. But Parliament cannot misuse this power, because the special procedure for their removal must be followed.

(2) Salary of judges fixed, not subject to vote of legislature

The salaries and allowances of the judges of the Supreme Court are fixed by the Constitution and charged on the consolidated fund of India. They are not subject to the vote of the Legislature. During the term of their office, their salaries and allowances cannot be altered to their disadvantage, except in grave financial emergency.

(3) Parliament can extend, but cannot curtail the jurisdiction and power of the Supreme Court

In respect of its jurisdiction, Parliament may change the pecuniary limit for appeals to the Supreme Court in civil cases, enhance the appellate jurisdiction of the Supreme Court, confer supplementary power to enable it to work more effectively, confer power to issue directions, orders or writs, including all the prerogative writs for any purpose other than those mentioned in Article 32. The point to be noted in all these provisions is that the Parliament can exceed but cannot curtail the jurisdiction and power of the Supreme Court. [Article 138]

(4) No discussion in the Legislature on the conduct of the judges

Neither in Parliament nor in a state legislature can a discussion take place with respect to the conduct of a judge of the Supreme Court in the discharge of his duties (Article 121).

(5) Power to punish for its contempt

The Supreme Court and the High Court have the power to punish any person for their contempt (Article 129 and 215). This power is very essential for maintaining the impartiality and independence of the judiciary.

(6) Separation of the judiciary from the Executive

Article 50 directs the state to take steps to separate the judiciary from the Executive in the public service of the state. It emphasizes the need to secure the judiciary from interference by the Executive.

(7) judges of the Supreme Court are appointed by the Executive with the consultation of legal experts

The Constitution does not leave the appointment of the judges of the Supreme Court to the unguided discretion of the Executive. The Executive is required to consult the judges of the Supreme Court and High Court in the appointment of the judges of the Supreme Court [Article 124(2)]. The independence of the Supreme Court is emphasized by Article 229, which provides that the appointment of officers and servants shall be made by the Chief Justice or such other judge or officer as he may appoint.

(8) Prohibition on practice after retirement

Article 124(7) prohibits a retired judge of the Supreme Court to appear and plead in any court or before any authority within the territory of India.

Thus, the position of the Supreme Court is very strong and its independence is adequately guaranteed. However, there are certain disturbing trends at present, which are likely to threaten the independence of the judiciary.

Threat to the independence of the judiciary

The independence of the judiciary means, in main, independence during the post-appointment period. The concept of independence of the judiciary at the pre-appointment stage is primarily to appoint the best persons, who have integrity and a sound knowledge of the laws, persons who will not succumb to pressures of any kind from any quarter. This independence alone secures justice for all and creates the confidence of society in judges. The judges of our country have proved worthy of the privilege for decades. The quality of justice depends upon the independence enjoyed by the judiciary.

The main causes for danger to the independence of the judiciary are as follows:

(1) Firstly, although judges are appointed by the Executive with the consultation of legal experts, the word 'consultation', as has been held in the judges Transfer Case, does not mean concurrence and the Executive is not bound by it. The Government may completely ignore the advice of legal experts. Thus, the power of appointment of the judges of the Supreme Court is solely vested in the Executive, from whose dominance the judiciary is expected to be free.

(2) Secondly, the power of the of President under Article 222 to transfer a judge from one High Court to another might also be used to undermine the independence of judiciary.

(3) Thirdly, the practice of appointing retired judges in various capacities might pose a serious danger to judicial independence.

So far as the appointment of judges is concerned, our founding fathers did not leave the power to appoint judges in any single quarter, be they the Chief Justice of the High Court, the Chief Minister and the Governor of the state, the Chief Justice of India and the President of India, besides the fact that each constitutional functionary has an effective role in the 'consultation process'. While calling this the "middle course", Dr. Ambedkar rejected the concept of a collegium, suggested by the Ad-hoc Committee of Jurists. He said that "there can be no difference in the House that our judiciary must both be independent of the Executive and must also be competent in itself". "Dr. Ambedkar made minor changes in the recommendations made by the conference of chief justices before giving final shape to the existing process of consultation provided in the Constitution of India for the appointment of High Court and Supreme Court judges. Several legal luminaries who intervened in the debates of the Constituent Assembly repeatedly assured the House that they were committed to an independent judiciary.

The question is therefore simple. Who should play the decisive role in the appointment of judges of High Courts and the Supreme Court? This involves the interpretation of Article 124(2) and 217(1) of the Constitution of India, insofar as appointments are concerned. Article 222 of the Constitution of India deals with the transfer of High Court judges.

The seven judges bench in the SP GUPTA case, AIR 1982, SC 149 interpreted the constitutional provision and delivered a judgment by a majority of 4:3, holding that the Chief Justice of India did not enjoy primacy over the Chief Justice of a High Court. I will discuss the case elaborately but before that, it is better to see the constitutional provision:

Article 124: Establishment and Constitution of the Supreme Court

(1) There shall be a Supreme Court of India, consisting of a Chief Justice of India and, until Parliament by laws prescribes a larger number, of not more than seven other judges.

(2) Every judge of the Supreme Court shall be appointed by the President by warrant under his hand and seal after consultation with such of the judges of the Supreme Court and of the High Courts in the States as the President may deem necessary for the purpose and shall hold office until he attains the age of sixty-five years:

Provided that, in the case of the appointment of a judge other than the Chief Justice, the Chief Justice of India shall always be consulted, provided further that:-

(a) a judge may, by writing under his hand addressed to the President, resign his office;

(b) a judge may be removed from his office in the manner provided in clause (4).

The age of a judge of the Supreme Court shall be determined by such authority and in such manner as Parliament may by law provide.

(3) A person shall not be qualified for appointment as a judge of the Supreme Court unless he is a citizen of India and

(a) has been for a least five years a judge of a High Court or of two or more such Courts in Succession; or

(b) has been for at least ten years an advocate of a High Court or of two or more such Courts in succession; or

(c) is, in the opinion of the President, a distinguished jurist.

EXPLANATION I- In this clause, "High Court" means a High Court which exercises, or which at any time before the commencement of this Constitution, exercised jurisdiction in any time part of the territory of India.

EXPLANATION II- In computing, for the purpose of this clause, the period during which a person has been an advocate, any period during which a person has held judicial office not inferior to that of a district judge after he became an advocate shall be included.

(4) A judge of the Supreme Court shall not be removed from his office, except by an order of the President passed after an address by each House of Parliament, supported by a majority of the total membership of

that House and by a majority of not less than two-thirds of the membership of that House present and voting, has been presented to the President in the same session, for such removal on the ground of proved misbehaviour or incapacity.

(5) Parliament may by law regulate the procedure for the presentation of an address and for the investigation and proof of the misbehaviour or incapacity of a judge under clause(4).

(6) Every person appointed to a judge of the Supreme Court shall, before he enters upon his office, make and subscribe before the President, or some person appointed in that behalf by him, an oath or affirmation according to the form set out for the purpose in the Third Schedule.

(7) No person who has held office as a judge of the Supreme Court shall plead or act in any authority the territory of India.

Article 220: Restriction on practice after being a permanent judge

No person who, after the commencement of this Constitution, has held office as a permanent judge of a High Court, shall plead or act in any Court or before any authority in India, except the Supreme Court and the other High Courts.

EXPLANATION- In this expression, "High Court" does not include a High Court for a state specified in Part B of the First Schedule as it existed before the commencement of the Constitution (Seventh Amendment) Act, 1956.

Article 222: Transfer of a judge from one High Court to another

(1) The President may, after consultation with the Chief Justice of India, transfer a judge from one high Court to any other High Court.

(2) When a judge has been or is so transferred, he shall, during the period he serves, after the commencement

of the Constitution (Fifteenth Amendment) Act, 1963, as a judge of the other High Court, be entitled to receive, in addition to his salary, such compensatory allowance as may be determined by Parliament by law and, until so determined, such compensation allowance as the President may by order fix.

Article 224 A: Appointment of Additional and Acting judges

(1) If, by reason of any temporary increase in the business of a High Court or by reason of arrears of work therein, it appears to the President that the number of the judges of that Court should be for the time being increased, the President may appoint duly qualified persons to be additional judges of the Court for such period not exceeding two years as he may specify.

(2) When any judge of a High Court other than the Chief Justice is, by reason of absence or for any other reason, unable to perform the duties of his office or is appointed to act temporarily as Chief Justice, the President may appoint a duly qualified person to act as judge of that Court until the permanent judge has resumed his duties.

(3) No person appointed as an additional or acting judge of a High Court shall hold office after attaining the age of sixty-two years.

Article 225: Appointment of retired judges at sittings of High Courts

Notwithstanding anything in this Chapter, the Chief Justice of a High Court for any State may, at any time, with the previous consent of the President, request any person who has held the office of a judge of that Court or of any other High Court to sit and act as a judge of the High Court for that State, and every such persons requested shall, while so sitting and acting, be entitled to such allowances as the President may by order determine and have all the jurisdictions, powers and privileges of, but shall not otherwise be deemed to be, a judge of that High Court:

Provided that nothing in this Article shall be deemed to require any such person as aforesaid to sit and act as a judge of that High Court unless he consents so to do.

Jurisdiction of existing High Courts

Subject to the provisions of this Constitution and to the provisions of any law of the appropriate legislature made by virtue of powers conferred on that legislature by this Constitution, the jurisdiction of, and the law administered in any existing High Court, and the respective powers of the judges thereof in relation to the administration of justice in the Court, including any power to make rules of Court and to regulate the sittings of the Court and of members thereof sitting alone or in Division Courts, shall be the same as immediately before the commencement of this Constitution:

Provided that any restriction to which the exercise of original jurisdiction by any of the High Courts with respect to any matter concerning the revenue or concerning any act ordered or done in the collection thereof was subject immediately before the commencement of this Constitution shall no longer apply to the exercise of such jurisdiction.

Power of High Courts to issue certain writs

(1) Notwithstanding anything in Article 32, every High Court shall have power, throughout the territories in relation to which it exercises jurisdiction, to issue to any person or authority, including in appropriate cases, and Government, within those territories directions, orders or writs including writs in the nature of *habeas corpus, mandamus, prohibition, quo warranto* and *certiorari,* or any of them for the enforcement of any of the rights conferred by Part III and for any other purpose.

(2) The power conferred by clause (1) to issue directions, orders or writs to any Government, authority or person may also be exercised by any High Court exercising jurisdiction in relation to the territories within which the cause of action, wholly or in part,

arises for the exercise of such power, notwithstanding that the seat of such Government or authority or the residence of such person is not within those territories.

(3) Where any party against whom an interim order, whether by way of injunction or stay or in any other manner, is made on, or in any proceedings relating to, a petition under clause (1), without

(a) furnishing to such party copies of such petition and all documents in support of the plea for such interim order; and

(b) giving such party an opportunity of being heard, makes an application to the High Court for the vacation of such order and furnishes a copy of such application to the party in whose favour such order has been made or the counsel of such party, the High Court shall dispose of the application within a period of two weeks from the date on which it is received, or from the date on which the copy of such application is so furnished, whichever is later, or where the High Court is closed on the last day of that period, before the expiry of the next day afterwards on which the High Court is open; and if the application is not so disposed of, the interim order shall, on the expiry of that period, or, as the case may be, the expiry of the said next day, stand vacated.

(4) The power conferred on a High Court by this Article shall not be in derogation of the power conferred on the Supreme Court by clause (2) of Article 32.

Article 227: Power of superintendence over all courts by the High Court

(1) Every High Court shall have superintendence over all courts and tribunals throughout the territories in relation to which it exercises jurisdiction.

(2) Without prejudice to the generality of the foregoing provision, the High Court may

(a) call for returns from such courts;

(b) make and issue general rules and prescribe forms and regulations the practice and proceedings of such courts; and

(c) prescribe forms in which books, entries and accounts shall be kept by the officer of any such courts.

(3) The High Court may also settle tables of fees to be allowed to the sheriff and all clerks and officers of such courts and to attorneys, advocates and pleaders practising therein:

Provided that any rules made, forms prescribed or tables settled under clause(2) or clause (3) shall not be inconsistent with the provision of any law for the time being in force, and shall require the previous approval of the Governor.

(4) Nothing in this Article shall be deemed to confer on a High Court powers of superintendence over any court or tribunal constituted by or under any law relating to the Armed Forces.

By going through the provisions of the Constitution of India it is clear that the judges of the Supreme Court are appointed by the President. The Chief Justice of the Supreme Court is appointed by the President with the **consultation** of such of judges of the Supreme Court and the High Courts as he deems necessary for the purpose. But in appointing other judges, the President shall always consult the Chief Justice of India. He may consult such other judges of the Supreme Court and High Court as he may deem necessary.

Though the President is required to 'consult' legal experts, he is not bound to act in accordance with such consultation. The meaning of the word 'consultation' came for the consideration of the Supreme Court in the Sankal Chand Sheth case (AIR 1977, SC 2328), which was related to the scope of Article 222 of the Constitution. It was held that the word 'consultation' meant full and effective consultation. For a full and effective consultation, it is necessary that the three constitutional functionaries "must have for its consideration full and identical facts", based on which they would be able to take a discussion. Consultation does not mean concurrence and the President is not bound by it. In the Judges Transfer case (AIR 1982, SC 149), the court unanimously agreed with the meaning of the term 'consultation' as explained by the majority in the Sankal Chand Sheth case. The meaning of the word 'consultation' in Article 124 (2) is the same as the meaning of the word 'consultation' in Article 212 and Article 222 of the Constitution. The only ground on which the decision of the government can be challenged is that it is based on *mala fide* and irrelevant considerations. This means that the ultimate power to appoint judges is vested in the Executive, from whose dominance and subordination it was sought to be protected.

Under Article 124 (2), the President, in appointing other judges of the Supreme Court, is bound to consult the Chief Justice of India. But in appointing the Chief Justice of India, he is not bound to consult anyone. Till 1973, the practice was to appoint the senior-most judge of the Supreme Court as the Chief Justice of India. This practice had virtually been transformed into a convention and was followed by the Executive without any exception. In 1973, the old practice was suddenly broken by the government within few hours of the delivery of the judgment in the Fundamental Rights case.

As a matter of fact, the specific question framed in the SP Gupta case was: "Does the advice given by the Chief Justice of India have primacy over that rendered by the Chief Justice of the High Court? The Court considered this question and answered in the following terms: "A point has been raised whether on a difference of opinion between them, the advice of the Chief Justice of India can be said to enjoy primacy over that tendered by the Chief Justice of High Court. Nothing is laid down on the matter in express terms in clause (1) of Article 217. If by 'primacy' is meant that the opinion of the Chief Justice of the High Court can alone be considered, it is clearly against the provisions of clause (1) of the Article 217, for the clause intends that the President should consult both judicial functionaries, besides the Governor. The Chief Justice of India does not sit in the appellate judgement over the advice of the Chief Justice of the High Court and the fact that the former has given his advice cannot imply that the advice given by the latter must be ignored."

Looking at the issue of unity amongst judges, events from the SP Gupta case onwards go to show that the Supreme Court itself has failed to take a united stand on the issue of the primacy of the Chief Justice of India in the matter of judicial appointments. Seeing the sensitivity of the issue, the SP Gupta care was reopened in the Subhash Sharma case [(1990) Suppl-(2) SCR 433], stating that it should be considered by a larger bench constituting nine judges to examine the two questions, viz. the position of the Chief Justice of India with reference to the primacy and justiciability of the fixation of judges' strength. The order states: "In the event of the amendment being carried and the National Judicial Commission being set up, the correctness of the ratio in SP Gupta's case, on the status of the Chief Justice of India, may not be necessary to be examined in view of the fact that, by the amendment, the Chief Justice of India would become the chairman of the commission. In case the commission is not constituted, the two questions indicated above, which are vital importance to the efficient functioning of the judicial system in the country, require consideration and there is an element of immediacy in the matter".

The reading of the order creates an impression that the bench, headed by Justice Ranganath Mishra, then Chief Justice of India, wanted a clear decision upholding the primacy of the Chief Justice of India in the appointment of judges. But the order says that, in the event of the setting up of a National Judicial Commission, the Chief Justice of India would become the chairman of the commission and therefore the correctness of the ratio in SP Gupta's case may not be examined. It is difficult to agree that if the Chief Justice of India is made chairman of an appointment commission, it would automatically give primacy to the Chief Justice of India. However, the Supreme Court of India did not take up the matter early, even though the court had considered it to be of vital importance to the efficient functioning of the judicial system. Justice MN Venkatchaliah took over as Chief Justice of India and constituted the nine-judge bench in 1993, to decide the points mentioned in the referring order quoted above.

The nine-judge bench did not strictly limit the scope of hearings to the two issues, i.e. the position of the Chief Justice of India with reference to the primacy and justiciability of the fixation of judges' strength as framed in the referral order. The Supreme Court once again opted to interpret Article 217(1) and 124 (2) of the Constitution of India in the post-SP Gupta scenario, to further insulate the appointment of judges. Again, the court was divided and by a majority of 6:3, they did not give primacy to the Chief Justice of India in the appointment of judges. The interpretation of the consultation process by the majority judgment is that the Chief Justice of India shall consult two senior-most judges in writing and send their views to the President of India, along with his own recommendations. In the case of unambiguity between the three judges, their recommendations are almost binding on the President of India, unless he sends them back for reconsiderations for specific reason. On such reconsideration, if three judges reiterate their earlier recommendations, they would be binding on the President of India. The majority decision, therefore, interpreted the relevant constitutional provisions not strictly in favour of the primacy of the Chief Justice of India but laid down a new consultation process. Recently, when Shri Punchchi, then Chief Justice of India, recommended the name of a few judges for appointment without the consultation of the two senior-most judges, the President refused the recommendations and asked the Chief Justice of India to reconsider the name as per the prevailing norm of consultation. In the case of a division of opinions among the three judges, the Supreme Court decision permits the President of India to make his choice from amongst the names proposed by the Chief Justice of India and two other judges. This is indeed a departure from the decision in the SP Gupta, case where the role of the judiciary was not so decisive. The Supreme Court decided, even after the nine-judges bench was informed by the Department of Law and Justice, that since 1985, the government had appointed only such persons as judges as were recommended by the Chief Justice of High Court and the Chief Justice of India. In no case would a person be appointed as judge if the Chief Justice of India did not agree to his or her appointment, even though recommended by the Chief Justice of the High Court and the Governor of the State. This unwritten rule has worked well and has promoted judicial independence.

In SC Advocates-on-Record Assn. vs. Union of India, AIR 1994, S.C. 268, the court said that the Consultation of the Chief Justice of India contemplated under the Constitution in the appointment of judges has to be meaningful and not illusory, and that the Chief Justice of India's (CJI) opinion enjoys primacy. Giving the simile of the Pope, who enjoys supremacy in ecclesiastical and temporal affairs, the Court said that the CJI being the highest judicial authority has a right of primacy, if not supremacy, to be accorded on the affairs concerning the "Temple of Justice". The Court observed:

"The judiciary may be the weakest among the constitutional functionaries, for the simple reason that it is not possessed of the long sword (that is the power of enforceability of its decisions) or the long purse (that is financial resources), but if the opinion of the Executive is to prevail over the opinion of the CJI in matters concerning the judiciary on account of that reason, then the independency judiciary which a power of strength for all- particularly for the poor, the down-trodden and average person confronting the wrath of the government, will be a misnomer".

Today there is a need to realise that judicial appointments are different from other types of appointments. Some argue that the Executive is entitled to take into consideration the mental outlook or the social philosophy of judges. This means that judge should subscribe to the social philosophy of the ruling party. It is true that in deciding cases, the social philosophy of the judge plays an important role. But the question arises as to what kind of social philosophy a judge is to subscribe to. Evidently, the philosophy of the Constitution. The preamble in the Constitution embodies social philosophy. Thus, it is clear that the Supreme Court judges are bound to adhere to the social philosophy of the Constitution.

The independence and impartiality of the judiciary is one of the hallmarks of the democratic setup of government. To give to the Executive unfettered discretion to decide the philosophy of judges is to make the judiciary subservient to the Executive. Every judge who desires to be elevated to the highest post of the Chief Justice of India will try his best to become a 'forward looking judge' in the eye of the government.

On the second issue of question of transfer of High Court judges, it should be remembered in the first place that High Courts are the highest courts in the states. They have the power of superintendence and control over the subordinate courts and tribunals. The judges of High Courts occupy a prestigious position in the administration of justice. Thus, the transfer of High Court judges has a strong bearing on the independence of the judiciary and judicial discipline. Even the transfer of a single High Court judge would attract criticism from several quarters. The Constitution of India does not empower the Supreme Court or the chief Justice of India to transfer the High Court judges. As a matter of fact, the Supreme Court does not enjoy any administrative control over the High Courts in our country. Only on the judicial matters is the Supreme Court a superior court to the High Courts. The role of the Chief Justice of India under Article 222 of the Constitution of India is to protect the interest of judges against arbitrary transfers by the Executive. He is the link between the judge and the President, to oversee that the transfer is not punitive and also to hear the concerned judge before rendering his advice to the President on the transfer. This process of consultation must be effective and full data has to be placed before the Chief Justice of India while seeking his views. After the joint conference of chief justice and chief ministers endorsed the policy of having one-third of the judges from outside in each court, in December 1993, the Chief Justice of India MN Venkatachaliah desired to implement the policy through the Peers Committee of three judges of the Supreme Court and two Chief Justices of the High Courts. He wanted to keep the government completely outside the consultation process and left it to the Peers Committee. The Government agreed to implement the transfer policy, based on the recommendations of the Chief Justice of India. Large scale transfers did cause hardship to judges. No norms were followed in the Peers Committee or by the Chief Justice of India. However, the government had faith that the judiciary would give justice to its judges.

So far as the subordinate courts are concerned, the Constitution secures the independence of subordinate judiciary from the Executive. Article 233 provides that the appointment, posting and promotion of district judges shall be made by the Governor of the state in Consultation with the High Court. The Governor is not bound to act on the advice of the High Court. The High Court recommends the names of the persons for appointment, but it is not obligatory on the Governor to accept the recommendation. Nor is the government bound to give reasons for not accepting the recommendations of the High Court. (MS Jain vs state of Haryana, AIR 1977, SC 276).

Appointment of persons other than district judges to the judicial service of a state shall be made by the Governor of the state in accordance with the rules made by him on behalf of public service, the State Public Service Commission and with the High Court of the state (Article 234). At present, the State Government exercises administrative control over the district and subordinate magistrates. The law commission has also suggested the strengthening the control of the High Court over district judges and the subordinate judiciary in a state. To ensure the independence of the subordinate judiciary, separation from executive and control of the High Court over the district judge and the subordinate judiciary is required. In a significant judgement in the case of the All India Judges Association vs. Union of India (1992), ISCC 119, the Supreme Court has directed the union government to establish an All India Judicial Service and to bring about uniformity in service conditions of members of the subordinate judiciary throughout the country. It is yet to be implemented by the government.

So far as the practice of appointing retired judges in various capacities is concerned, obviously it is a danger to the independence of the judiciary. The law commission has pointed out the dangers of the prevailing practice in the following words:

"It is clearly undesirable that the Supreme Court judges should look forward to other government employment after their retirement. The government is a party in a large number of cases in the highest court and average citizens may well get the impression that a judge, who might look forward to being employed by the government after his retirement, does not bring to bear on his work that detachment of outlook which is expected of a judge in case in which government is a party. We are clearly of the view that the practice has a tendency to effect the independence of judges and should be discontinued.

Recommendations

In order to uphold the independence of the judiciary, a meaningful unity and mutual respect must exist within itself. There are a few recommendations, which may create the independence without any controversies:

(1) There is a need to establish an All India Judicial Service and to keep the uniformity in service conditions of members of the subordinate judiciary

(2) The state Governments' administrative control over the district and subordinate magistrates must be

abolished and control of the High Court over the district judge and the subordinate judiciary is to be strengthened.

(3) A judicial committee, consisting of the Attorney General, the Law Minister, the President of the Bar Association and the retiring Chief Justice of India may be constituted and authorised to suggest a panel of names for the appointment of judges of the Supreme Court and High Courts.

(4) To bring about uniformity in service conditions of members of the judicial subordinate judiciary throughout the country, there is a need to establish an All India Judicial Service.

(5) There is a need to chalk out a syllabus for the professional degree of law, which must be applicable throughout the country and of course, the classes/ courses of law must be taught in one language throughout the country.

(6) There should be an institute or academy for the training of judicial officers to be set up by the central government with the Chief Justice of India as a chairman. The functioning of the institute or the academy should be under the supervision of the governing body to be constituted in consultation with the Chief Justice of India. The Chief Justice shall also be the chairman of the governing body. The governing body will determine whether and in what place branches of the institute or academy should be set up for such training.

(7) There is a need to take immediate action to upgrade the infrastructure facilities for the judiciary.

(8) There is a need to set up a judicial disciplinary authority over the misconduct of judges, which must be under the control of judiciary.

In the 50th year of the Independence of India, we, the law makers, lawyers and judges, must do some introspection. It is our duty to bring justice within the reach of the common man without any favour or disfavour. In the United States of America, judicial independence has developed into a set of institutions that ensure that judges decide according to the law, rather than according to their own whims or the will of others, including the other branches of the government. The components of judicial independence comprise the constitutional protection enjoyed by judges in the United States of America.

We must achieve the independence of the administration of the judiciary and judicial disciplinary authority over the misconduct of judges. Together these components combine to assure an independent judiciary that is the basis for a society in which the people and the government behave according to the law. India accepts the concept of security of tenure for judges in our Constitution but there is no provision for judicial control over the misconduct of judges. The procedure for impeachment is very cumbersome and is ultimately not in the hands of judiciary. Judicial independence is the foundation on which the whole concept of justice is based. There is no doubt that the Indian judiciary has served the country well even in difficult times. It has produced judges of outstanding integrity and ability. There is a need to maintain this independence with proper administration of justice without interference. If this can be ensured, India will be able to proclaim proudly that we not only judge the judges but also provide the justice for all.

Bibliography

1. *Pandey, Dr. JN, constitutional Law of India.*
2. *Bhardwaj, HR, The Law, Lawyers and Judges.*
3. *Kumaramanglom, Judicial Appointments.*
4. *Advani, Poornima, Indian Judiciary: A Tribute.*
5. *Dhawan, R, Khurshid, S and Sudharshan, R, Judges and Judicial Power.*
6. *Iyer, VR Krishna, Justice and Beyond.*
7. *Iyer, VR Krishna, Judicial Justice: A New Focus.*

9

Justice and Judgements

*- Dr. P. Bhaskara Mohan**

Jurists say that "Justice hurried is justice buried" and "Justice delayed is justice denied", which implies that there should be justice in the judgment rendered by the courts.

Inspite of all the difficulties faced in courts by the litigant public and delays caused in the adjudication of cases, the volume of litigation in Indian courts is on the increase. In both the High Courts and the Supreme Court, litigation is increasing year by year, which implies that most people turn to the courts seeking justice. Thus, a very high responsibility is cast upon the Indian judiciary, right from the Court of Munsiff Magistrate to the Supreme Court.

The Indian judiciary has proved, in an ample number of cases[1], that it provides protection and relief to the needy and downtrodden where the Executive miserably fails in its duties and/or causes severe hardship to the people due to mal-administration. Thus, judicial activism today, within a particular parameter, is felt as the need of the hour. At this crucial juncture, especially with the existing political instability in the country, the Indian judiciary plays a very effective and balanced role.

With the development of public interest litigation, any number of examples can be given about judicial activism. However, it is also necessary to uncover the other side of the

* Advocate, High Court of A.P., Part-time lecturer Post Graduate College of Law, Osmania University, Hyderabad, A.P.

coin, in order to make the system more foolproof and effective. As the popular saying goes, "Justice should not only be done but it also should also appear to have been done". Using this perspective, this study will therefore examine a few judicial decisions.

Case Studies

Case I: A finance firm by the name of Vijaya Credit Corporation was run by nine partners, of which one member was male and eight were female. The company collected several lakhs of rupees as fixed deposits and finally closed down the firm without paying several depositors either the principal or the interest due on maturity of the deposits. Aggrieved by this, some of the affected depositors filed consumer complaints[2] before the AP State Consumer Disputes Redressal Commission. Among these partners/ respondents, respondents 4,5 and 6 contested the matter on the ground that their signatures were forged and that they were never partners of the firm. On 7 June 1994, the State Commission passed a common order in both the C.D. Nos. 51/93 and 84/93, allowing the claim of the complainants to the extent of their principal, along with 18% interest and costs and held all the partners jointly and severally liable to the complainants. Since the respondents did not comply with the order, the complainants filed EP No. 5/94 in C.D. No. 84/93 and EP No. 6/94 in C.D. No. 84/93 under Section 27 of the Consumer Protection Act, 1986.

Subsequently, respondents 4,5 and 6 informed the State Commission that since they preferred appeals[3] before the National Consumer Disputes Redressal Commission against the orders of the State Commission, the EPs may not be proceeded with until the National Commission decided the matter. They also sought time to move the N.C.[4] for the granting of a stay. The N.C. refused and since no stay was granted, on 3 December 1994, the State Commission passed a sentence of imprisonment and a fine under section 27 of the Consumer Protection Act, 1986. Then, the three respondents moved the High Court of Andhra Pradesh[5], under the contention that women cannot be arrested as provided under Section 56 of the Code of Civil Procedure 1908. The High Court declared that the appeals were pending before the N.C. and dismissed the writ petitions[6]. It argued that it would not be proper for the High Court to entertain the writ petitions under Article 226 of the Constitution of India. Against this order, these partners filed SLP (Civil) Nos. 23264-65/94 before the Supreme Court and on 21-12-94, the Supreme Court ordered an interim stay of the arrest of these respondents. (R-4, 5 and 6 in the C.D. Nos. 51/93 and 84/93).

Subsequently, on 20 March 1995, the Supreme Court observed that the counsel for the petitioners (partners) prayed for four weeks time, so that in the meantime they could approach the National Commission for taking up the said petitions filed by the petitioner (appeals against the orders of the State Commission) pending before the National Commission and directed to list the SLPs after four weeks. This order was passed since, by that time, the appeals against the orders of the State Commission were already pending before the National Commission. The National Commission heard these Appeals, Nos. 594 and 595 of 1994, and on 25 October 1995 dismissed the appeals by awarding costs. Thus, the orders of the State Commission in the Consumer Dispute Nos. 51/93 and 84/93 became final. However, the sentence (which had been ordered in EP Nos. 5/94 and 6/94) was stayed by the Supreme Court. The SLPs had earlier been listed for hearing on 2 January 1996 and the counsel for the complainants (Respondents Nos. 2-9 before the Supreme Court) informed the complainants that the SLPs had been dismissed. But they were taken by shock and surprise when they received the actual copy of the order, which reads as follows:

> "The learned counsel for the respondents Nos. 2-9 state that the National Consumer Disputes Redressal Commission has dismissed the appeal filed by the petitioners against the main order of the State

Commission and that he further states that the respondents would withdraw E.P 5 and 6 filed under section 27 of the Consumer Protection Act pending before the State Commission. In view of the said statement of the learned counsel, the petitions have become infructuous. The special leave petitions are dismissed as infructuous".

It is respectfully suggested that the basic question before the Supreme Court was whether women can be sentenced to imprisonment under section 27 of the Consumer Protection Act. Now, by the dismissal of the appeals by the National Commission, the orders of the State Commission became final. Then there was no necessity to withdraw the EPs before the State Commission. Further, in the EPs, the State Commission had already passed sentences against all the partners against whom the writ petitions were filed and the present SLPs were filed against their dismissal. Hence, the Supreme Court ought to have set aside the sentence passed in the EPs, if it felt that women cannot be arrested, by the analogy of applying CPC How could complainants withdraw the EPs which were already ordered and for which warrants were issued for imprisonment? The counsel has made such a statement for the best reasons known to him and the Supreme Court ought to have appreciated the legal position of the complainants, that they could not withdraw the EPs in which sentence was already pronounced. Hence, the complainants were put in a very awkward position. When they wanted to question their counsel about his commitment made before the Supreme Court, they learnt that he had gone abroad.

The very peculiar problem for the complainants now is that if they do not move the State Commission for withdrawal of the EPs, it will amount to committing contempt of court. If they have to withdraw, must they withdraw the EPs against all the other respondents also, who did not approach the Supreme Court, or against only the three who moved the Supreme Court? More so, how can the State Commission permit the with withdrawal of EPs in which sentence was already pronounced? To seek clarification, the complainants filed review petition Nos. 409-410 before the Supreme Court in 1996, bringing to its notice all the above queries and the said review petitions were dismissed on 13 March 1996. Left without any option, the complainants filed a memo, seeking permission to withdraw the EPs before the State Commission against these three partners alone and the State Commission, on 2 April 1996, recalled the warrants and dismissed the EPs on 5/94 and 6/94, as withdrawn against the three partners who had approached the Supreme Court.

It is submitted that these three partners, whose appeals were dismissed by the National Commission, again filed SLP (Civil) Nos. 1782-1783/96, against the order of dismissal of their appeals. These SLPs were dismissed by the S.C. on 7 February 1996. Hence at this juncture, the order of the National Commission became final and for its execution M.P. Nos. 145/96 and 146/96 were filed before the National Commission. On 20 August 1996, the National Commission ordered that, as regards the execution of the order passed by the State Commission, the complainants would have to approach the State Commission. Again, the complainants filed a fresh EP (Nos. 23 and 24/96) against these three partners for payment of the deposit amounts before the State Commission. The three respondents again contended that women cannot be arrested as under Section 56 of the Code of Civil Procedure and further that, since the earlier EPs were withdrawn against them, the doctrine of *res judicata* applies. The State Commission heard this matter and reserved for orders on 6 February 1997. However, the orders were not pronounced and after a long time passed, the then Chairman of the State Commission retired and these fresh EPs were reopened on 9 September 1998 and are still pending.

On close examination of the case, it seems reasonable to submit that, when the orders of the State Commission became final, the adjudication on the EPs ought not to have been prolonged. It would be an ordeal for the complainants, who, for over a period of five years, have had to run to different authorities to seek justice for having lost their hard-earned money. The Supreme Court, at the very outset, ought to have decided on the question of whether a woman can be sentenced and arrested for imprisonment under Section 27 of the Consumer Protection Act. As it happened, this question was not decided at all and, because of the order passed in SLP Nos. 23264 and 23265/94, a multiplicity of further litigation was shot up. In fact, it is advisable now that, whenever any counsel seeks permission to withdraw any case before any court, such a court may have to ask for an affidavit being filed, sworn in by the concerned party.

The Consumer Protection Act stipulates only three months time for adjudication. In the present case, the complainant's grievance is yet to be resolved and they have been struggling for over five years. It seems clear that the respondents have the money of the complainants to use in litigation against the complainants and the complainants are spending good money against bad money. A proper appreciation of the facts and adjudication would have cleared the whole issue long ago. Today in the Andhra Pradesh High Court, several writ petitions are pending, in which the same question has been raised as to whether women can be arrested and sentenced under Section 27 of the Consumer Protection Act. It is submitted with great respect that, had the Supreme Court decided this question in the first series of SLPs Nos. 23264-65 of 1994, the entire controversy would have been closed all over the country, as the question involved is recurrent and hence very important.

Case II: In the year 1991, a Mrs. R Jayalakshmi of Hyderabad filed a claim petition before the Land Acquisition Officer, since the Government of Andhra Pradesh had acquired her land, along with that of several others. The Land Acquisition officer referred her claim to a civil court, under Sections 30 and 31 of the Land Acquisition Act, under the pretext that, as per the sale deed, the total extent was stated as 586 sq. yds., whereas as per the plan attached to the sale deed and also as per the layout, the extent was stated as 568 sq. yds.. She gave an undertaking that, since in the plan attached to the registered sale deed and also in the layout the extent was stated to be 568 sq. yds., she would restrict her claim to 568 sq. yds. But the Land Acquisition Officer neither paid her compensation nor sent her file to civil court. Then she filed a writ petition No. 8599/92, praying the High Court of Andhra Pradesh to direct the Land Acquisition Officer to pay her compensation immediately for 568 sq. yds. She also gave an undertaking to restrict her claim to 568 sq. yds., foregoing her claim on 18 sq. yds. However, the High Court passed the following order: "The Land Acquisition Officer referred the matter under Section 30 of the Land Acquisition Act to the Civil Court, as there is a disparity in the extent of the land shown in the sale deeds produced before him and according to the layout. The prayer in the WPMP 10616 of 92 in W.P. 8599/92 is to direct the payment of the compensation amount to the petitioner as per the award. Whenever the compensation amount is deposited, it is open to the petitioner to withdraw the amount. The learned counsel for the petitioner submits that the Land Acquisition Officer has not sent the records to the Civil Court after reference in Section 30 of the Land Acquisition Act. Under these circumstances the G.P. shall instruct the Land Acquisition Officer, to send the records to the Civil Court at an early date".

The claimant was aged 70 years at that time and her 85-year old husband was very sick and bedridden. The Land Acquisition Officer should have accepted her undertaking to restrict her claim to 568 sq. yds., foregoing 18 sq. yds. He was stiff for reasons best known to him. Subsequently, the High Court ought to have accepted her plea and directed the Land Acquisition Officer to pay her compensation for 568 sq. yds., instead of 586 sq. yds.. In fact, the mistake crept in only in the sale deed but the plan attached to the sale deed tallied with the layout plan, which showed 568 sq. yds.. The error was apparent on the face of the document. But the order of the High Court caused further delay, as the Land Acquisition Officer took his own time sending the file to Civil Court. Further, even though there was a direction of the High Court that the claimant could withdraw the compensation amount when it was deposited, the civil court followed a lengthy procedure and conducted a full trial as per Civil Procedure. The lady received her compensation after two years. Receiving compensation amounts from the courts is in fact a terrible experience to many persons, since a very lengthy procedure and many intricacies are involved. The High Court ought to have called for the records from the Land Acquisition Officer and ascertained the correctness of the undertaking of this poor senior citizen, so that she would restrict her claim to extent of 568 sq. yds., and on examination of the documents it could have ordered the payment by the Land Acquisition Officer. The lady could then have comfortably and immediately provided proper medical care to her ailing husband. This old couple had to wait for years to receive their compensation.

Thus, the application of equity in judicial decisions would avoid the multiplicity of litigation and also delay in reaching justice. India is now facing multi-dimensional problems. The high-tech phenomenon is ruling the government. The entry of foreign firms, the MNCs, in India has already created an impact, good as well as bad. In fact, the import of "terminator seeds" created several problems and agitations among farmers in several villages of Andhra Pradesh[7]. One of the hottest issues for discussion among lawyers is the question of whether to allow foreign law firms and their panel lawyers to prosecute several cases involving crores of rupees in Indian Courts. Thus in the 21st century, the Indian judiciary should have to play a very pragmatic role in the protection of democracy and the rights of the people, as enunciated by the Constitution of India. Any judgement rendered in haste or out of any inadvertence would prove catastrophic to the people, in the light of the fast-changing socio-economic and cultural scenario and also the in the context of the unstable political situation in India. No doubt, an innumerable number of examples can be given about the justice done by the Indian judiciary but the above two cases have been cited to depict that one would look at the other side of the coin also, so as to look forward to more effective and equitable judicial decisions. At least the Higher Courts in India, with the enormous powers they have been vested with as provided under the Indian Constitution, can do away with several lengthy procedures and formalities, be guided by equities and render judgements which would depict only justice.

The feeling of the majority of the seekers of justice is that "before they reach the ends of justice, their end should not reach them".

References

1. (a) *Municipal Council, Ratlam vs. Vardhichand, AIR 1980, SC 1622.*

   (b) *People's Union for Democratic Rights vs. Union of India, AIR (Asiad Case) 1982, SC 1473.*

   (c) *Bandhu Mukti Morcha vs. Union of India (Bonded Labour Case), AIR 1984, SC 802.*

   (d) *DS Nakra vs. Union of India (Pensioners Case), AIR 1983, SC 130.*

2. *C.D. Nos. 51/93 and 84/93.*
3. *F.A. Nos. 594/94 and 595/94.*
4. *National Commission.*
5. *W.P. Nos. 21397/94 and 21398/94.*
6. *On 13 December 1994.*
7. *News published as cover story in Andhra Jyothi, a Telugu daily paper, dated 13 December 1998.*

10

Indian Judiciary:
Role and Responsibility

*- V.P. Srivastav**

The law is an instrument for establishing justice and freedom in the community. The very end of the law is to promote liberty, to attempt to promote maximum freedom by suppressing discordant elements in the society and by promoting harmony through its organ. Since this kind of responsibility rests on the shoulders of the judiciary, the existence of a free judiciary becomes vital. Without an independent judiciary, the system may be termed 'democratic centralism', which is practically equivalent to despotism or dictatorship. In any healthy democratic state, the independence of the judiciary is sought to be maintained through certain norms in appointing judges, along with a complicated procedure for removing them from office. Furthermore, their salaries and allowances are not changeable at the whim of the executive or the legislature. Above all, a free judiciary can exist only in a political system in which democratic principles are truly believed in and acted upon by all alike: the executive, the legislature and the citizenry at large. Reciprocally, the judiciary in a democracy should have the courage to protect its independence and deliver impartial

* Ex. Addl. Public Prosecutor, NCT Delhi, Currently Copyright Information Officer, Ministry of HRD, Department of Education, Shastri Bhawan, New Delhi - 110 001.

judgments free of fear of repercussions on career and prospects.

Certainly, a balance between the three organs of democracy is to be desired; but immature bickering over respective powers should be avoided. David Selboume observes that "the judiciary is attacked in the name of the sovereignty of the parliament while sovereignty of the parliament is attacked in the name of democracy and the people; also democracy and people are being attacked in the name of national discipline and the struggle against conspiracy and subversions". To my view, the independence of the judiciary means mainly independence during the post-appointment period. The concept of the independence of the judiciary at any pre-appointment stage is primarily to appoint the best persons with integrity and a sound knowledge of laws, persons who will not succumb to pressures of any kind from any quarter. The quality of justice depends upon the independence enjoyed by the judiciary. This independence alone secures justice for all and creates confidence of the society of judges. The judges of our country have proved worthy to the privilege for decades.

The principle that judicial independence is a privilege for the protection of the people and not the judge's own applies to India and all democracies based on the rule of law. However, in order to uphold the independence of the judiciary, a meaningful unity and mutual respect must exist within itself. If fissures are developed in the judicial fraternity, it is likely to lose its independence to the liking of vested interests and to the detriment of society. Judicial principles should unite the judiciary, not its men. In the USA, judicial independence has developed into a set of institutions that ensure that judges decide according to the law, rather than according to their own whims or the will of others, including that of other branches of the government. There are five components of judicial independence: constitutional protection, independent administration of the judiciary by the judiciary, judicial disciplinary authority over the misconduct of judges, the manner in which conflicts of interest are addressed and the assurance of effective judicial decisions. Together, these components combine to assure an independent judiciary that is the basis for a society in which people and the government behave according to the law. India accepted the concept of security of tenure for judges in our constitution. However, there is no provision for judicial control over the misconduct of judges. The procedure for impeachment is very cumbersome and is ultimately not in the hands of the judiciary.

The judiciary and judicial system in a welfare state should be welfare-oriented and liberal. Justice should be dispensed without along wait or a long purse otherwise the poor masses will be deprived of it. In a welfare state judiciary need be regarded as social service and not a more department of the judicial administration.

The courts have been vested with the jurisdiction to adjudicate upon the validity of laws made by the legislature and the Constitutional and the legal validity of the acts of the executive. To ensure independence of the higher judiciary, the process of appointment of judges must have transparency. So long as the executive has a voice in the selection of judges, extraneous influence is bound to prevail in the selection. Persons of questionable antecedents, either from the bar or the subordinate judiciary, should be screened effectively by the some independent agency not amendable to political pressure. There is a fairly good system of law but we cannot vouch for invariable impartiality in its enforcement, not because of any intrinsic problem but because of political, bureaucratic or other such intrusion into its domain, to subjugate it to the needs of expediency.

In India, it is disturbing that the executive and the legislature have combined to demoralise the judiciary on the one hand and make it 'committed' on the other. The service conditions of the judiciary at the lower levels are deplorable. Imagine a situation in which the judicial officers in Bihar and Delhi are forced to stage a protest march to focus attention on their plight. What type of justice can the public expect from a judiciary that has itself failed to get justice? Moreover, the politics of supersession, transfer, demotion, extension of terms of judges on a monthly ***adhoc*** basis, non-confirmation of High Court judges etc. are disturbing trends. There are also examples where judges have been threatened publicly by ministers and legislators. Again, whenever the judiciary declares any law passed by the legislature constitutionally invalid, there has been a lot of hue and cry in parliament. For example, some of the judges of the Supreme Court were criticised when their decisions in the cases of Golak Nath (1967), Bank Nationalisation and Privy Purses (1970), Keshavanand Bharti (1973) and Minerva Mills (1980) etc. were not to the linking of the ruling party. The judges were ridiculed by the being called backward-looking and their philosophy was considered to be out of step with the times. In the Shah Bano case, the court verdict was nullified by constitutional amendment.

To my view, the subordinate judiciary constitutes on important tier of judicial administration and it is only on the strength of the officials, their ability, sincerely, honesty, diligence, wisdom and conduct that the entire edifice of the whole judicial system stands. For the majority of the seekers of justice, the subordinate courts are the first and last courts and only a negligible percentage among them go to the courts of the higher and the highest judiciary. The lower court decisions become final verdicts for most people and as such, any casual approach to the issue of cases could never mean justice rendered. If the functioning of the lower judiciary shows any let-up or slackness, the damage will be too vast. On appeal, we find enough instances of lower courts judgment being modified, set aside or of the accused person being exonerated by the higher courts. However, until the lower judiciary is insulated from the evil effects of society, it cannot be completely free from the general pattern of the behaviour of men and women, good or bad, to which it is susceptible.

Against all these odds, the Indian judiciary has served to stabilise, consolidate and protect the independence of the judiciary by giving many important verdicts. A representative verdict was in the Keshanand Bharti case, where the Supreme Court held that the Constitution has a certain basic structure which cannot be amended. This concept of 'basic structure' limited the amending power of parliament. Again, in the Minerva Mills case, by striking down clauses 4 and 5 of Article 368, the Constitutional Bench of the Supreme Court has rightly restored the doctrine of judicial review, which the 42nd constitutional Amendment Act, 1976 had very substantially curtailed. More recently, we have had striking verdicts on the anti-defection acts.

It cannot be denied that ours is a welfare state, with social justice as the main line of the Constitution. In the welfare state, the law does not permit the government to deprive the citizens of constitutional rights. The state has to guard the rights of its individuals irrespective of their caste, creed, sex and religion. But in practice, people without resources are defenseless and arrangements of revision and appeal are beyond their means. The only way available to them for striking back against injustice is to resort to violence or to become recidivist irrespective of the fact, whether they are outside or inside of the stone walls of the prison. Further, it is said that equality of justice in our country should never depend upon the defendant's wealth or lack of resources. But we must admit that we have failed to achieve such ideals. The economic, social and political status of a person permeates the judicial process.

The law is more than an aggregate of rules. No doubt, the law must govern life; but neither life nor the law falls neatly into slots. When a court starts laying down rules enumerated (1.) (2) (3) & (4) or (a) (b) (c) & (d), it is arranging traps and pitfalls. Categories, classifications and compartments, which the statute does not mention, all tend to make the law "less flexible, less sensible and less just" (Ayodhya Dube and others vs. Ram Sumer Singh, AIR 1981, SC 1415).

Above all, the judiciary and the judicial system in a welfare state must be welfare-oriented and liberal. Justice should be dispensed without a long wait or a long purse, otherwise the poor masses will be deprived of it. Today, the judiciary need be regarded as a social service and not a mere department or constituent body of the Constitution.

By tradition, the legal scope and purpose of the law had been limited to the extent the law itself imposes. But this limited purpose of the law has undergone a violent change under judicial review in recent times. One strange aspect of judicial review is that it is never based on any doctrine with specific scope and philosophy. Apparently, judicial review sets itself no limits. It punishes officials for lapses, admonishes the bureaucracy as a class, pulls up other organs of the Constitution and checks and regulates admission to professional colleges. It issues orders on pollution control matters, issues decrees on investigation and enquiry on crimes and custodial deaths; in short, in almost all matters connected with law and order, the law enquires into temple administration protects against human rights violation and adjudicates almost on all matters of legal disputes. Judicial review seems to be a growing power of the judiciary, with the danger of being in excess. The judicial reviews so far pronounced, however, are quite judicious and necessitated by the facts of the disputes and the compulsion of the circumstances.

The concept of legality is based on the concept of enforceability. This task has not been assigned to the judiciary. The legislature controls the purse and lays down laws and the executive holds the sword. It is for the judiciary to decide that these two wings function according to the Constitution. The judiciary alone has the capacity and mandate to adjudicate on the validity of laws and executive actions. There are fears in some quarters that the judiciary is overstepping its authority that it is trespassing into spheres reserved for parliament and the executive. Policy-making and administration or carrying on the business of government is the executive's job; to legislate (or change the law) is the prerogative of the legislature, after due debate and discussion of public interest involved. In the present wave of judicial activism prompted by public interest suits, ranging from cases such as that of out-of-turn allotment of government houses without proper reason, discretionary allotment of petrol pumps and LPG connections to those having influence with highly placed bureaucrats/politicians, the fraud involving animal husbandry seen in Bihar and, of course, the famous 'hawala cases', the Supreme Court had given firm decision. True, in some cases the court has assumed the role of issuing directions (telling the CBI to investigate thoroughly and not close any case without the Court's order), a job of the executive. It may also be pointed out that, as the law stands regarding the CBI, there is a provision in the law that the agency should report to a court and not to the minister concerned. The CBI is also under law not empowered to investigate cases in a state without the state government's permission. The law, as it stands, may be productive of abuse but changing that law is the business of the legislature not the courts. So here the judiciary is actually legislating!

The authenticity of the law courts depends upon public confidence. The interests of society demand that judges should do nothing to shake this confidence. In spite of the fact that the judiciary is not elected by the people, the functions assigned to it are vital to the sustenance of the rule of law and democracy. Lawyers and judges are meant to serve litigants. It is their duty to do nothing that may hamper the litigant's access to courts of justice. The judiciary has a duty to decide matters between man and man and man and the state. It enjoys the security of tenure, the conduct of judges is immune from discussion in the legislature. It is therefore incumbent upon judges that they should be true to their oath of office and the high traditions that are well-established in our country. Their independence, impartiality and integrity enables them to administer justice without fear or favour. Judges who seek publicity not only erode the credibility of the judiciary but they also themselves become controversial at a certain point of time. They have to function within the framework of the Constitution and the laws while interpreting the Constitution. Judges do inject philosophies to expand the meaning of law. This power should not be issued to propound philosophies against the Constitution and the laws.

Viewed from different angles, an efficient and impartial judiciary seems to be the only ray of hope to save democratic norms from peril and maintain the rule of law, safeguarding the rights and liberties of the common man. Justice must reach the doors of the common man without being too costly. This responsibility is the first priority of the judiciary.

11
Judicial Positivism

- *Justice R.M. Sahai**

Recently, the style of judicial functioning, which has been more liberal and forward looking to problems of public law as compared to the past, has come up for comment and criticism. This criticism has not come from the people, who have and always had unflinching faith in the judicial system and admiration and respect for judges for the responsible role they have played in shaping society and giving it much needed direction. Criticism has come from some jurists, a few academicians, interested media and now politicians, by labeling it judicial activism. If one feels that the court should refrain from interfering with political wisdom and public policy, the other advises the court to proceed cautiously. Is this justified? They ask whether the courts, particularly the higher judiciary, that is the apex court and the high courts, have deviated from their primary duty of operating as a court of law. If they have, then is this deviation substantial or marginal, and why and how has it happened? Did the courts resort to it for societal development and growth or was it judicial extravaganza and the assertion of power under the veil of judicial activism? Or it has succeeded in energizing various organs of the government and awakening the conscience of the people. Is the exponential thrust in public

* Former Judge, Supreme Court of India, 28-A, Hashimpur Road, Allahabad, U.P.

law jurisprudence unwarranted and unjustified and have the courts crossed the forbidden line?

Judicial activism appears to be a fashionable expression, an expression that has also captured our imagination. The literature on this issue is overflowing. Debate galore is being carried on in every part of the country. So much so, that even the judiciary has come up in defence of it. Former Chief Justice of India, Mr. Justice Ahmadi, while delivering the Zakir Hussain memorial lecture, said, "the phenomenon of judicial activism in its aggressive role will have to be temporary one." The words sound like a political apology. But the propagandists of judicial activism ignore the fact that our courts are, and have always been, traditional in approach and conservative in outlook. This has undergone change in the judicial techniques, to cope with modern challenges posed by the transformation in social and political structure. Mr. Justice J.S. Verma, while inaugurating the P.K. Goswami memorial lectures, was pragmatic and realistic when he said that the expansion of the sphere of judicial review is another reason for the increase in the importance of the role of the judiciary. This is in addition to the significant role of the judiciary in the constitutional scheme of the separation of powers. Various factors have resulted in the increasing role of the judiciary: growing awareness of the rights of people; the concept of public interest litigation; the trend of judicial scrutiny of every significant government action; the readiness of the Executive to seek judicial determination of debatable and controversial issues.

Even the English judges who "grew to love their constitutional chains" did not remain immune in the latter half of the nineteenth century, which witnessed a welcome departure from the letter of law to purposive interpretation. What was considered to be "constitutional heresy" by the House of Lords became "obvious common sense" in 1952. The entire concept of natural justice and fairness was revolutionized, extending it to public authorities and even to private bodies if they exercised public power. The theory of unfettered administrative discretion, of which Lord Simon was the greatest exponent of his time, was replaced by the welfare of the people and fairness in approach by Lord Denning. His impact on the English judicial system was massive. The conventional wisdom was that it was undemocratic for the non-elected judiciary to act as law-makers, a view that emanated from "austere judicial literalism." But this has given way to courageous judicial law-making, breathing new life into English administrative law, reviving and extending the ancient principles of natural justice and fairness. Decisions such as that of Liversedge were castigated as an abdication of judicial responsibility. This progress in administrative law and the power of law-making has been hailed as the greatest achievement of the English courts. Even in America, there have been Supreme Court decisions on racial relations, legislative reapportionment and administration of criminal and civil law. Taken together, they add up at least to a strong suggestion, if not a command, by the judiciary to political branches of the government, regarding how they must behave in certain instances.

The judiciary of all institutions is soaked in traditionalism and slow to react. This is prominently reflected in the apex courts judgment rendered in earlier decades. Despite the breeze of liberalism in England and America, our courts remained, largely, conventional. But for a sprinkling here and there, and that too in freedom of speech and expression and property rights, the court refrained from making fresh inroad into law-making. The conservatism of the apex court was prominent, whether it was legislative competence or preventive detention or discrimination, legislative or Executive. Gopalan argues that the very first constitutional decision upheld absolute sovereignty of Legislature and forbade the courts from declaring an act as "void because in their opinion it is opposed to the spirit supposed to pervade the constitution". The majority further explained that "the procedure established by law meant the procedure established by the law of the state." In Sankari Prasad it was held that the word 'law' in Article 13 sub clause (2) of the constitution did not include constitutional amendments. In Hamdard Dawakhana, the court upheld that freedom of speech included constitutional guarantee of issuing advertisements but if the advertisement was commercial in nature then it was beyond the fundamental right of speech and expression. Article 14 was confined to classification and class legislation. Charanjeet Lal and RK Dalmia were concerned with action against one individual and with an inquiry against a single group of companies, yet it was upheld and the onus to assail the presumption of constitutionality was held to be on the person challenging it. Today, the judiciary has come a long way. Nothing appears to be beyond it. Not only are the spheres of the constitutional and the legal being reviewed, but also the social, economic, political, administrative, ecological, environmental and religious. Reason for this can be related to gradual changes in the social structure, resulting in a subtle march from the conventional approach, "thou shalt not," to "it must be done." This shift in approach is erroneously assumed as the assertion of authority or power. On the contrary, it is the call of duty, constitutional responsibility and obligation towards the society and people of the country. When the Constitution was framed, the members of the Constituent Assembly brought to the framing of the judicial provisions of the constitution idealism equaled only by that shown towards fundamental rights. Indeed, the judiciary was seen as an extension of rights, for it was the courts that would give force to rights. The judiciary was to be an arm of the social revolution. The judiciary was visualized, in the parliamentary government, as being wedded to the rule of law, to act as a living moral and intellectual force, protecting not only the individual against the legislative but also the social structure itself. It was entrusted with the dual responsibility of maintaining "the delicate balance" and promoting a welfare society by a people-oriented approach to socio-economic measures. For either the tool was and in judicial review founded on rule of law which is the proud heritage of National Indian Culture and Traditions. Manu said, "Law in fact, is the sovereign and leader and regulator of the society. The whole race of mankind is kept in order by law." Gettel in his book history of Political thoughts has summoned up thus. Hindu theory thus upholds a limited rather than an absolute monarchy, and a system of checks and balances was favoured. Many Hindu writers upheld democratic institutions, popular assemblies, communistic undertaking and personal liberty. The ideal of human brotherhood and personal equality was frequently expressed. Dr. Radhakrishnan one of the greatest philosophers and scholars, while speaking on the objective resolution in the constituent assembly on 13th December 1946, said, "We have held that the ultimate sovereignty rests with the moral law, with the conscience of humanity. People as well as kings are subordinate to that Dharma, righteousness is the king of kings." **"Dharmah, kshatrasya, kshatram"**. It is the ruler of both the people and the rulers themselves. It is sovereignty of law that we have asserted.

Therefore, the courts were required to function under the law for the betterment of society. Our Constitution is, foremost, "a social document." The preamble, the chapter on Fundamental Rights and Directive Principles, Right to Equality and Liberty, provisions for Religions Freedom, Protection of Minorities etc. are all directed, directly or indirectly, to promote the welfare of the common man, revolutionizing the entire social structure. In an enlightened democracy, the Legislature is obliged to undertake socio-economic measures, the Executive to implement it honestly and sincerely, and the judiciary to construe and interpret it liberally, so as to promote the constitutional goal of prosperity and happiness of the masses. Therefore, the role of judiciary was to be socially positivist. Numerous decisions on labour laws, land legislations, ceiling acts, rent control provisions, service matters in the earlier decades, eloquently pronounce the judicial anxiety of the common man. Even the striking down of enactments, for lack of legislative competence or for being discriminatory, did not escape severe comment. The echo was heard even in Parliament and the judiciary was criticised for being archaic in approach. When our Republic was constituted, it was an experience in heterogeneous democracy, multi-ethnic and multi-religious in character. Economic poverty, illiteracy and inequality were staring. The picture was frightening. Yet in the earlier decades, the country marched ahead, due to high standards of political statesmanship. The Nehru era, the golden period of our parliamentary democracy, was remarkable for respect and regard for the judicial decisions, irrespective of whether they were against the government's interest. The post-Nehru era was remarkable for slogans, and for attractive catchwords exploiting the emotions of the poor and downtrodden. Various legislations of far reaching consequences were enacted, avowedly to promote the welfare of society but succeeding in benefiting the few and the rich. The more dangerous trend, however, was the emergence of the political-bureaucratic nexus, a joint venture to squeeze the common man. The elected representatives did not keep the confidence of the people. The legislative activity and the constitutional amendments were not for the benefit of the society. The common man was bewildered by the growing apathy. He felt helpless. The danger to the society was more than apparent. With the passage of time, the neo-rich class surfaced, a class with no ostensible source of income. The monster of corruption raised its head. Work culture was on the wane and indiscipline was growing. The older generations of politicians was vanishing or receding. A new generation of executive, more conscious of power than duty, was emerging.

Yet it was not before 1975 that the courts, in the wake of the emergency and sensitized by the perpetration of large scale atrocities, awakened to its constitutional obligations to human rights jurisprudence. The courts did not sit idle when dereliction of constitutional duties and gross violations of human rights were brought before it by interested individuals and organizations. The public law jurisprudence necessitated a dynamic approach. This was possible as, in the meantime, a new breed of judges had been inducted, who had been indoctrinated in welfare jurisprudence, trained and tuned for a fresh look at constitutional problems. The people, therefore, through public interest litigation, approached the courts for redress. It was this constitutional conscientiousness which persuaded the court to develop the theory of the basic structure of the constitution in Keshwa Nand Bharati. Otherwise the constitution would have been defaced beyond recognition. If the 50's and early 60's were known for a more expansive approach to Article 19 and 31 of the constitution, the beginning of the 70's ushered in an era of liberalism and justice for the common man. The Supreme Court of India was becoming, after 32 years of the Republic, the Supreme Court for Indians. For too long, the apex court had become an arena of legal quibbling for men with long purses. Now increasingly, the court was being identified by justices as well as the people as the last resort for the oppressed and the bewildered. The transition from a traditional captive agency with a low social visibility into a liberated agency with a high socio-political visibility is a remarkable development in the career of the Indian appellate judiciary. The liberal judges expanded the horizon of Article 14 and extended the concept of arbitrariness to be included in it. Royappa, Menaka Gandhi, Ramanna and Ajay Hasia, all strengthened the hands of the courts to do justice and relieve the common man of executive agony. Krapiak obliterated the decades-old controversy about quasi-judicial and administrative functions. All this led to a judicial renaissance. The judiciary had come of age, willing to take up the social revolution to the masses. Even though emergency was short-lived, it generated all kinds of evils and brought in its wake the criminalisation of politics. The politico-criminal nexus, beginning in 1976, blossomed in later 80's and has now become a social order. Corruption, which was in its infancy in the Nehruvian era, has spread like cancer and has overtaken every organ of society. In public life, it has become the order of the day. This is not a new phenomenon; but earlier, the corrupt indulged in it surreptitiously. Now there is no sense of shame or fear of social censure. From individual trade, it has become institutionalized business. The effect of institutionalized corruption results in the protection of each other, by keeping secrets guarded. The result is disillusionment and dismay all around. Thanks to investigative journalism and an interested approach by a few individuals and social organisations, willing to remove the lid and expose the corrupt, some headway has been made. That is why the court dockets, whether in the high courts or the apex courts, are overflowing. The judges, who are drawn from society, could not remain oblivious. They could not remain immune to the social and economic changes in the country. The decade beginning from 1990 saw the courts in a new role. Its interpretations of Article 122, Article 356 and Article 142 of the constitution in the judges case, SR Bombai and Nadiad case has profoundly altered the vision of the court's duty and performance. Even the claim of hospital to establish a clinic in a place reserved for a public park was not accepted in the Bangalore Medical Trust case. The recognition of primary education as a fundamental right, noted in the Unnikrishnan case, is a milestone. The judgment in the Mandal case has given a refreshing look to the directive principles of the constitution. The law of accountability of public servant is highlighted in MK Gupta. Furthermore, the responsibility of the government for compensation to the wrong done to the common man in numerous decisions has infused new life in an otherwise despondent society. The recent judgements on the environment and the penalties imposed on those who were responsible or remiss in their duty, or on those who deliberately bent the rules, has restored the confidence of the common man in the judicial system. If the court of 1980 expanded the judicial horizon and ushered in the judicial renaissance, then it was the court of 1990 which enhanced the majesty of the law by extending its arm to the mightiest, establishing the supremacy of the law by reasserting that no one was above it. Prior to the

Emergency, the judiciary was an interpreter of law; after the Emergency it became a forum for redressal for the common man; and since 1990, it has assumed the role of enlightened law making. The judicial graph on the national canvass has thus been moving up, as a consequence of the social and political atmosphere prevailing in the country. It is not an activist movement but the result of the social and political atmosphere prevailing in the country. It is also the outcome of the compulsion to meet the new challenges thrown up by society. It is this positive approach to day-to-day problems that has come up for criticism. Such criticism is primarily due to lack of knowledge. The reasons why there is no system of judicial review in England is because they have no written constitution or fundamental rights; in addition, they have the advantage of highly educated and developed public opinion. Our constitution is federal and derives inspiration from America, where judicial review is the essence of the constitution. Judicial review is not judicial supremacy but judicial nationalism, to bring about all round progress of the country. No constitution in the world has a provision similar to Article 141 and 142 of the Indian constitution. Our founding fathers, who drafted the constitution after thoroughly studying the constitution of advanced countries, were apprehensive of our political setup and social backwardness. Therefore, they thought it proper to empower the superior courts not only to interpret the law but also to legislate, if necessary, to ensure that the country's progress was not impeded. Judicial review is not a usurpation of power but a part of the grand design, to ensure the supremacy of the constitution. Our courts are not political because the courts are entrusted with responsibility of examining all issues social, economic or political.

Thus the bold judicial thrust has emanated from the social, political and economic climate prevailing in the country. Such judicial development is not uncommon. It has taken place in every society. In the United States, the Warren court, as an instrument of reform vigorously used the constitutional adjudication. Yet no one thought of amending the constitution. Therefore in the present prevailing social circumstances, free movement of the judiciary in wider orbits, for sake of rule of law, is healthy for society.

12

Defective Judgements?

A Question Mark on the Face of the Judiciary

*- B. Ratnakara Rao**

JUDGEMENT : 1. The decision of a Judge, Opinion.
2. Sentence of Court of Justice.[1]
3. The determination by a Court of Competent Jurisdiction of a Controversy between two or more persons, which is brought before the Court by proper procedure.[2]

DEFECTIVE : 1. Faulty, not complete.
2. Having defect(s), incomplete, faulty, wanting or deficient (in some respect), (Gram.) not having all the usual inflexions.[3]

In the Consumer Protection Act, 1986 (Act No. 68 of 1986) Chapter I, II & IV of which are made to commence with effect from 15th April, 1987 and Chapter III of the Act with effect from 1st July, 1987.[4] Indian Legislature elaborately dealt with the word "defect", "deficiency" and the word "service".

S.2(f) of the Consumer Protection Act defines "defect" to mean any fault, imperfection or shortcoming in the quality,

* Director/Founder, Chambers of Protection of Rights, First Street, No. 10-39-10/B, Janathapet North, Kavali - 524 201, Nellore Distt. A.P.

quantity, potency, purity or standard which is required to be maintained by or under any law for the time being in force, or as is claimed by the traders in any manner whatsoever in relation to any goods.[5]

S.2(g) of the Consumer Protection Act defines "deficiency" to mean any fault, imperfection, shortcoming or inadequacy in the quality, nature and manner of performance which is required to be maintained by or under any law for the time being in force or has been undertaken to be performed by a person in pursuance of a contract or otherwise in relation to any service.[6]

S.2(o) of the Consumer Protection Act defines "service" to mean service of any description which is made available to potential users and includes the provision of facilities in connection with banking, financing, insurance, transport, processing, supply of electrical or other energy, board or lodging or both, entertainment, amusement or the purveying of news or other information, but does not include the rendering of any service free of charge or under a contract of personal service.[7]

The High Court is an institution constituted by the Indian citizenaire through their constitution, popularly known as "The Constitution of India", thrusting on it the pious obligation and stringent duty of rendering services to Indian society by receiving plaints, writs, writ appeals, complaints, original petitions, etc. and to process them, and to call upon the defendants, respondents, accused etc. to appear before it and state their own case or their defence against the case registered by it against them; and after bearing the arguments on both sides, to read and study every bit of paper filed before it and to go through each and every line on paper and the arguments advanced by the parties to litigation before it and to prepare and deliver an order or judgment in accordance with the law laid down by the Parliament or the State Assembly of the concerned state, as the case may be, and to apply the principles laid down by the Supreme Court of India on the subject matter of dispute, and to deliver the same to the parties of the dispute. The High Court is not entitled to, and is not constituted by, the citizen of India through their constitution to deliver judgments, impregnant with any fault, imperfection or shortcoming in the quality, quantity, potency, purity or standard which is required to be maintained by or under any law for the time being in force, in relation to any judgment delivered by it. Any judgment delivered by the High Court, if it is impregnant by means of any fault, imperfection, short-coming or inadequacy in the quality, nature and manner of performance, which is required to be maintained by or under any law for the time being in force, is called "delivering defective judgement".[8]

As already submitted above, even to recognise the certified copy delivered by the High Court for which it has already charged word-rate, again-avariciously demands to pay fee, i.e. to purchase "COURT" Labels and affix on them.

Thus the High Court not only charges for delivering the words of services, but also charges to recognise the words of its own service by itself.

Thus, therefore, the High Court does not fall within the frame of words "But does not include the rendering of any service free of charge" occurring under Chapter-I Section 2(o) of the Act 68/1986.

The High Court, therefore, conveniently comes within the purview of the Consumer Protection Act (Act 68/96) and the jurisdiction of the District Forum, since the High Court is working for gain and claim against the High Court before a District Forum under the Consumer Protection Act sustains, under the law of the land.[9]

"The purveying of news or other informations" and "but does not include the rendering of any service free of charge"[10] occuring in Sec.2(o) of Act 68/86 is the JUICE.

Services by Public Bodies

"Standard of living does not merely signify being successful in keeping the body and the soul together or being able to consume newer and newer products and services but also being able to consume with a difference, in terms of accepted (implying decent) values of life. Since the public sector owns the bulk of the service sector, it has the immediate and ultimate responsibility to provide a good quality of life in relation to services. There is an urgency to provide this quality of life to the Indian people for two important reasons. Firstly, when the people are paying (as they are made to pay) tax on income, on wealth, on purchases and sales, paying high and ever-increasing prices for almost all commodities and services for both households and industry, and are bearing the brunt of shortages and forced sacrifices, they have every right to expect the normal standard of delivery of services that are so basic. After all, there is a limit to one's patience after 40 years of independence. The present generation has a full right to a good quality of life, and the public sector has an obligation to provide it. It is time that India should entitle herself to be counted among the developed countries of the world.

Secondly, the quality of life is indispensable in order to cope with fast changing values and life styles, such that, according to Toffler, push society forward towards a historical crisis of adaptation, to create an environment so ephemeral, unfamiliar and complex as to threaten millions with adaptive breakdown (Toffler, Alvia, "The Future Shock", Random House, 1970).[11]

Judicium non debit hssh illusorium; suum effecti, jabere debet - A judgement ought not be illusory; it ought to have its consequence.

Judex est lex locunes - A Judge is the law speaking.

Justitea non est neganda, non differenda - Justice is neither to be denied nor postponed.[12]

Some of the civil and criminal matters falling under the "Defective Judgements" are quoted. Judgements falling under the head "Defective Judgments" are not closed. They are ever increasing. As the judgments are delivered round the clock, so are defective judgements.

Defective Judgements:

1. Judgements delivered before the case has been heard. [See S.33 of C.P.C. (P.471), AIR Manual (4th Edition)]
2. Judgement not supported by cogent reasons. [See AIR 1969, Supreme Court 1167 (1169, 1170)]
3. Judgement in a case pronounced without hearing the case fully.
   [See (1907) 4 Low Bur rul 256 (258) (DB).
   (1875) 23 Suth WR 77 (77) IB]
4. Judgement delivered without giving the parties an opportunity of putting their case before him.
   [See AIR 1964, ORISSA 185 (186)
   AIR 1959, A.P. 212 (214) (D.B.)
   AIR 1920, LAHORE 246 (247)]
5. Judgement containing a direction that the preparation of the decree be stopped until the payment of deficit court fees or until the disposal of the application by the judgement-debtor for scaling down the debt.
   [See AIR 1957, PUNJAB 65 (68)
   AIR 1932, PATNA 228(231) (IB)]
6. Judgement delivered not noticing the provisions of S.66-C of the Wakf Act.
   (See AIR 1985, ANDHRA PRADESH 127 (129)
   AIR 1985 ANDHRA PRADESH 127 (135)]
7. Judgement pronounced by Court not in accordance with the S.353 Cr. P.C.
   (See AIR 1942, LAHORE 100(101)
   AIR 1960, MAD 507 etc.
   AIR 1963, RAJASTHAN 104 (105)
   1963 (1) Cri LJ 615
   1974 SC 1880 (1881) 43 Crl LJ 619
   1974 CriLJ 1291

8. Judgement (Single Judgement) delivered disposing separate appeals arising out of separate trials.
   [See ILR (1972) 2 ALL 309 (Overruled on another point in 1977 Cri LJ 2000]
9. Judgement of the Appellate Court
   a) failed to avert to the fact that the trial court, in convicting the appellants, overlooked the inordinate and unexplained delay in dispatching the First Information Report to the Magistrate, and/or
   b) failed to avert to the fact that the trial court, in convicting the appellants overlooked the differences in the account given by the prosecution witnesses among one another, and/or
   c) failed to avert to the fact that the trial court, in convicting the appellants, overlooked the differences in the account given by the prosecution witness/witnesses and as appearing from the first information of the occurrence, and/or
   d) failed to avert to the fact that the trial court, in convicting the appellants, overlooked the absence of any statement in the First Information Report as to the injuries received by some of the accused, and/or
   e) failed to avert to the fact that the trial court, in convicting the appellants, overlooked the non-examination of material witnesses.

   Note: Appellate Court includes the High Court.

   [See AIR 1976 SUPREME COURT 2423 (2428)

   1976 Cri LJ 1888]
10. Judgement pronounced by a judge or magistrate that has not held the trial.

   (See 1889 AN 181 (184

   AIR 1948, ALL 339 (340) (341)

   49 Cri LJ 457

11. Judgement pronounced by a magistrate who has gone on leave in a trial held by him.

    [See AIR (1981) 3 ALL (565) (FB)

    AIR 1932, ALL SRI 582 (582)

    34 Cri LJ 112 AIR 1924, CALCUTTA 192 (193)]

12. Judgement pronounced by a magistrate who has been transferred to another district and has handed over charges.

    [See AIR (1881) 3 ALL 563(565) (FB)

    AIR 1932, ALL 582 (582)

    54 Cri LJ 112

    AIR 1924, CALCUTTA 192 (193)]

13. Judgement is prepared and delivered by the presiding officer in the absence of the other members of the bench, where the court consisted of a bench of magistrates.

    [See AIR 1954, MADRAS 1172 (1173)

    29 Cri LJ 973]

14. Judgement delivered by a judge of a High Court Bench consisting of two judges, in a criminal appeal that was purported to write a joint judegment, which was prepared, signed and sent to him by the other judge, who died before the judegment was delivered.

    [See AIR 1954, Supreme Court 194 (196, 197)

    1954 Cri LJ 475]

15. Judgement pronounced, but was not signed.

    [See 1978 ALL Cri R 287 (288)

    1971 ALL Cri R 578 (579)]

16. Judgement pronounced after the closing of the case with a delay in between the closing of the case and pronouncement.

    [See 1961 BLJR 282 (283) (Pat):

    (1892) 5 CPLR Cr 24 (24)]

"It is open to anyone to express fair, reasonable and legitimate criticism to any act or conduct of a judge in his judicial capacity, or even to make a proper and fair comment on any decision given by him, because justice is not a cloistered virtue and he must be allowed to suffer the scrutiny and respectable, even though out-spoken, comments of ordinary man.[13]

"Lawyers and litigants every day express opinions about the validity of orders passed by courts. Such an expression of opinion could not become contempt of court because the Superintendent of Police had expressed such an opinion."[14]

"The object is to maintain public confidence in the fairness and impartiality of the court. Vindication of prestige is not the object. The discretionary power is not available as a cloak for judicial authorities to cover up their inefficiency and corruption, or to stifle criticism made in good faith against such officers.[15]

"One has right to express fair criticism of act or conduct of a judge in his judicial capacity.[16]

"The Supreme Court, by its decision, never shuts the mouth of any counsel, and the counsel is always entitled to make a comment on the judgment of the Supreme Court, if he does not agree in principle with the decision.[17]

"Areopagition", namely, the freedom of press and religious liberty was published on 23rd November, 1644 to protest the licencing order of Parliament issued on 16th June, 1643.[18]

"Milton's homily is built upon the one-fold argument clearly stated in the proposition and developed in the course of the pamphlet with the aid of efforts of reasoning. Milton asks the Parliament to consider, first, that the inventors of licencing are those whom the Parliaments should not be willing to own. Secondly, he says that the order does not specify the criteria for calling a book before supposing it. Thirdly, he says that in effect, the order becomes a severe discouragement of all learning and the suppression of truth.

According to him, censorship is a development of the papacy and has been used by the church to the design of ownership. It is not only to deny freedom of the press but also to deny freedom of the pursuit of truth. Milton's freedom is the freedom of the pursuit of truth. Milton's definition of the good book has become the most popular quotation on it. According to him, many people live as burden to the earth, but a good book is "the precious life-blood of a master spirit embalmed and treasured upon a purpose to a life beyond life". Milton then turns to his second argument that all books, good as well as bad, serve the cause of truth. Bad books may serve, in many respects, to discover, to confute, to forewarn, and to illustrate. He further argues that lack of knowledge of and warble of bad will make a person incapable of fighting against evil.[19]

"A probe into the complicity and the unconstitutionality of the Art. 124(4) of the Constitution of India would prove to the entire satisfaction of the reader of the Article that the Barristers-at-Law who have drafted the Constitution have taken the convenience of their closeness to the drafting and passing resolutions in the Constituent Assembly to safe-guard the future of their community.

Art. 124(4) of the Constitution of India

reads thus:

> "(4) A judge of the Supreme Court shall not be removed from office except by an order of the President passed after an address by each House of Parliament supported by a majority of not less than two-thirds of the membership of that House present and voting has been presented to the President in the same session for such removal on the ground of proved misbehaviour or incapacity.

Those Barristers-at-Law, their minds influenced by politicianism and communalism, have drafted and resolved Art. 124(4) of the Constitution of India in satisfying their egos and their communalism and in safeguarding their own and professional descendants as could be found hereunder.

Therefore, a judge of either a High Court or the Supreme Court, though impregnant of proved misbehaviour and/or incapacity, can continue to be in the office.

In addition to the above, a judge of either a High Court or the Supreme Court, though impregnant of proved misbehaviour and/or incapacity, can continue to be in office since no discussion shall take place in Parliament with respect to the conduct of any judge of the Supreme Court or of a High Court in the discharge of his duties, except upon a motion for presenting an address to the President praying for the removal of the Judge under Art. 121 of Constitution of India.[20]

Article 121: Restriction on discussion in Parliament: No discussion shall take place in Parliament with respect to the conduct of any Judge of the Supreme Court or a High Court in the discharge of his duties except upon a motion for presenting on address to the President praying for the removal of the Judge as hereinafter provided.[21]

"Further, it is surprising to note that the Constitution which said under Art. 121 that no discussion shall take place in Parliament with respect to the conduct of any Judge of the Supreme Court or a High Court in the discharge of his duties except upon a motion for presenting an address to the President praying for the removal of the Judge has failed to prescribe and remained silent although as "how and the manner in which the misbehaviour or incapacity provided" to form a "ground for removal" to be placed for "voting". This is a gap and lacuna prominently appearing on the face of the Constitution of India.[22]

"1. Non-liability to suit of Officers acting Judicially for official acts done in good faith and of Officers executing Warrants and orders:

> No Judge, Magistrate, Justice of the Peace, Collector or other person acting Judicially shall be liable to be used in any Civil Court for any act done or ordered to be done by him in the discharge of his Judicial duty,

> whether or not within the limits of his jurisdiction; provided that he at the time, in good faith, believed himself to have jurisdiction to do or order the act complained of; and no officer of any Court or other person, bound to execute the lawful warrants or orders of any such Judge, Magistrate, Justice of Peace, Collector or other person acting Judicially, shall be liable to be sued in any civil Court, for the execution of any warrant or order, which he would be bound to execute if within the jurisdiction of the person issuing the same.[23]

Now, a question mark on the face of the judiciary is "Why should a citizen subjected to the misconduct and incapacity of a judge be moulted with the exertions and expansion for complying with the necessary formalities prescribed under the Supreme Court Rules?"

Who is to serve and save the common citizen of India?

"My Lords, Parliament makes the Law, the executives carry the law into effect and the judiciary enforces the law. The expression, 'the Crown', has two meanings; namely, the monarch and the executive. In the 17th century, parliament established its supremacy over the crown as monarch, over the executive and over the judiciary. Parliamentary supremacy over the crown as monarch stems from the fact that the monarch must accept the advice of a Prime Minister who is supported by a majority of parliament., Parliamentary supremacy over the judiciary is only exercisable by statute."[24] (Lord Templeman).

A Bachelor of Arts in English Literature, Kumari B Prasanthi, my young and enthusiastic personal secretary, who also helps in comparing, said the Book *Errors of Magistrates* is a compilation of a self-asserted statements of the Magistrate that have committed errors and that was even prior to Shakespeare's century.

The Constitution of India is the basic law for the governance of our country and, according to Dr. Babasaheb, is a mechanism for the purpose of working various organs of the State. It defines the various organs of the State, specifies their respective functions and demarcates the fields of their operations. "It is a vehicle of a nation's progress, reflecting the best in the past traditions of the country, to cope up with and respond to the needs of the present and possess enough resilience to the needs of the future. At the same time, it must be a living organ, not for one or two generations, but for succeeding generations to come"[25]

"The writers have conveniently drafted the Constitution of India to satisfy their ego and their communities. As everyone knows, the freedom struggle was lead by Barristers-at-Law and the inherent desire of any Barrister-at-Law is to retire safe as the Supreme Judge of his country."[26]

Consider the fact of the convenience of their closeness to the drafting and passing of resolutions in the Constituent Assembly. To safeguard the future if their community, they failed to prescribe and remained silent although "how and the manner in which the misbehaviour or incapacity proved" to form a "ground for removal" to be placed for "voting" to take place in parliament, with respect to the conduct of any judge of the supreme court or a high court in the discharge of his duties, and have brought into force Art. 121, restricting even the parliament and enforced Art. 124(4), drafting it with such complicity that amounts and equal to "unconstitutional". They have not repealed Act XVIII/1850.

As seen above, erred judges are above the Lok Ayukta, Sub Lok Ayukta, the Bar Council of India and the Law Commission of India. Parliament is restrained,. And as far as impeachment is concerned, we know the fact of impeachment proceedings in India as is evident from the affair of Justice V Ramaswamy.

Then Writher The Sufferer Go?

"Moreover, the judicial process must also remain unpolluted by personal pride or an erroneous sense of dignity. As it is very rightly said, the best guarantee of justice is the personality of the judge. It is the judge who must bring honour to the seat of justice rather than claim that the seat of justice must honour him. Trust and confidence of the bar and the people must constitute his greatest asset. It is good to remember that respect and dignity are better commanded rather than demanded; and the road to dignity is humility. Though it is not possible for everyone to become a great judge, there should be no difficulty in every judge trying his best to be a good judge. Greatness may not be destined for all but goodness certainly is within the reach of all on the bench. There is no reason why one should not, indeed as a matter of duty, try to be a good judge.[27]

The Writ Petitioner in W.P. No. 8885/81 on the file of the High Court of Andhra Pradesh affirmed that the failure and compliance to take cognizance of the offences committed by the judges by ordering an elaborate enquiry on the part of the Indian judiciary is an absolute an unrebutted admission that the conduct and character exhibited proves beyond all reasonable doubt that the Supreme Court of India is executed by and controlled by culprit judges for the sake and safety of the culprit judges and thus is anti-national in all respects.

The Writ Appellant in W.A. No. 1318/87 on the file of the High Court of Andhra Pradesh confirmed that the failure and compliance to take cognizance of the offences committed by the judges by ordering an elaborate enquiry on the part of the Indian judiciary is an absolute and unrebutted admission that the conduct and character exhibited by the Supreme Court of India in living on order X Rule 6 (I) of the Supreme Court Rules and not ordering the institution of elaborate enquiry into the offences committed by the judges immediately on receipt of the complaint against the judges amounts to polluting the judiciary and the due course of justice and the lawful process of Court.

The Complainant Petitioner in C.D.S.R. No. 7523/91 on the file of the State Consumer Disputes Redressel Commission of Andhra Pradesh hastened forward and said that the failure and compliance to take cognizance of the offences committed by the judges by ordering an elaborate enquiry on the part of the Indian judiciary is an absolute and unrebutted admission that the conduct and character exhibited by the Supreme Court of India in living on order X Rule 6 (I) of the Supreme Court Rules amounts to "bad."

Meanwhile, having been aggrieved by the dismissal of his Special Leave Petition in No. 11372/91 on the file of the Supreme Court of India on 11.8.1989 states that, "The dismissal order is arbitrary, not a speaking order and is in one line, "The special leave petition is dismissed". This one-line judgment of the Supreme Court should not be a Fate-Line on my forehead. The Supreme Court "dismissed" my right to life guaranteed under Art. 21of the Constitution of India, viz. livelihood. The Supreme Court has gone against its own judgment reported in AIR 1986 Supreme Court 180(193) and she has deprived me the right to livelihood and thus deprived me of my life in a non-detailed judgment in a single sentence, "The special leave petition is dismissed". In so doing, the Supreme Court ought to have delivered a detailed judgment that all the aforementioned persons are not guilty of any administrative and judicial misconduct and misbehaviour and their conduct and character in delivering an order in a Writ and a judgment in the Writ Appeal is either "good" or "satisfactory" in the eye of the Hon'ble Supreme Court of India. The Supreme Court is not constituted to deliver scraping judgments. It is patronised and maintained by the citizens of India through their Exchequer, to deliver not one-line judgment scraping the fate of the approacher of it spending time and money both in it and in the lower Courts in addition to his patronising and maintaining through the taxes paid to the Exchequer and also giving them utmost respect and keeping them in high dignity in the society, but to deliver, and the Supreme Court is bound to be responsible, gracious and dutiful to its Patrons, Judgments explaining the merits. The failure to give a detailed judgments, writing down the merits and demerits of the case in disposal, amounts to unfaithfulness to the mother whose breast milk we feed on, since it is WE, THE PEOPLE OF INDIA, and particularly the aggrieved lot at the hands of lower Court judges.

And, the Supreme Court lacks "Stamorality" (Stamina + Morality = Stamorality), i.e. Moral Stamina. "Judgment" is as it is an exhibit or "Mentality of the Judgement", being drawn from the word "mentality" and suffixed to "judge".

Mr Y Janaki Ramaih, a gold-medalist, a very well known and versatile gentleman practising civil law in this town, said that judgements of the lower courts fall within the frame of defective judgements when the judgements have been passed in the following manner:

1) Not following the latest legal position and trying to rely on some obsolete decisions;
2) Improperly construing the effect and merits of the documents;
3) Not properly interpreting the terms of the documents;
4) Not following the established legal presumptions;
5) Erring on a question of law;
6) Not going by the record of the case;
7) Delivering a judgment in slipshod manner without looking into the documents;
8) Wrong conclusions based on no reasons;
9) Disposing of matters without hearing both parties completely and without giving adequate opportunity;
10) Not rendering substantial justice by relying on technicalities, viz. by refusing to condone delays, etc.
11) Basing judgements on the contents of the Appendices and not looking into and quoting the contents of the documents, viz. tax receipts, land revenue receipts, etc.

Mr B Siva Kumar, advocate and lecturer in the Law College at Ongole expressed that the judgment devoid of *ratio decidendi* and *obiter dictum* proceeding the operative portion of the judgment and/or contradicting each other in the judgment renders it "defective".

Mr V Lakshmi Narayan, an advocate practicing in the office of his father, Mr Venteru Remana Reddy, leading criminal lawyer of Kavali, says that "Decisions of civil courts are binding on criminal courts. The converse is not true."[28] He states that judgment delivered by a criminal court refusing to give effect to the judgment delivered in a civil court on the subject matter of the case can be safely called a "defective judgment". "The judgment must contain points for determination, the decision thereon and the reasons for decision.[29] Admission has to be taken as a whole and the Court cannot accept one part and reject the other."[30]

As has already been submitted, judgments falling under the head "defective judgments" are not closed. They are ever increasing. As the judgments are delivered round the clock, the defective judgments too add themselves to the list of "defective judgements".

"It is the bounden duty of an author that he should do justice to the article he writes. To do justice he not only has to exhibit both sides of the coin, but has also to be sincere in showing a practicable solution for the ills that are prevalent in society. Then only he will be discharging his responsibility as an author; otherwise, he shall be treated as a partisan.[31]

Equity follows the law. Let punishment be in proportion to the crime. Let right be done though the heavens should fall. Justice is neither to be denied nor postponed. These are some legal maxims which show what is expected of the judiciary.

At this juncture, one would wish to address the entire legal community: the Chief Justice of India and his companion judges; the Chief Justices of all the High Courts in India and the Union Territories; High Court judges; the Law Commission of India; the Vice Chancellors of the law universities in India; retired judges; the Legislatures of the states; the Parliament; the Prime Ministers; the President of

India and other legal bodies and luminaries. They must come to the rescue of the aggrieved citizen of India, who are often betrayed at the hands of judges and magistrates and do justice by bringing about the following proposed effects in the field of law and justice:

(1) "A DEFECTIVE JUDGMENTS (PROHIBITION) ACT" may be brought into force.

(2) To "CANCEL" the G.Os and/or provisions relating to "obtaining prior permission of the government or higher authority" to sue or proceed against judges/magistrates/gazetted officers/public servants/ministers of states and central/elected political persons and thereby raise all immunities available to persons possessing public authority establishing equality among all as is guaranteed in the Constitution of India.

(3) To REPEAL "The Judicial Officers Protection Act (Act XVIII) of 1850 forthwith.

(4) To SCRAP Art. 121 of the Constitution of India.

(5) (a) To AMEND the rules framed under the Act and the Contempt of Courts Act, 1971 in such a manner as to enable any and every person to directly file a complaint petition under the Act against any judge or magistrate.

(b) To AMEND the rules framed under the Act and Contempt of Courts Act, 1971 scrapping the requirement of the consent of the Advocate General or the Solicitor General in the State or at the Centre which is now a pre-condition or qualification for the Courts to take cognizance of the Contempt and to take action, BECAUSE:

(i) It restricts the power of the Court to take cognizance of the contempt and to take action against an alleged contemner.

(ii) No Advocate General or no Solicitor General is superior to a court to take cognizance or to take action on a subject that has come to their notice and knowledge, irrespective of whether received by post or by filing.

(iii) During the course of the growth of democracy in India, the constitutional validity of the office of Advocate General created and the purity attached to it in the Constitution of India in practice is erased and, substantially, we, the people of India, have taken the office of the Advocate General as a political post, similar and as is adapted in the United States. The person filling the office of the Advocate General offering his resignation to the government as soon as the party in power and/or the Head of the Ministry runs down and the Prime Minister or the Chief Minister in the state nominating his party's affiliated person to the office of the Advocate General that fell vacant due to resignation consequent on political changes in power, simply turned it out as a political office. Since the purpose and sanctum sanctorum of the office of the Advocate General is used with dirty politicianism, the essence of S.15 of the consent of the Advocate General for filing a contempt petition is no more a good law to exist in India.

(6) (a) "UNITS", as is now counted or added to the Personal Record of the magistrates/judges as is in vogue in the State of Andhra Pradesh, should be implemented all over the country, bringing out specific rules and regulations, therefore, within the purview and under the guidelines, to be framed in THE DEFECTIVE JUDGEMENTS (PROHIBITION) ACT, for each and every order pronounced or judgement delivered by him that which is dissented or quashed by the appellate court/forum.

(b) Suitable directions should be issued to all the appellate courts/forums in the country that every judgment delivered and every order pronounced in appeal should not only contain the reasons for allowing the appeal, but also should state therein the grounds of dissent from the opinion or operative portion of the lower court judgement, very specifically, in clear terms and words and to note"THE NUMER OF UNITS THAT HAVE TO BE MISUSSED OR ADDED TO THE PERSONAL RECORD OF THE MAGISTRATE/JUDGE" that delivered the lower courts judgment.

(7) (a) Based on the "UNITS" acquired for delivering DEFECTIVE JUDGEMENTS, the concerned judge/ magistrate should be reduced in rank and suitable punishment be meted out to him at the end of every five year period of service.

(b) A last number such as 100, should be "fixed" in the total service, i.e. (1) counting from No.1; (2) irrespective of the reduction of rank and/or punishment suffered; (3) namely, from the date of joining in the judicial service either as a magistrate or judge. Automatic compulsory retirement should be enacted and introduced for having delivered defective judgements and the same judge/ magistrate should not be allowed pensionary benefits on such retirements, so that the public exchequer will be relieved and/or reduced of the burden of patronizing defective judges/defective magistrates in our country.

(8) (a) A Defective Judgements Controller PostOffice may be established under the Defective Judgements (Pro hibition) Act, its office to be located at the Supreme Court and all the High Courts. It should be headed by a retired judge or persons drawn from the seniormost judges in office, vesting them with all the powers required to control defective judgements and to punish the defective judges/magistrates.

(b) The costs and expenses incurred by the appellants for going in appeal against defective judgements may be compensated from the Consolidated Fund of the State and/or the Consolidated Fund of India.

(c) The Defective Judgements Controller may be vested with the power to take on file the complaints and/or appeals over the defective judgements falling within the purview of the definitions and/or provisions of the Defective Judgements (Prohibition) Act and to award costs and expenses to the appellants under the Act.

(9) A Defective Judgements Commission may be established under the Defective Judgements (Prohibition) Act, on the lines of the Law Commission, to submit proposals to the legislature to add and amend the Defective Judgements (Prohibition) Act, at regular intervals of about three or five years.

(10) A text book on the defective judgement should be introduced and classes may be conducted for students of law during their bachelorship. Also, doctorates on defective judgments should be produced, examining the effects the defective judgements on the individual and society.

(11) In the interest of maintaining judicial sanctity and constitutional validity, Chapter IV of the Constitution of India, Art. 124(4) is as follows:

Establishment and Constitution of Supreme Court

(1) There shall be a Supreme Court of India, consisting of a Chief Justice of India and, until Parliament by law prescribes a larger number, of not more than seven other Judges.

(2) Every Judge of the Supreme Court shall be appointed by the President by warrant under his hand and seal, after consultation with such of the Judges of the Supreme Court and of the High Courts in the States as the President may deem necessary for the purpose and shall hold office until he attains the age of sixty-five years:

Provided that in the case of appointment of a Judge other than the Chief Justice, the Chief Justice of India shall always be consulted; provided further that:

(a) a Judge may, by writing under his hand addressed to the President, resign his office;

(b) a Judge may be removed from his office in the manner provided in clause (4).

(2.A) The age of a Judge of the Supreme Court shall be determined by such authority and in such a manner as Parliament may by law provide.

(3) A person shall not be qualified for appointment as a Judge of the Supreme Court unless he is a citizen of India; and

(a) has been for a least five years a Judge of a High Court or of two or more such Courts in Succession; or

(b) has been for at least ten years an advocate of a High Court or of two or more such Courts in succession; or

(c) is, in the opinion of the President, a distinguished jurist.

EXPLANATION I - In this clause "High Court" means a High Court which exercises, or which at any time before the commencement of this Constitution exercised, jurisdiction in any part of the territory of India.

EXPLANATION II - In computing for the purpose of this clause the period during which a person has been an advocate, any period during which a person has held judicial office not inferior to that of a district judge after he became an advocate shall be included.

(4) A Judge of a High Court or the Supreme Court shall be removed from his office by an order of the President passed after receiving a recommendation made by a majority of the Judges in a Bench of the Supreme Court consisting of the Chief Justice of India and eight more sitting Judges of the Supreme Court passed in a Writ Petition filed by any aggrieved citizen of India or in a proceeding *suo mottu* moved by the Supreme Court on

a representation received from any aggrieved citizen of India on the ground of incapacity or misconduct or misbehaviour or malpractice or corruption or violation of the contents of the oath or affirmation prescribed in Schedule IV or VIII of the Constitution of India.

Provided, however in a Writ Petition against the Chief Justice of India himself, the Bench of the Supreme Court shall be headed by the seniormost Judge of the Supreme Court and eight more sitting Judges; and for this purpose the Seniormost Judge shall have all the powers of the Chief Justice of India.

Provided, however, in a Writ-Petition filed by any aggrieved citizen of India or in a Proceeding *suo mottu* moved by the Supreme Court or a High Court on a representation received from any aggrieved citizen of India on the ground of incapacity or misconduct or misbehaviour or malpractice or corruption or violation of the contents of oath or affirmation prescribed in Schedule IV or VIII of the Constitution of India against an officer discharging the judicial duties and function under any description or designation shall be removed from his office by an order of the Chief Justice of the High Court of the concerned State/Union Territory as a result of the judgement made by a majority of the Judges of the High Court of the State/Union Territory consisting of the Chief Justice of the State/Union territory and eight more sitting Judges of the said High Court.

EXPLANATION- The judgement of the Chief Justice of the Bench shall be treated as a Judgement of an ordinary Judge for the purpose of counting and deciding the majority Judgement of the Bench. The Chief Justice of India and the Chief Justice of the State, as the case may be, shall act in accordance with the judgement of the majority of the Judges in the Bench.

The aforesaid proposed amendment to Art. 124(4) and the substitution of the same will remove the difficulty to the aggrieved citizen of India and the unconstitutional phenomenon which has taken place in the Constitution of

India.[32]

The Writ Petitioner in W.P.No. 8885/81 complained that the registrar and other court officers to whose desks his papers are reaching are either not placing them before the Hon'ble Chief Justice of India or the Chief Justice of India is not proceeding against the deliverers of defective judgements.

"The tradition of selecting law officers and Judges of the High Courts from among the leading members of the bar known for their integrity has already been abandoned over the years. Successive Chief Justices found it difficult to resist pressures from the executive. The 121st Report of the Law Commission records the helplessness of a former Chief Justice of India, who said, "The Government has a great power of filibustering. I will tell you what happens; I say this man must be appointed Chief Justice. The Government has got the power of appointing an acting Chief Justice. The Government says, we are not doing anything against you. But you see, he deserves to be appointed. Let us consider it. Now I find that the administration of the High Court is suffering grievously. Then what to do I do? I have to give in. I have to give in not because I am under the Government's pressure but in the interest of the institution. Or else what happens is this: supposing there is no agreement between me and the Government on certain appointments to the Supreme Court or to the High Court, no appointments are made." Such compromises on appointments have lowered the standards of selection.[33]

"Borrowing the words of Chief Justice of Madhya Pradesh Shri Shivdayal, the interests of the nation are paramount and supreme.[34]

In this context, I may also quote the observations of one who eminently adorned our Supreme Court, Mr. Justice MR Khanna:

"We in the world of law, have for long taken for granted the respect of the people. There is a stir today, a spirit of skepticism and to some extent, of iconoclasm. There is also much greater awareness of rights and people are acquiring a new consciousness of the strong points and shortcomings of different human institutions Many of us in the world of law have so far been allergic to criticism. There is, perhaps, a need today for change in our mental attitudes. If weaknesses have crept into the system, they cannot be wishfully brushed under the carpet, nor can criticism be silenced even by threat of contempt of court. Contempt of court is no answer to genuine criticism of the functioning of our courts.[35]

"The rule of law is the foundation of democratic society. The judiciary is the guardian of the rule of law. Hence, the judiciary is not only the third pillar, but the central pillar of the democratic State.[36]

"The foundation of the judiciary is the trust and the confidence of the people in its ability to deliver fearless and impartial justice. When the foundation itself is shaken by acts which tend to create dissatisfaction and disrespect for the authority of the court by creating distrust in its working, the edifice of the judicial system gets eroded.[37]

"In a democracy like ours, where there is a written constitution which is above all individuals and institutions and where the power of judicial review is vested in the superior courts, the judiciary has a special and additional duty to perform, viz. to oversee that all individual and institutions including the executive and the legislature act within the frame work of not only the law but also the fundamental law of the land. This duty is apart from the function of adjudicating the dispute between parties which is essential to peaceful and orderly development of the society. If the judiciary is to perform its duties and functions effectively and true to the spirit with which they are sacredly entrusted to it, the dignity and authority of the courts have to be respected and protected at all costs. Otherwise, the very cornerstone of our constitutional scheme will give way and with it will disappear the rule of law and civilised life in society.[38]

References

1. *Oxford Dictionary, p. 617.*
2. *Dhiraj Pal Narula & Hari Mohan Sinha, Legal Dictionary (Including Legal Maxims, Terms and Phrases), Pioneer Publications: New Delhi.*
3. *Ibid-6, p.296.*
4. *Dr. Gurbax Singh, , Law of Consumer Protection, Bharat Law Publications: Jaipur, 1991, p. 23.*
5. *Ibid-4, p.25.*
6. *Ibid-4, p.25.*
7. *Ibid-4, p.26.*
8. *"High Court: Whether falls with in the Jurisdiction of a District Forum?" National Outlook, (Vol.1 No.1), p.6.*
9. *Ibid-8, (Vol.2 No.2), p.12.*
10. *Ibid-4, p.26.*
11. *Ibid-4, pp. 49, 50.*
12. *Ibid-2, pp.335, 336.*
13. *AIR 1971, Supreme Court 221 (230).*
14. *1971, ALL Cri. R. 257 (260) (260).*
15. *1970, ALL W.R. (HQ) 280.*
16. *1971, Supreme Court 221.*
17. *1987, MAH.L.R. 210 (BOMBAY): 1995(1) Journal F.1 A.L.D.(P.1).*
18. *Milton, "Areopagitica". Sri Venkateshwara, "Amoral Literature".*
19. *Ibid., (No. 18) pp. 65, 66.*
20. *VP Srivastav, ed., Crime, Justice and People of India, Delhi: Indian Publishers Distributors, pp. 169 & 170).*
21. *Constitution of India.*
22. *Ibid, (No.20), p.171.*
23. *The Judicial Officers Protection Act (Act IVIII) of 1850.*

24. *The House of Lords in "Re: MV Home Office", (1994, 1 AC 377), observed (as per Lord Templeman).*
25. *Justice K Ramaswamy (Judge, Supreme Court of India), "Dr. BR Ambedkar, Bharat Ratna: The Cornerstone of the Constitution". Paper presented in the National Seminar on the life, mission, contribution and relevance of Baba Sahed Dr. BR Ambedkar at New Delhi on the 15th April, 1991.*
26. *Ibid, (No. 20), p.169.*
27. *Justice S.C. Pratap, "Relationship between the Bar and the Bench", High Court, Bombay, pp.11 & 12.*
28. *AIR 1971, Supreme Court 1244: 1989 Cr. L.J. 2358 (As found in MR Reddy, Compendium of Criminal Law, Secunderabad: Jyotsna Publications, p. 290.*
29. *AIR 1954, Supreme Court 436: 1969 Cr LJ 580 (Ibid No. 59).*
30. *AIR 1968, Supreme Court 147 (Ibid No.89).*
31. *VP Srivastav, ed., Police, Law and Indian Reality, New Delhi, Manas Publications.*
32. *"Constitutional Validity of Art. 124(4) of the Constitution of India", AIR (Journal Section) August, 1993, p.121.*
33. *PP Rao (senior advocate and former President of the Supreme Court Bar Association), "Transfer of Judges", The Hindu (AP Edition), 20.8.1996, p.12.*
34. *Ramacharan Ehare, Distt. & Sessions Judge, Rewa, "Training the Judicial Officers", AIR 1977, Journal 18 & 19.*
35. *Justice S.C. Pratap (High Court, Bombay), "Relationship between the Bar and the Bench" Journal Section of A.I.R. 1980, pp. 11 & 12. This is a lecture delivered to the Members of the District Court Bar Association, Nagpur, on Wednesday, the 2nd January, 1980.*

36. *AIR 1995, Supreme Court 2348 (2366), Para 13.*
37. *Ibid No. 97 (P.2366).*
38. *Ibid No. 97. (P.2366).*

13

Constitutional View on Human Rights and Justice in India

*- Dr. Gokulesh Sharma**

These days society is confronted with the problems of human rights. Every individual in the world is facing human rights problems of some kind every day. Various attempts have been made to solve the problem. In the present forum, we shall take up only the subject of constitutional guarantees of human rights. It would be not only for the benefit of society, but perhaps a national service to share this knowledge with others who are interested in the field of human rights.

Today's demand for human rights is essentially the product of a democratic pattern of governance of society, which has, over the ages, been through five stages: 1. Primitive rights. 2. Feudalistic rights. 3. Industrialized rights. 4. Civil and Political rights. 5. Social and economic rights. Lastly, human rights in the present form were formulated. Let us consider each of these stages.

(i) **Primitive Rights:** Man had no notion of human rights at all, though he did have limitless freedoms which no civilised man can even dream of. His freedoms were without

* IInd Civil Judge (Sub. Div.) ACJM, Kanpur Dehat, Civil Courts, Kanpur, U.P.

restrictions. Actually speaking, these freedoms had absolute anarchic form. It is a unique feature of the history of political institutions that the progress towards organised society was not a movement toward attainment of rights in the absolute sense but toward the suppression of the absolute and anarchric freedom of primitive man.

(ii) **Feudalistic Rights:** When we look at feudal society, we find that there was nothing left of the primitive man's freedom and liberty. The feudal society was total negation of the human rights. It was only human rights of the rulers, princely classes such as the clergies and other nobility.

(iii) **Industrialised Rights:** In the 16th and 17th century we find the middle class flanked by lawyers, doctors (physicians, artists, teachers) and other men of letters. These classes of persons were intelligent, and were mostly dissatisfied with the feudal system. They opposed the system. Hence, industrialization started. If industrialization was to survive, the feudal system would have to go, including the feudal social order. Hence, there emerged a new school of natural law, which declared that there existed certain inherent, inalienable, immutable and inviolable freedoms and rights of man, which cannot be taken away by any authority whatsoever. As Rousseau, a great thinker, said, "All men are born free but everywhere they are in chains."

(iv) **Civil and Political Rights:** Armed with this metaphysical reasoning, a new philosophy took birth. They asserted that the positive law (the law made by king or government) was subordinate to natural law. Hence, the new Goddesses of "Equality, Liberty and Fraternity", was installed. It started the era of the doctrine of civil and political or fundamental rights of human rights in an indirect sense. These rights manifest themselves in the political and governmental sphere by replacing absolutism with Constitutionalism. The supremacy of fundamental rights implies that the government has the duty to refrain from a course of action which may result in the infringement of these rights.

(v) **Social and Political Rights:** The great economic depression of the thirties struck a heavy blow on the above philosophy of natural law. Social reality came to the fore. It was then realised that beneath this lofty idealism lay hidden the most ugly aspect of capitalism. Sir Julius Stone said, "One third of our population, the overwhelming majority of which is in industry and agriculture, is ill-nourished, ill-clad and ill-housed". This led to some new thinking. If fundamental or human rights were to have any meaning, it was necessary that their contents must change. If human rights or fundamental rights were considered to be conditions for the fulfillment of purpose of life, then not merely the capitalistic class but also the working class and the other poor and weaker classes should have these conditions guaranteed to them. It was the start of social and economic rights. In due course, people realised the importance of these social and economical rights and they compelled their ruler (king or government) to codify all these rights in the Constitution for their guaranteed enforcement to the public, so that the state may feel bound to comply with them in case of their violation.

In the modern Constitutions of many States, these civil and political, social and economical rights, have been recognised in some or the other form. The Indian Constitution is no exception. The Preamble of the Constitution, Part III of Fundamental Rights and Part IV of the Directive Principles of state policy, jointly and severally, constitute the consitutional guarantee of human rights in India. All civil and political, local and economic rights and all other ideal provisions for the betterment of human beings have been included.

Let us now come to the Indian sphere how human rights are constitutionally guaranteed.

The entire platform of human rights provisions of the Constitution of India are based on the ancient Indian Vedic concept, whose Sanskrit version, with English translations, is as follows:

(All should be happy, all should be free of diseases and want. All should see the welfare of the world at large. No one should be sick and worried.)

A careful examination of the Indian scriptures and cultural heritage shows us that Indian society is duty-based and had no place for rights Lord Krishna preached in holy book Gita:

You are supposed to do your duties. Do not expect for results. God will do the needful.

This does not mean that in India rights were exploited or not considered. It simply means that rights and duties are correlated but duties should be performed first, and rights should be asked for later.

Looking into Indian thinking, cultural heritage and the then prevalent constitutional position in the world, our founding fathers established a constituent assembly to draft a Constitution for a free Republic of India. It was taken for granted that fundamental rights were going to be an integral part of the Constitution. Throughout the freedom struggle, the demand for fundamental rights was always in the forefront. A resolution was adopted at the forty-third annual session of the congress at Madras (in December 1927) to draft "a swaraj Constitution for Indian on the basis of the declaration of rights." The Moti Lal Nehru committee submitted its report in August 1928. It observed that "it is obvious that our first care should be to have our fundamental rights guaranteed in a manner which will not permit their withdrawal under any circumstances." When the Constituent Assembly met, it appointed a sub-committee on Fundamental Rights. The terms of reference of the sub-committee included the task of drafting a Bill of Rights.

The country was unanimous that we should include all human, political, civil, economic, cultural and social fundamental rights. But in what shape and in what form should we adopt them was a matter of considerable debate and discussion. When we were drafting our Constitution, the Declaration of Human rights had already been made. Ultimately, a compromise was struck. These rights were, broadly speaking, divided into two: (i) political and civil rights and (ii) social and economic rights. The former are termed fundamental rights and enshrined in Part III, and the latter are called Directive Principles of State Policy as enshrined in

Part IV of the Constitution under Part III. The following are included as fundamental rights:

1. Right to equality (Article 14 to 18)

II. Right to six freedoms (Article 19)

i) Freedom of speech and expression

ii) Freedom to assemble peacefully and without arms

iii) Freedom to form association or unions

iv) Freedom to move freely throughout the territory of India

v) Freedom to reside and settle in any part of the territory of India

vi) Freedom to practise any profession or to carry on any occupation, trade or business

III. Rights to life and personal liberty (Article 20 to 22)

IV. Right to freedom of religion (Article 24 to 28)

V. Cultural and educational rights (Article 29 to 30)

VI. Right to property (this has been deleted from the 44th Amendment Article 31 and has been re-enacted it in Article 300 A as part of constitutional rights.

VII. Rights against exploitation (Article 23 to 24)

VIII. Rights to constitutional remedies (Article 32 to 35)

Cultural, Social and Economic Rights under the Directive Principles

Part IV of the Indian Constitution, detailing the Directive Principles of State Policy, lays down the following rights:

a) Right to adequate means of livelihood

b) Right against economic exploitation

c) Right of both sexes to equal pay for equal work

d) Right to work and education

e) Right to leisure and rest

f) Right to public assistance in case of unemployment, old age, sickness and the like

Part IV also contains some directive principles of economic and social justice and certain ideals which the state should strive to attain. Article 38 directs the State to bring about a social order where justice, social, political and economic, shall inform all the institutions of national life. It directs the State to create conditions where there will be no concentration of wealth and means of production to the common detriment, and where the ownership and control of the material resources of the community are so distributed as best to serve the common good.

In the words of K Subba Rao "What American and other highly developed democratic countries have achieved through judicial decision and pragmatism has been crystalized, embodied and improved upon by the Indian Constitution. The basic distinction between the Fundamental Rights and the Directive Principles is that the former are justicable, in the sense that any person entitled to these rights can enforce them in a court of law. While the latter are not justiciable, in that no individual can enforce them in a court of law. But nonetheless, the Directive Principles are as much part of the Constitution as Fundamental Right. The state is duty-bound to give them effect. They are, in a sense, a command to the state to bring about the necessary conditions so that they can become effective.

There are some other rights of individuals which are enacted in some other articles of the Constitution or are inferred from the constitutional limitations on governmental powers. Thus, Article 265 lays down that no tax shall be levied or collected except by the authority of law. This implies that a person has a right not to be taxed except under a law. Similarly, Article 301 guarantees freedom of trade and commerce throughout India. The freedom of trade and commerce can be regulated only under certain conditions specified by law. Article 300A guarantees that no person shall be deprived of his property save by the authority of law.

Fundamental rights under the Indian Constitution are not enacted in absolute terms; limitations have been enumerated along with each fundamental right. This has led one critic to remark that Part III of the Constitution of India should be entitled "Limitations on Fundamental Rights." The founding fathers worked on the ideology that, in the interest of securing social justice, these rights could be abridged. Not merely this, there are certain constitutional provisions under which the enforcement of fundamental rights can be suspended or prevented. Article 34 lays down, "Notwithstanding anything in the foregoing provisions of this part, Parliament may by law indemnify any person in the service of the union or of a state or any other person in respect of any act done by him in connection with maintenance or restoration of order in any area within the territory of India, where material law was in force or validate any sentence passed, punishment inflicted, forfeiture ordered or other act done under martial law in such area. Another constraint is imposed on fundamental rights when the proclamation of emergency is in operation. The original Article 359 laid down that "Where a proclamation of emergency is in operation, the president may by order declare that the right to move any court for the enforcement of such of the rights conferred by Part III as may be mentioned in the order and all proceedings pending in any court for the enforcement of the rights so mentioned shall remain suspended for a period during which the proclamation is in force or for such shorter period as may be specified in the order." The original Article 358 provided for the suspension of the operation of Article 19 during the period the proclamation of emergency was in operation. It enacted: "While a proclamation of Emergency is in operation, nothing in Article 19 shall restrict the power of the state as defined in Part III to make any law or to take any executive action which the state would but for the provisions contained in that Part be competent to make or to take, out any law so made shall, to the extent of the incompetency cease to have effect as soon as the proclamation ceases to operate except as respect to things done or omitted to be done before the law so ceases to have effect." How sweeping could be the combined effect of these provisions was made amply clear by the Supreme Court in ADM Jabalpur vs. Shukla. The Supreme Court held that when the right to enforce fundamental rights is suspended under Article 359(1), then any claim to a writ of *habeas corpus* for the enforcement of fundamental rights under Article 21 is not maintainable. It is also not competent for any court to go into the malafides of the order of detention or the *ultra vires* character of the order of detention or whether the order was passed on the satisfaction of the detaining authority. The bar created by Article 359, the Supreme Court observed, applies to petitions for the enforcement of fundamental rights mentioned in the presidential order, whether by way of an application under Article 32 or under Article 226. The 44th Amendment has drastically amended Articles 358 and 359. Articles 20 and 21 cannot be suspended in any proclamation of emergency. The 44th Amendment has also provided some further safeguards to the citizens during the proclamation of emergency.

All the above devices for safeguarding and securing fundamental rights have been adopted in the Indian Constitution. It is basically a democratic Constitution, which envisages the judiciary as the final arbiter of the Constitution, as the sentinel and guardian of freedom and liberty, and as a citadel against any misuse of power.

The device of judicial review has been enacted in clause (2) of Article 13. The clause runs: "The state shall not make any law which takes away or abridges the rights conferred by this part and any law made in contravention of this clause shall to the extent of the contravention be void". Clause (1) of the Article deals with the existing laws. It runs: "All laws in force in the territory of India immediately before the commencement of the Constitution, in so far as they are inconsistent with the provisions of this part, shall, to the extent of such inconsistency, be void".

The remedial fundamental rights is enshrined in Article 32, which was called by Dr Ambedkar as the very heart and soul of the Constitution. This article confers a right on a person whose fundamental right is violated to move the Supreme Court directly. In Ramesh Thapar vs. State of Madras, the Supreme Court very aptly said that the remedial right contained in Article 32 is itself made fundamental, thereby making the Supreme Court the protector and guarantor of fundamental rights. Article 32 empowers the Supreme Court to issue any writ, order or direction for the enforcement of fundamental rights. A similar power is conferred on the High Courts under Article 226.

Article 226 confers power on the High Court to issue to any person or authority including any government or its agency, department or office, any direction, order or writ, including writs in the nature of *habeas corpus, mandamus prohibition, certiorari* and *quo warranto,* for the enforcement of (i) any of the fundamental rights, and (ii) any other legal right or for any other purpose.

The writ jurisdiction of the High Courts, under Article 226, is fairly comprehensive. The reason for conferring this jurisdiction on the High Courts seems to be this: the makers of the Constitution, having decided to provide for certain safeguards for the people in the new setup, evidently thought it necessary to provide also a quick and inexpensive remedy for the enforcement of such rights. Finding that prerogative writs, which the courts in England had developed and used whenever urgent necessity demanded immediate and decisive interposition were peculiarly suited for the purpose, they conferred, in the state sphere, new and wide powers on the High Courts, of issuing directions, orders or writs primarily for the enforcement of fundamental rights. The power to issue such directions, etc. for any other purpose was also included, with a view apparently to place all the High Courts in this country in somewhat the same position as the courts of the King's bench in England.

The provisions of Article 226 were interpreted to contain twofold limitations. The writs issued by a High Court could not run beyond its territorial jurisdiction and the person or the authority to whom the writ was issued must be within those territories. This obviously caused great hardship to persons who wished to proceed against the Government of India or another state government. Consequently, the 15th Amendment amended Article 226 by inserting a new clause (IA), under which jurisdiction was conferred on the High Court on the basis of cause of action.

It is apparent that the writ jurisdiction of the High Court is fairly wide and ample to redress all grievances of the citizens against any organ of the government. The High Courts have very wide discretion and this discretion has been, in practice, exercised judiciously. For instance, ordinarily, the High Court would not issue a writ if there was an adequate, alternate remedy available to the petitioner, yet this was a rule of policy convenience and discretion rather than a rule of law.

Many a time, a writ of *certiorari* was issued, in spite of the fact that the aggrieved party had other adequate legal remedies, as in cases were there was a patent want of jurisdiction, denial of natural justice, infringement of the vires of a statute or infringement of fundamental rights. In short, this jurisdiction proved adequate in redressing the grievances of citizens and other individuals, particularly the High Court's jurisdiction of issuing writs, orders and directions for the enforcement of non-fundamental rights of citizens. It also proved satisfactory in containing administrative excesses. Any person, who claimed a legal right and its infringement by any organ of the government, could seek speedy redress from the High Court. The High Court jurisdiction comes into clear relief when it is realised that no other court, including the Supreme Court, has such a power.

The directive principles of state policies are definitely social and economic human rights under Constitution. It is a fact that these have not been made enforceable in the court of law but the state is duty-bound to give them effect. On the political platform, the government in power is also answerable to the public for not enforcing these directive principles.

The latest trend of the Supreme Court and various other High Courts is that directive principles are enforced under the garb of fundamental rights or equality, freedom and particularly fundamental rights of life and liberty, which has very vital clause of the due process of law. So far as question of Constitution position of human rights is concerned, the contribution of the preamble cannot be ignored. The concept of equality, liberty and fraternity has been incorporated to include the people of India. It starts with "We, the people of India." This shows that this nation has been made to be a welfare state. Welfare of the nation is only possible when its citizens and residents think that their welfare is being considered by the competent authorities and various steps are being taken to ensure the same. It may be concluded that, in India, human rights are sufficiently protected and various safeguards have been provided, under constitutional remedies, to the people in case of violations.

Apart from constitutional remedies, various legislative enactments have also protected human rights. The Protection of Human Rights Act, 1993, has further fortified the position of human rights in India. The present day contribution of the National Human Rights Commission under the Chairmanship of Justice JS Verma, which has been constituted under the aforesaid Act of 1993, is worthy of appreciation. Various other state human rights commissions have started functioning and we are hoping for the best of human rights from them. No doubt, our human rights are well protected under various constitutional provisions as discussed above, as they are under various other laws also, with the inspiration of the protection of the human rights of the public. Our international standard of human rights are definitely on the increase and there shall be a day when our human rights standard shall shine in the world.

Voting Human Rights of Prisoners

A prisoner may become an M.P. or an M.L.A but cannot cast his vote. The Constitution of India and the Representation of the Peoples Act provides basic foundation of the electoral system in India. Since India is a democratic country leaning towards federalism, the office of the Chief Election Commissioner plays a vital role in the election system of the nation. It is a fact that a person who is not convicted and who is simply undertrial as a prisoner cannot cast his vote from jail or from another place where he is detained but he can contest elections from jail. Is it not a mockery of the law that one who cannot cast his vote can become an M.P./ M.L.A. or Minister but cannot cast a vote during election period? There are several instances in our country where people have contested elections while in jail, and some of them have also won and become MLAs and MPs. Emphatically speaking, it has raised serious questions on the viability of the existing electoral system. It can very safely be said that those persons who cannot manage to get bail or are not able to raise the amount required or the surety required for getting the bail and thus remain in jail, cannot exercise their right to a vote. Likewise, those who are in lawful or unlawful custody of the police cannot vote. Hence, it can be provides immunity to the police for any action but robs the aggrieved person of the right to vote. Now, the question is whether a person who, convicted or not, is confined in jail can be barred from casting his vote. Would such a restriction violate his fundamental rights given to him under Articles 14,19, and 21 of the Constitution, and should such a provision be declared *ultra virus* and void to the Constitution? Now, the further question is that if such persons are supposed to surrender their right to vote as provided in u/s 62(5) of the Representation of the Peoples' Act, then this principle should be applied to all kinds of prisoners, but it is not so. How is a person who is detained in any provision of Preventive Detention laws, such as N.S.A, eligible to vote? It is no doubt true that the criminalisation of politics is a matter of hot discussion throughout the nation and all attempts are being made to check it and ensure that at least no criminal should be allowed either to contest elections or to cast his vote. Very recently, pushing ahead with its agenda of keeping criminals out of politics, the Election Commission has suggested that any person convicted of a crime for more than six months should be debarred from contesting elections for six years. In a letter to the then Prime Minister IK Gujral, the commission has recommended changes in a number of clauses, to fine-tune the existing Representation of Peoples Act (RPA), to plug the loopholes that have enabled even history-sheeters to contest elections.

The letter, sent in mid-September, urges that the amendments to the RPA be pushed through in the winter session of Parliament.

Two months ago, the Commission has stirred up a nation-wide debate on the issue of checking criminalisation of politics, by suggesting that those convicted up to six months be barred form contesting elections, even if they have appeals pending in the higher courts.

Election Commissioner GVG Krishnamurthy's revelation, in early August, that up to 40 MPs in the current parliament and nearly 700 out of the 4,072 legislators in state assemblies have criminal records, has raised a storm in political circles. The question that agitated the politicians was whether the axe would fall on sitting MPs or MLAs.

Though the commission's clarification that the new rules would apply to future elections was some consolation, that the Election commission meant business became evident soon after, when it issued a directive that any person convicted by a court under Section 8 of the Representation of People's Act would be debarred from contesting elections.

It was the first time in the recent Rajya Sabha elections that nomination forms were required to be accompanied by affidavits declaring that the candidate did not have a criminal past.

Another long-pending issue is that of imposing a limit on election expenses, fixing a limit of Rs 15 lakhs for parliamentary constituencies and Rs 6 lakhs for assembly constituencies. Calling for flexibility in fixing the ceiling for election expenses, the EC has recommended that the power to suitably amend these limits for smaller or larger constituencies should rest with the commission.

A significant recommendation relates to the politician seeking entry to the Rajya Sabha by giving false declarations on their addresses and enrolling themselves in the electoral rolls of the state. This problem could be eliminated altogether if the laws are amended to permit anyone to contest Rajya Sabha polls from any parliamentary constituency in the country, so long as he or she is a valid voter.

I would like to mention here also that first of all these general reforms do not have any legislative support. It is further important that this general order is silent on the question of the fate of undertrial prisoners. The Chief Election Commissioner should make efforts to abolish this kind of discrimination and to ensure that the right to adult franchise is made available to all concerned. The constitutional provisions of Articles 14, 19, and 21 of fundamental rights elaborate the position that a person should not be discriminated against and should be assured to exercise all his rights. The right to adult franchise has been guaranteed to every citizen of India. How, them, it is possible to put restriction on this right by any other subordinate authority? Let us examine the Constitutionality and legality of this issue.

The Supreme Court has already made its view clear on the diabolical nexus between politicians, bureaucrats, big industrial houses with great mophias and underworld dons. The Supreme Court has directed to the Union Government to set up a body of eminent personalities and jurists, having crystal-clear and upright reputations, to look into this nexus. It is highly unfortunate that very little progress has been made in this direction so far. The Supreme Court has described the criminalisation of politics as the bane of society and a negation of democracy. Recently, the then Chief Justice of India, JS Verma, said the criminalisation of politics is subversive of free and fair elections which is a basic feature of the Constitution." The Supreme Court noted the importance of free and fair elections and the right to adult franchise but I am afraid to say that sometimes the court undermines the significance of free and fair elections while it dismisses a petition which had challenged section 62(5) of the Representation of the People's Act. In this writ petition it was challenged that section 62(5) is violative and *ultra vires* to the Constitution and it was urged to the court that the right to vote should be extended to all undertrial prisoners also but the court dismissed this plea and held that the expression "or otherwise" has very wide connotations. It denies voting rights to the undertrials and other persons detained in prison for any reason including an inability to furnish bail. This restriction applies even to those persons who are in the custody of the police lawfully or unlawfully. It will include a person detained during investigation, or in police custody through the order of the court, before a charge-sheet has been filed against him.

Yet a person, even one convicted or sentenced or undertrial, who is released on bail is permitted the right to vote. The court held that it shall not be a discrimination. With due regards and apologies, I do not share this view. When right to adult franchise has been guaranteed to all, then certainly each and every person (citizen) who has right to vote should tender it and there should not be any unreasonable legal bar prohibiting the use of this right. Further, it is also to be noted that there should not be any discrimination, at least within a group of persons who are undertrial but under preventive detention. Otherwise, it shall be a clearcut violation of Articles 14,19 and 21 of the Constitution.

Now a days, the human rights movement is gaining momentum. We have to preserve human rights at all costs. The right to vote is a very valuable human right. It is the basic foundation not only of the democracy but also of the present legal system. A person may be found innocent, then what shall happen. Is there any provision for compensation to be paid from stopping him to tender his vote, whether the undertiral who is deprived from his right to vote can be compensated easily either way, if it is found that he was quite innocent and he remained in jail without an reasonable and probable cause. Fortunately, the Supreme Court has armed all the lower courts with the power that if a person, who is deprived of his liberty without any reasonable and probable cause, the court can compensate him in terms of money for his grievances. I think this facility should be extended to those undertrials who have been deprived of the right to vote. All Indian citizens, unless they are convicts, or insolvent, or otherwise disqualified from voting, or if their right has been taken away expressly under any law for the time being in force, should be permitted to cast their vote during the election process as a goodwill gesture for human rights. The Apex Court has tried to distinguish between undertrial prisoners under ordinary criminal laws and their counterparts detained under preventive laws. It has been said that preventive detention such as under the National Security Act is meant to prevent any breach of the law, while persons in jail after conviction or during investigation and trial subsequent to the commission of crimes are on a different footing. I think this distinction is not sufficient by itself. The proceedings of the preventive detention laws are taken against those offenders or criminals who are beyond the reach of ordinary criminal laws or against those who are highly criminal or mischief mongers but have made their escape from the courts on legal technicalities and they are likely to cause terror in the society. The Supreme Court, in the case of Sangram Singh vs. Union of India, held that right to vote was a statutory right and not a common law right. The right to vote or to stand as candidate for election is not a right but is a creature of state or special law and must be subject to the limitations imposed by it. Then Court kept in view the

Representation of the Peoples Act and various other election laws prevalent in this country.

I think that it is a universal truth that, in all democratic countries, the right to adult franchise has been assured fundamentally. Although it may not be a very ancient right, it can safely be said to be a fundamental right for the foundation of society nowadays. The present day legal position is that a prisoner cannot vote but can be an MLA, MP or Minister. This legal position should be changed and parity should be maintained. All undertrial prisoners should be permitted to vote, irrespective of their crime, unless they are specifically barred or disqualified from tendering a vote. Looking into the human rights movement and Article 14, 19 and 21 of the Constitution, this restriction upon the right to vote of prisoners should be removed by the government itself. If not, then our courts, specifically the apex court, should not hesitate in declaring these provisions null, void and ultravires to the Constitution. The court should also show its regard and respect to human rights as shown by it in the past so that right to adult franchise can be utilized by all citizens of India, whether they are in jail or not, because they are citizens of India.

Whether the right to education, the right to know and knowledge should be a fundamental right

In India, at present, the right to education is not a fundamental right and the right to know and knowledge is not constitutionally protected under any of the provisions of the Constitution, while the constitutional provisions of the various foreign nations have guaranteed the right to education and the right to know and knowledge to its residents or citizens. Let us undertake a comparative study of the provisions of the Indian Constitution vis-a-vis the constitutional provisions of various other foreign nations.

Under Chapter IV of Directive Principles of State Policy within Article 45, provisions have been made for free and compulsory education for children. It has also been provided that the state shall endeavour to provide, within a period of ten years from the commencement of the Constitution, for free and compulsory education to all children until they complete the age of 14 years.

Eire Article 42 states: The State shall provided for free primary education.

Burma Article 33 states: When in particular, the State shall make provisions for free and compulsory primary education.

Article 44 states: The State shall pay special attention to the young and promote their education.

France The preamble in the 1946 Constitution of the Fourth French Republic states: The establishment of free, secular, public education on all levels is a duty of the State.

Czechoslovakia Section 12 - (i) All citizens have right to education.

(ii) Elementary education is uniform compulsory and free.

Germany Section 39 States:

(i) Every child must be given opportunity to develop thoroughly his physical, mental and moral powers. Attendance at the technical and secondary schools and at the institutes of higher learning shall he made possible for all sections of the Nation.

(ii) Schools shall be free of charge. Learning aids in compulsory schools shall be supplied without payment.

Costa Rica Section 78 States: Primary education is compulsory.Primary, pre-school and secondary education are free and are provided at national expense. The State shall facilitate the higher studies of persons who lack the necessary funds. The Ministry of Education shall be responsible for the awarding of scholarships and grants-in-aid, through a body appointed by law.

Section 82: The State shall provide food and clothing for needy pupils in accordance with law.

UNO

Article 23 (i) says elementary and fundamental education shall be free and compulsory. Likewise, the Constitution of Nepal has also promised free education to children. The Constitution of Nepal has also guaranteed the right to know and knowledge (U/S 16 of the Constitution of Nepal).

Now, the perusal of these provisions of the various Constitutions of foreign nations has shown us a path for free and compulsory education, although certain riders have been imposed. Hence, the right to free education has been made a fundamental right and the State is bound to oblige. In some foreign nations, this right to education has been made compulsory and free completely to all kinds of children, but in certain nations, it has been made free up to primary education. The position of France is quite unique, which has provided for the establishment of free, secular public education at all levels as a duty of the State. The position of India is different. The framers of the Constitution have directed the State for free and compulsory education and the State is made responsible under the directive principles of state policy. However, it is not for the people to get this right enforced in case of non-compliance by the State.

In the last 50 years, constitutional experience has shown us that the expected progress of education has not taken place, either due to the State's negligence of or non-compliance with the directive principles of state policy, or due to administrative or other offenses prevailing in the education system. Justice PN Bhagwati, in Sheila Barse vs Union of India, AIR 1986 SC 1773, has observed that a child is a national asset. It is the duty of the state to look after the child with a view to ensure full development of its personality. The right to education under the directive principles was supposed to be fulfilled within ten years of the commencement of the Constitution, but nothing concrete has been done so far. The framers of the Constitution might have thought that, within a span of ten years, the educational standard of the nation shall be uplifted by the State and the State shall be obliged to fulfill its obligation and responsibility. At the time of independence, there was about 84% literacy. Now the position is that 2/3 of the population is still illiterate and 1/3 is only literate. It shows very slow progress. In the last 50 years, the position has not improved and now we are tempted to wonder why the right to education and the right to know and knowledge should not be made a fundamental right. In Mohini Jain vs State of Karnataka (1992) SCC (666) the Supreme Court held that the right to education at all levels should be a fundamental right. However, next year in Unnikrishann vs. State of Andhra Pradesh 1993, SCC page 645, the Supreme Court limited the scope for the right to education by holding that, due to the non-availability of wide resources and keeping in view the limited sources of the government, children's education up to the age of 14 years must be regarded as a fundamental right. In this case also, the court showed great regard to the right to higher education, also assuming it to be a fundamental right.

The present legal position is that the right to primary education up to the age of 14 years has been presumed by the Supreme Court to be a fundamental right. The last 50 years' experience has shown us that generally in all states of India, the right to primary education for students, specifically for girls up to the age of 14 years, has been provided with prime importance and the State itself is bearing all the expenses of education for children.

Practical experience has shown us that middle class people do no want to send their children to these schools because of the poor quality of education, inefficient staff and the lack of an academic atmosphere. People are compelled to spend more and more on the education of their children. If due care and attention had been brought by state governments on educational standards, then certainly the position could have been otherwise today. If the government tries to improve, it may do a lot even today. Unless the right to education is made a fundamental right completely, in all respects and at all levels of education, the welfare of the nation and society is not possible and feasible.

It remains a question as to why, given that other nations have made education a fundamental right, the right to education in India was not made a fundamental right at the time of inception of the Constitution. The framers of the Constitution might have thought it that it should be better to place promises of education under the directive principles of state policy as a responsibility of the State, to be fulfilled within ten years of the Constitution.

Now it is felt that the right to education must be a fundamental right, along with the right to know and knowledge. In 1990, the Acharya Ram Murthi Committee recognized, for the first time in free India, that the right to education should be made one of the fundamental rights of Indian citizens. The committee recommended an amendment in the Constitution to that effect. It is also a fact that, when India became a signatory to the United Nations Convention on the rights of the child, it accepted the obligation of making education compulsory. But making education compulsory has always been opposed by the Central Advisory Board of Education, New Delhi which even declared that compulsion in education is unnecessary. The Board also stated that compulsion shall be ineffective and useless. I think the Central Advisory Board of Education forgets its responsibility of educating the masses, which is not only its duty towards this nation but also a obligation towards individuals. Education opens vistas towards fertilization and progress. Unless education is made compulsory, the progress of the nation shall never take place. The board should not forget its responsibility to educate every individual, particularly children, to make them good citizens. It is not a compulsion, but a benefit for society and towards the welfare of all. I know that the fundamental right to education shall create greater responsibilities for the State. Compulsory education shall compel the State to spend more on education, by opening new schools and colleges, including for adults. We know that State shall have to bear a greater burden in the establishment of these schools, colleges and other materials and paraphilia relevant to education.

We thank Maharaja Sayaji Rao Gaikwad of Baroda, who introduced compulsory education in his kingdom in 1906.

Likewise, Vitha! Bhai Patel pursuing the efforts of Gopal Kishna Gokhale, got the Bombay Education council to adopt in law for compulsory education in 1918. By 1930, all the provinces in British India covered under the Bombay Legislative Council have adopted compulsory education acts. Gokhale had desired these acts and he made local bodies responsible for introducing compulsory education in respective areas. Hence, it is wrong to say that a compulsory education system to children, adults and even to elders shall be ineffective, unnecessary, and useless. I emphasis the fact that when the compulsory education system had proved fruitful in the earlier states of Baroda and Bombay, then why should it not be effective and useful for the rest of contemporary India. The State's budget for education is now nearly 4%. The state will have to increase its budget if a compulsory education system is introduced.

Furthermore, it is clear that the educational system is somewhat backward and we are still following the old British education system; this should be Indianised. It should be made to suit Indian conditions and needs. In May 1997, the Union Government has decided to bring legislation to regulate private educational institutions, including their fee structure, to check commercialization of the educational system. The Ministry of Human Resource Development had prepared a bill to make education a fundamental right and it was expected that the Union Government would do the needful in this regard. Unfortunately, that Government is no longer in office. In May 1997, it was expected that to create the requisite infrastructure for achieving full literacy, Rs. 40,000-/ crores would be needed and, if found necessary, an education tax may be imposed to mobilise resources for compulsory education. Now, all these proposals are merely dreams, unless these proposals are adopted by the new prospective government.

In this regard, various non-governmental organisations should be consulted on how to improve the education system. The Kothari Commision report should always be considered and government agencies like NCERT and NIEPA should also be asked to submit their suggestions. After full discussion in this regard, a proper law for making the right to education a fundamental right should be made. Complete enforcement of these rights should also be made responsibility of the State, for the benefit of society and the individual.

The question is whether the right to education should be made a fundamental right only up to primary education or in the complete sense. This question may be decided by inviting the opinions of various educationists and jurists and with reference to different case laws of the Supreme Court. In the Mohini Jain case (1992), the right to education has been made to be a complete fundamental right to education at all levels, while in the Unnikrishanan case (1993), the court limited the scope of fundamental rights to education up to the primary level only. Ideally, the right to education should be made fundamental right in the complete sense but, for the sake of convenience and looking to the limited resources of the government, a phase-wise implementation should be ordered. At the first stage, primary education should be made effective. At the second stage, intermediate education should be taken into consideration; and at the third stage, university level education should be considered. Lastly, scientific research education should be taken up. All these programmes should be executed equally by time bound schemes and programmes.

If the right to education is made a fundamental right, then each individual shall be able to get this right enforced through court.

Now we have also to see whether the newly appointed government adopts the recommendations of the previous government, of making the right to education a fundamental right. Importantly, we have also to see whether the recommendation of the previous government were made to camouflage the government's responsibility, cast upon it by the Supreme Court in 1992 and 1993, to the aforesaid cases, or whether the government is sincerely looking into the interests of education. It might be possible that by enacting the judgment of the Supreme Court into legislation, the Government may be able to postpone any kind of implementation. If the right to education is made a fundamental right in view of the decisions of the Supreme

Court, then the government shall be the first to take the credit. If no sincere steps are then taken by the government in this regard, the right to education shall be futile and of no use. Hence, two things are required: first, education should be made a fundamental right under Part III of the Constitution; and second, there should be a will of government to get this right enforced, by providing sufficient funds for the establishment and the machinery to make it work. To make this right more effective, monitoring by all should be permitted. In case of violation and noncompliance, these rights may be enforced at the behest of the court. So far as the question of necessary funds is concerned, the government may levy taxes and invest its own money. Other semi-government authorities or welfare societies may be invited for free and easy education to all. Lastly, education should be free from interference and control of government or its local bodies. This does not mean that government will not be in a position to say anything. Government shall supervise and, in due course, shall take suitable steps, looking into the prevalent needs and according to the various suggestions prescribed by the educational institutions. A permanent body of eminent personalities and educationists should be made to supervise the educational system in India, to make it more effective.

Along with the right to education, the right to know and knowledge should also be made fundamental rights. Nowadays, right to secrecy along with right to privacy, are two major impeding factors, with are adopted by all public servants and even by government to curtail their misdeeds. If we want to crush and eliminate completely corruption, mismanagement and inefficiency, then Indian citizens should be authorized and permitted to have the right to know and knowledge as a right to information. Nowadays, public life and public dealings require transparency. Whatever is being done by any public servant or government functionary, except in cases where national integrity and unity is in danger and where it affects the foreign policy of the nation, there should be no secrecy. Section 5 of the Official Secrets Act and sections 123, 124 of the Indian Evidence Act should also be scrapped. There should be no public documents which are confidential, except those which affect national unity or foreign policy. Secrecy breeds corruption and inefficiency, while openness provides greatness, confidence and sincerity. Hence, the veil of secrecy should be removed and transparency should replace it. In November 1997, the Bombay High Court has delivered a very important judgment on the petition of Sanjeev M Gowadkar vs. State of Maharashtra. The Bombay High Court has directed Maharashtra, and the Union of India that all laws, enactments and legal provisions should be made available to the public at large and at reasonable prices. The Court ordered that, under Article 21 of the Constitution, every citizen has a right to know and it is the duty of the State and the Union that all necessary facilities should be provided while making this right to know an effective right. The Court also directed the publication department of the State of Maharashtra and the Union of India that all legal provisions and laws should be published and made available to the individual at reasonable cost. The Court has further directed that if any legal provision is found in the English Language, then its Hindi version or its version in the local language of the State should also be made available.

Hence, I expect that right to education at all levels and the right to know and knowledge shall not only be made fundamental rights but that these rights should be duly implemented by the government in the near future. It is also expected that all the members of society shall cooperate with the government in this regard, for the welfare of the individual and the nation as a whole.

14

The Onward March of Justice in Fifty Years

- Justice A.D. Mane*

At first, let me tell about the concept of law. The study of jurisprudence and history reveals what ends law has served, though what ends it should serve is a question for legal philosophy. To know what is law, it has to be defined; and yet, it is not a physical object that can be defined so easily. It has multifarious dimensions. A definition of law again may be either in the terms of judicial process, or in its perspective of social engineering.

Lord Sankey, Lord Chancellor, has said, "The rule of law is the condition of liberty. Amid the cross-currents and shifting sands of public life, the law is like a great rock upon which a man may take his seat and be safe, while inevitable inequalities and private life are not so dangerous in a country where every citizen knows that in the law courts, at any rate, he can bet on justice."

As Paton says, a definition of law should have two aims, firstly to make precise the meaning of law and secondly to call up in the minds of the reader a true picture of law and its operation.

Goodhart defines law as those rules of conduct on which the existence of society is based and the violation of which in consequence tends to invalidate the existence of society.

So, law prescribes what is considered necessary for the time being in the interest of a civil society. That means law is

* Judge, High Court of Aurangabad, Aurangabad.

an instrument of justice. Therefore, law should be used as an instrument of social control and social engineering. Sometimes, confusion arises as to the relationship between law and justice. Law and justice are however, two different concepts. They are interrelated but each has a distinct sphere of its own. The concept of justice is even older than that of law. Justice is the legitimate end of law. It must necessarily precede law, because the people thought of law as they wanted justice. Justice is ideal, though it is difficult to attain. Like the pole star, it guides us to move in the right direction. However, Justice Krishna Iyer has described the law and justice as distant neighbours.

Role of Judges

One of the cardinal principles is that a judge must articulate his judgment in obedience to the fundamental interest of the society. He must recognize the role of the ideals of right and justice in giving shape to the law in accordance with experience developed by reason. Roscoe Pound said, "Experience teaches decisions that prove to satisfy the demands of justice. Reason shapes and orders and develops decision to ideals of justice and so into the principle of law. The principal function of administration of justice is to adjust the relations of individuals with each other so as to accord with the general moral sense. Progressive positive law is the law which utilizes the scientific discoveries of the law of social development for the welfare of mankind."

Salient and Silent Features of our Constitution

No sooner that the World War II ended in 1945, the question of India's freedom assumed priority. The British government sent a three-member delegation to suggest the ways and means for the smooth transfer of power. The delegation was called the Cabinet Mission; it announced its proposal on 16th March, 1946, in which it was suggested that the Constituent Assembly be set up to frame a Constitution for the future governance of India. Accordingly, elections to the Constituent Assembly were held, to which members were elected by the Provincial Legislative Assemblies. The Constituent Assembly started its work of framing free India's Constitution on 9th December, 1946. The Drafting Committee was appointed by a resolution passed by the

Constituent Assembly on 29th August, 1947. Dr. Babasaheb Ambedkar was elected Chairman of the Drafting Committee. The report of the said committee was submitted on 20th August, 1947. The Draft Constitution was introduced by Dr. Babasaheb Ambedkar to the Constituent Assembly on 4th November, 1948.

There were several readings of the draft Constitution. The draft Constitution was discussed clause by clause. The discussion concluded on 17th October, 1949. Again, on 14th November, 1949, the Constituent Assembly sat for the reading of the Constitution. That was finished on 26th November 1949, when the Constitution was declared as passed, and thereafter, the Preamble of the Constitution was signed out. On the day of the adoption of Constitution of India, Dr. Ambedkar said, "Constitution of our country would be found to be bulky. It would be difficult for those who have been through it to realize its silent and special features" Speaking about article 32 of the Constitution, Dr. Ambedkar said, "If I was asked to name any particular article in this Constitution as the important one, without which this Constitution would be nullity, I would not refer to any other article except this one......" He further said, "It is the very soul of the Constitution and the very heart of it......"

Another quotation which I would like to mention at this stage is the answer given by Dr. Ambedkar to various amendments suggested by the members in the draft constituent assembly, in regard to the provision contained in part IV- directive principles of State Policy.

You know that fundamental rights are followed by what are called directive principles. That is novel feature in the Indian Constitution framed for parliamentary democracy. Since the fundamental rights and directive principles find place in two different chapters or Part III and Part IV, obviously they are separate and independent.

Fundamental rights recognize the importance of the individual in the affairs of the State and seek to assure other citizens full freedom to enjoy life, liberty and happiness.

The idea with which the fundamental rights are embodied in the Constitution in Part III was essentially a negative idea.

These rights were carved out with an idea where the individual was to be supreme. They raise a procedural barrier to unwarranted intrusions. They assume that in this realm the citizen has no claim upon the government, except to be let alone. It is this negative which lies at the bottom of fundamental rights.

The story of the evolution of fundamental rights, as enforced in the courts of law, is a long one. In substance, fundamental rights, like natural rights, are intended to be limitations on governmental powers of state actions, including the Legislature. It is to protect fundamental rights from legislative enactment.

The effect of granting human rights in the written Constitution is to ensure that any state action inviting legislation, which violates or is inconsistent with fundamental rights, shall be struck down by the courts, because the Constitution is the fundamental and supreme law of the land. Powers of all other organizations and government are considered to be limited by its provisions. It follows that not only the Legislature but also the Executive, in all administrative authorities, are equally governed by its provisions, so that any legislative Executive or administrative act which contravenes that provision of the Constitution must summarily be avoided.

It is agreed that the rights included in Part III in particular and those included in Part IV of the Constitution are distinguishable. The former are justiciable, while the latter are not. That is why the former are called fundamental rights while the latter are called directive principles.

Most members of the Constituent Assembly agree that directive principles are superfluous, or mere guidelines, or pious principles or instructions. They have no binding force on the State. In his speech, Dr. Ambedkar answered, "The directive principles are like instruments of instructions which were issued to the Governor General and Governors of colonies and to those of India by the British Government under the 1935 Act under the Draft Constitution. It is proposed to issue such instructions to the President and Governors . The text of these instruments of instructions shall be found in schedule IV to the Constitution of India. The directive principles are instructions to the Legislature and the Executive. Such a thing is, to my mind, to be welcomed, wherever there is grant of power in general terms for peace, order and good government, it is necessary that it should be accompanied by instructions regulating its exercise."

Dr. Ambedkar further said, "The inclusions of such instructions in the Constitution such as proposed in the draft becomes justifiable for another reason. It is said that the directive principles have legal force. I am prepared to admit it. But I am not prepared to admit that they have no sort of binding force at all.[1] Nor I am prepared to concede that they are useless because they have no binding force in law.....The draft Constitution, as framed, only provides for machinery for the government of the country. It is not a contrivance to install any particular party in power, as has been done in some countries. Who should be in power is left to be determined by the people as it may be; if the system is to satisfy the test of democracy. But whoever captures power will not be free to do what he likes with it. He may not have to answer for their breach in the court of law but he will certainly have no answer for them before the electorate at election time."

This answer given in the speech of Dr. Ambedkar is read as the only consequence from the political plane for the failure to implement the directive principles. I, therefore, make an attempt to delve in his subconscious mind, to trace whether that was the only consequence that was in the mind of Dr. Ambedkar, or whether he wanted to suggest some hidden consequences which he had in mind, when he spoke of Article 32 of the Constitution of India.

It was never intended by Dr. Ambedkar that the directive principles had no legal force but had moral affect, while he was educating members of the Government and the Legislature, nor can it be said that the answer referred to necessarily implied that the directive principles had no legal force. If we have regard to the further speech of Dr. Ambedkar while introducing the Draft Constitution, it would be clear what Dr. Ambedkar had in mind was the primacy of Directives Principles over fundamental rights. The directive principles were enacted for the socially proved laws and implementing directive principles should prevail over the laws designed to protect the fundamental rights of the individuals.

Dr. Ambedkar had also said that, "What great value these directive principles possess will be realized better when the forces of the right contrive to capture power. Thus, it has no binding force, is no argument against their inclusion in the Constitution. There may be difference of opinion as to the exact place they should be given in the Constitution. I agree that it is somewhat odd that the provisions which do not carry positive obligations should be placed in the midst of the provisions which do carry positive obligations. In my judgment the proper place is in schedule UIA and IV which contain the instruments of instructions to the President and the Governors for, as I have said, they are really instruments of instructions to the Executive and the Legislature as to how. they should exercise their powers but there is only a matter of arrangement. . . ."

He also said that, "Having regard to the fact that there are various ways by which the directive principles may be brought about, we have deliberately introduced in the language that we have used in the directive principles something which is not fixed or rigid. We have left enough room for people of different ways of thinking with regard to reaching the ideal of economic democracy to strive in their own way, to persuade the electorate that it is the best way of reaching education. The fullest opportunity to act in the way in which they want to act. That is the reason why the language of the Articles in part IV is left in the manner in which the Draft Committee thought it fit to leave it.... It is no use to give a fixed rigid form to something which is not rigid, which is fundamentally changing and must, having regard to the circumstances and the times, keep on changing. It is therefore no use saying that the directive principles have no value. In my judgment, the directive principles have a great value, for they lay down that our ideal is economic democracy because we did not merely adopt the parliamentary form of the government to be instituted through the various mechanisms provided in the Constitution without any directions as to what our economic ideal is, and what is our social order are to be, we deliberately included the directive principles in our Constitution."

It is clear from the above speeches read together that Dr. Ambedkar, in clear terms, was firm in his conviction that the directive principles have a binding force on the State, in as much as they are in one way mandatory in nature. Therefore, he did not concede to the criticism that directive principles are useless because they cannot be enforced by individuals in the court of law as in the case of fundamental rights.

Till recently, there was different opinion as to whether Part III overrides Part IV, or whether Part III has supremacy over Part IV, but that controversy has been minimized by the decisions of the Apex Court. The directive principles have now received increasingly greater importance since the Constitution was enacted. The Supreme Court, in a series of cases, interpreted that Part III includes further fundamental rights on reading Part IV. That means the rights are not only natural rights to be conferred by the Constitution. Public interest litigation is the outcome of this. The directive principles of state policy contained in Para IV does not achieve the socialistic role envisaged in the Preamble of the Constitution. The democratic ideal of justice raised on the foundation of equality, liberty and minimum control of the government is thus a promise to promote the fraternity, assuring dignity to the individual and unity to the nation. What Dr. Ambedkar had envisaged 50 years ago, his dream of the close relationship of fundamental rights and directive principles, the Supreme Court has realised. Thanks to the higher judiciary, it has demolished the wall between these two immediate neighbours and has built a bridge between them, so that the concepts in the Preamble can now ply to and fro without any conservative hindrance.

Dr. Ambedkar, while explaining the word 'strive' as used in the directive principles, has said:

"...In my judgement it is very important. We have used it because our intention is that even when there are circumstances which prevent the Government or which stand in the way of the Government giving effect to these directive principles they shall always strive in fulfillment of these directives, that is why we have used the word strive. Otherwise it would be open for any Government to say the circumstances are so bad, finances are so inadequate that we cannot even make effort in the direction in which the Constitution asks us to go. Ours is a welfare state, significantly Part HI read with part IV is to support the development of the nation as a welfare state and preserve the rights. In the recent judgment in case of Dalmiya (1996(10) SCC 104), the Supreme Court has explained the concept of socio-economic justice. The word "justice" as envisaged in the Preamble is used in broad spectrum to harmonse individual rights with the general welfare of the society. Justice ends to promote the general well-being of the community as well as individual excellence. The principle aim of the society is to protect the rights of the individual; subject to social order, social justice is the comprehensive forum to remove social imbalances of law, harmonizing rival claims and interest, without which it would not be possible to build up the welfare state. The ideal of economic justice is to make equality of status meaningful and give worthy living at its best, removing inequality or studying the socio-economics of politics.

It is heartening to note that in the post-Maneka era, the judiciary has changed its grammar of interpretation with social awareness, thus generating new thoughts of judicial activism. The judiciary has shown a progressive approach in the areas of dispensation of justice. The right to free legal aid, as contained in article 39-A, has been read into the fundamental right to life and liberty as a part of a just, fair and reasonable procedure and hence made enforceable.

The expression "socio-economic justice" is the flame of the Constitution and the courts, being the guardians of the Constitution, are catalysts of social revolution. It is the duty of the courts to apply the directive principles in interpreting the Constitution and laws. In the case of ABSK Sangh vs. Union of India[2] A.I.R 1981 SC 298, it was held that the directive principles serve as the code of interpretation for the Judiciary.

I may remind you that during the first two decades of the commencement of the Indian Constitution, the Apex Court subscribed to the outmoded dogma of the analytical school. They treated fundamental rights as the sanctum sanctorum of the constitutional temple and placed them beyond the reach of parliament. Thus, the pace of socio-economic justice was halted. But in recent years, the Apex Court entered into the dilemma of studying the relationship of supremacy over the directive principles. Till 1980, the importance of the directive principles was not fully recognized. In Kasturi Lal vs. State of J&K [3] (AIR 1980 SC 1992), directive principles are held as reasonable restrictions in the public interest on fundamental rights.

Though the court may not be able to actively enforce the directive principles by compelling the state to apply them in the governance of the country or in the making of laws, the court can, if the state commits a breach of its duty by acting contrary to these directive principles, prevent it from doing so. This was also said in Central Inland Water Transport Corporation Limited vs. Brojo Nath[4] (AIR 1986 SC 1571). The success of socio- economic democracy will come only after the Part III and part IV of our Constitution are interpreted harmoniously and people become the main focus.

Looking at the issue from another angle, though the directive principles are not enforceable in a court of law, they have an important position in the scheme of the Constitution. Article 37 shows that it shall be the duty of the State to apply these principles in the making of laws. It must be noted that the Supreme Court, while interpreting the Constitution, also makes law. It is a constitutional obligation upon it to see that, while interpreting any provision of law, goals enunciated in Part IV are kept in view. Article 38 is mandatory, which shows that the State shall endeavour to bring social order, social justice, economic justice and political justice to the individual and minimize the inequality of individuals. Due to social and economic inequalities, a large segment of our society does not have food, clothes and shelter. For them, individual liberties have no meaning. The problem of bonded labour and discrimination based on rich and poor are some glaring examples of social realities, which make the socio-economic justice only a paper parchment and a constitutional anathema. Women, who constitute almost half of the Indian population, children and the youth, on which depends

India's future, still continue to be downtrodden segments of society.

Scheduled castes and scheduled tribes, as also other weaker sections of society, suffer from social and economic inequalities. The role of the directive principles in providing socio-economic justice to the working class, the right against exploitation and bonded labour, the right to work in a human condition, the right to a fair wage, participation of the workers in the management of the industries, are the items covered under Part IV of the Constitution. Similarly, various questions of the educational and economic interest of the scheduled castes, scheduled tribes and other backward classes, the upliftment of humans, the prohibition of child labour, public health and a healthy environment, equality in the dispensation of justice etc., are items falling under chapter IV. In various decisions, the Supreme Court interpreted part IV, giving new birth to fundamental rights in Part III of the Constitution.

A silent revolution has taken place within the court halls of the judiciary. The non-justicable directive principles embodied in Part IV of the Constitution have now been resurrected as enforceable fundamental rights by the magic wand of judicial activism playing on Article 21 of the Constitution. Prior to the decision in the Maneka Gandhi case, Article 21 was construed narrowly as the guarantee against Executive action in spirit by the law. The Maneka Gandhi case opened up new dimensions, which are that, while prescribing the procedure for depriving a person of his life or personal liberty, the procedure must be reasonable, fair and just.

The right to life enshrined in Article 21 means something more then survival or animal existence[5] (State of Maharashtra vs. Chandrabhan AIR 1983 SC 803). It would include the right to live with human dignity[6] (olga vs. Bombay Corporation AIR 1986 SC 180) and a right to minimum subsistence allowance during suspension (the Chandrabhan case cited above)[7]. It would include all those aspects of life which go to make a man's life meaningful, complete and worth living[8]. That which alone can make it possible to live must be declared to be an integral component of the right to live[9]

(Olga vs. Bombay corporation cited earlier). It would include all that gives meaning to a man's life e.g. his tradition, culture heritage and protection of that heritage in its full measure[10]. It would thus include:

(a) The right of a person not to be subjected to bonded labour or to unfair conditions of labour.[11]

(b) The right of a bonded labourer to rehabilitation after release.[12]

(c) The right to livelihood by means which are not illegal, immoral or opposed to public police. Hence, public employment cannot be taken away by any procedure which is not reasonable, fair and just.[13]

(d) An obligation upon the state to preserve the life of every person, by offering immediate medical aid to every patient, regardless of the question of whether he is an innocent or guilty. The criminal law shall operate after the life of the injured is saved.[14]

(e) Personal liberty has been given a wide meaning and the right to privacy is also considered a fundamental right.[15]

The Supreme Court has given expansion to the scope of Article 21, by giving an elaborate interpretation of the words "life" and "liberty." Article 21 has now came to be invoked almost as a residuary right to existence.

The public interest petitions have thus been on Article 21, to comprehend such diverse aspects as children in jail being entitled to special treatment[16], health hazards due to pollution[17], beggars interest in housing[18], health hazards from harmful drugs[19], the right to a speedy trial [20], handcuffing of prisoners[21], delays in execution of death sentences[22], immediate medical aid to injured persons[23] (Parmanand Vs. Union of India), starvation death[24], the right to know[25], the right to open trial[26], inhuman conditions in after-care homes.[27]

Similarly, the right to pollution-free water and air, the right to a reasonable residence, the right to food, clothing, a decent environment and even the protection of cultural heritage, the right of every child to a full development, the right of residents of hilly areas to access to roads, the right to education, are now become enforceable as fundamental rights, though these are included in Part. IV of the Constitution in the directive principles of State Policy.

The trend in the Supreme Court is that, when the constitutionality of a statute is challenged as arbitrary or unreasonable, the court has to test its validity on the anvil of Articles 14,19 and 21, read together[28].

It is now established that even where a person is convicted and imprisoned under the sentence of Court, he does not lose all the fundamental rights belonging to all persons under the Constitution, excepting those which cannot possibly be enjoyed owing to the fact of incarceration, such as the right to move freely, or the right to practice a profession. Hence, a prisoner can claim to exercise certain rights, namely:

(a) the right to acquire, hold and dispose of property

(b) the freedom of expression, reading and writing, except in so far as it is circumscribed by the fact of imprisonment

(c) the right, under Article 21, not be deprived of his life or personal liberty except according to procedure established by law

(d) the right against discrimination under Article 14. etc.

In the Unnikrishnan case[29], reference is given to several rights, which now fall within justifiable categories. To say that the directive principles of State Policy are not enforceable in a court of law is to indulge in sophistry. Part IV and Part III are not supposed to be exclusionary of each other; they are complementary to each other. The rule is as much a part of Article 14 as it is of clause (1) of Article 16. In the N.M. Thomas case[30], the Supreme Court made it clear that the directive principles and fundamental rights are construed in harmony with each other and every attempt should be made by the court to restore apparent inconsistency. The directive principles contained in Part IV constitute the stairs to climb the high edifice of a socialistic state and the fundamental rights are the means through which one can reach the top of the edifice.

The directive principles form the fundamental feature and social conscience of the Constitution and the Constitution enjoins upon the State to implement those directive principles. The directives thus provide the policy and the guidelines and the end of socio-economic freedom.

The Supreme Court has interpreted the provisions as contained in Part III and Part IV of the Constitution giving meaning to the intention of the framers of the Constitution. I have already referred to the statement that Dr. Ambedkar has made before the drafting committee of the Constitution, in regard to Article 32 and part IV of the Constitution, and it is a matter of pride that whatever he has said about 50 years ago is now becoming the truth.

Dr. Ambedkar emphasized that directive principles, though they are not legally enforceable, are legally binding on the State, as they are having governance of the Constitution and it shall be the duty of the State to apply them in making laws. The judicial activism in the field of socio-economic justice has made the Supreme Court the sentinel of people's rights. Responding well to the clarion call of the day, the judiciary has been playing an important role in regard to the Executive and Legislative inactions in pursuit of socio-economic justice which was foreseen by Dr. Ambedkar.

In this context, it is not out of place to refer to the observations of the Supreme Court in the case of Post Graduate Institute of Medical Education & Research, Chandigarh and others vs. KL Narasimha and others[31], K. Ramaswamy, speaking for the court, has supported the importance of Article 32 of the Constitution of India, as spoken to by Dr. Ambedkar. The Supreme Court observed;

"The faith of the Founding Fathers of the Constitution in the Supreme Court Judges was so high that they chose to describe Supreme Court Judges as "worthy Judges" to interpret the Constitution, to sustain social order, to integrate the people in united Bharat, to elongate constitutional rights, ensure the enjoyment of those rights and make these rights available to the dalits, tribes, poor, minorities and all sections in equal measure. It is repeatedly held by this Court that the interpretation of the constitutional provisions should always be such as to enable the availing of the rights given in the Constitution to the citizens, and not to deny or denude them by the process of interpretation. The Judges of the

Constitutional Courts, in particular, as judicial statesmen, would always endeavour to ensure enjoyment of the rights enshrined in the Constitution by every section of the society consistent with the policies and principles laid down in the Constitution. We are to keep at the back of our mind the above perspectives to reach the result."

The onward march of our law must continue. The right to privacy and certain socio-economic provisions also need to be brought under fundamental rights. Some socio-economic rights, which are in the directive principles chapter of the Constitution, should be put in the chapter of fundamental rights. Though the rights of education, health and medical care have been rendered as fundamental rights through the Supreme Court rulings, this should be expressly put in the fundamental rights chapter. In short, let us change the caption of Part IV and name the chapter the fundamental rights.

So, this is a march of law within 50 years of Independence, in fulfillment of the pious desire of Dr. Ambedkar, even though there is no end of the journey, as the goal of social justice is still to be achieved.

References

1. *1996 (10) SCC104.*
2. *ATR 1981 SC 298.*
3. *AIR 1980 SC 1992.*
4. *AIR 1986 SC 1571.*
5. *State of Maharashtra vs. Chandrabhan, AIR 1983 SC 803.*
6. *Olga vs. Bombay Corporation, AIR 1986 SC 180.*
7. *Ibid No.5,*
8. *Maneka Gandhi vs. Union, AIR 1978 SC 597.*
9. *Ram Sharan vs. Union.*
10. *Ibid No. 6.*
11. *Peoples Union vs. Union of India, AIR 1982. SC 802.*
12. *Neeraj vs. State of M.P., AIR 1984 SC 1099.*
13. *Board of Trustees vs. Dilip, AIR 1983 SC 109.*

14. *Paramanand vs. Union of India, AIR 1989 SC 2039.*
15. *Malkani vs. State ofMaharashtra, AIR 1973 SC 1571.*
16. *Sheela vs. Union of India, (1986) 3 SCC 596.*
17. *Mehta vs. Union of India, (1987) 4 SCC 463.*
18. *Kalidas vs. State of J&K, (1987) 3 SCC 430.*
19. *Vincent vs. Union of India, AIR 1987 SC 990.*
20. *Raghubir Singh vs. State of Bihar, AIR 1987 SC 149.*
21. *Alltemesh vs. Union of India, AIR 1988 SC 1765.*
22. *Triveniben vs. State of Gujarat, AIR 1989 SC 1335.*
23. *Ibid No. 13.*
24. *Kishen vs. State of Orissa, AIR 1989 SC 677.*
25. *Reliance vs. Indian Express, (1988) 4 SCC 592.*
26. *Keshar Singh vs. State, AIR 1988 SC 1883.*
27. *Vikram vs. State of Bihar, AIR 1988 SC 1782.*
28. *Minerva Mills vs. Union of India, AIR 1983 SC 1155.*
29. *(1993) I SCC 645.*
30. *(1976) 2 SCC 310)*
31. *(1997) 6 SCC 383.*

15

Human Rights and Judiciary

*- V.P. Srivastav**

Human rights are based upon identical fundamental conceptions. Most fundamental is the idea of human rights as pre-suppositions of a human life worth living, in whatever minimal sense. No life can be worthwhile without enforceable guarantee, against the state and others, to physical integrity, freedom of thought and action and minimal means of subsistence. Human rights are based upon identical fundamental conceptions. Most fundamental is the idea of human rights as pre-suppositions of a human life worth living, in whatever minimal sense. No life can be worthwhile without enforceable guarantee, against the state and others, to physical integrity, freedom of thought and action and minimal means of subsistence. To reiterate, human rights are expression of what is a life minimally worth living. The Universal Declaration of Human rights by General Assembly of the United Nations on 10th December 1948 states that one has the rights to life, liberty and security of person. It also states that every one has the right to a standard of living adequate for the health and well being of himself and of his family including food, clothing, housing and medical care and necessary social service and right to security in the event of unemployment, sickness, disability, widowhood, old age or other lack of livelihood in circumstances beyond his control.

The human rights are a product of history. Human rights should be covered by effective mechanisms and procedures to guarantee and protect them and to provide sanctions.

* Ex. Addl. Public Prosecutor, NCT Delhi, Currently Copyright Information Officer, Ministry of HRD, Department of Education, Shastri Bhawan, New Delhi - 110 001.

Only democracy within states and within the community of states can truly guarantee human rights The area of protection is punishment of genocide, suppression of genocide, abolition of slavery, efforts of discrimination based race, sex, religion or belief. Rights of people, protection of refugees, stateless persons, women, children, disabled persons, person with mental illness, prisoners, victims of enforced disappearance, protection of rights of migrant workers and their families and protection of indigenous people. With establishment of the U.N. there has been a considerable development of International law of human rights. The U.N. Charter in Article55 declared Universal respect for observance of human rights of human rights and fundamentals freedom of human rights of 1948 proclaimed that all human being are born free and equal in dignity and right and enumerated the basic right and fundamental freedom.

In spite of all this, we frequently hear about the violation of human rights all over the world. The situation of the world has become very shaky. Everywhere, it is full of dissatisfaction and restlessness. The Supreme Court of India is being identified by justice as well as people as the 93 Last resort of the oppressed and bewildered 94. Under-trial as well as convicted prisoners, women in protective and migrant laborers, unorganized laborers who fall prey to faulty mechanization, women who are bought and sold, slum dwellers and pavement dwellers, kins of victims of extra judicial executions these and many more groups now flock to Supreme Court seeking justice.

PUBLIC INTEREST LITIGATION:

The medium through which it has happened and is happening is public interest litigation. The most significant amongst the latest developments in judicial process under the leading national constitutions, which are even expanding the efficacy and enforceability of human rights, is Public Interest Litigation. In India, the justices of the Supreme Court Notably Krishna Iyer and Bhagwati began converting much of the constitutional litigation into Public Interest Litigation through a variety of techniques of judicial activism. The right is to life and personal liberty under procedure established by law in Article 21 was soon to encompass within itself the right to bail, the right to speedy trial, the right to dignified treatment in custodial institution, the right to privacy and the right to legal service to the poor prisons and places of detention. The various civil, political, economic, social and cultural rights as enshrined in the constitution of India are yet to be implemented and they have to serve useful purposes for the protection of human rights. However, due to dynamic interpretation of fundamental rights by the supreme court of India and introduction of the 93 Public Interest Litigation94 by it, has been possible to protect many of the human rights in the recent past.

The landmark judgment in the case of Public Interest Litigation is that of Justice Bhagwati in S.P.Gupta vs. Union of India (A.I.R.1982, S.C.149) popularly called the Judges case. The court found that the major impediment in bringing the problems of the under privileged before the courts and in the way of providing access to justice to the deprived and vulnerable sections of the society was the traditional rule of 93locus standi94. Rejecting the government plea that the citizens have no lucus standi to invoke the jurisdiction of the Supreme Court, Bhagwati (J), held that any public spirited individual can move the court in case where the person concerned seeks judicial redress in the cause of justice, provided the person moving the court is acting in the interest of public and not for personal gain, private profit, political motivation or other oblique consideration. Bhagwati (J), observed that where a legal injury is caused to a person or to a determined class of person, by reason of violation of any constitutional or legal rights and such person or determinate class of persons is by reason of poverty, helplessness or, disability or, socially or economically disadvantaged position, unable to approach the court for relief, any member of the public can maintain an application for an appropriate direction, order or, a writ.

Since the above judgments had been given, whenever any illegality or atrocities or inaction is brought to the notice of the Supreme Court or High Court, it becomes duty of the constitution to look into the same, get the matter investigated and grant proper relief to the needy persons who are really oppressed, illiterate and uneducated.

Here, we are mentioning few judgments pertaining to the human rights.

1.SUNIL BATRA V. DELHI ADMINISTRATION: AIR 1980 SC1559

This originated form a letter by a prisoner (Sunil Batra) Tihar Jail to a judge of the Supreme Court. The letter complained of a brutal assault by a head warden on another prisoner Premchand. Entertaining the petition Justice Krishna Iyer said 93 Rights-Jurisprudence is important but becomes an abstraction in the absence of remedial jurisprudence. True technicalities and legal niceties are no impediment to the court entertaining even as informal communication as a proceeding for Habeas Corpus if the basic facts are found. Finally, the court said that the writ of habeas corpus can be issued not only for releasing a person from illegal detention but also for protecting prisoners from inhuman and barbarous treatment. Whenever the rights of a prisoner either under the constitution or under the laws are violated, the writ power of the court can run and should run to rescue.

2.PEOPLES UNION FOR DEMOCRATIC RIGHTS V.UNION OF INDIA AIR1983 SC339

A petitioner sought an order to ensure observance of the various provisions of labour laws relating to workmen engaged in the construction work of various projects connected with the Asian games. The petitioner alleged that the violation of related laws resulted in the deprivation and exploitation of the workers employed. The court held that nonpayment of minimum wages to the workers employed in various Asiad Projects in Delhi was a denial to them of their basic right to live with basic human dignity and violative of Article21 of the Constitution. The court observed that the non-implementation by the private contractors and non-enforcement by the state authorities of the provisions of various labour laws violated the fundamental right of workers 93 to live with human dignity. 94 This decision has heralded a new legal revolution. It has clothed millions of workers in factories, fields, mines and project sites with human dignity.

3.BANDHUA MUKTI MORCHA VS UNION OF INDIA AIR 1984 SC 803

An organization dedicate to the cause of release of bonded labours informed the Supreme Court through a letter that they conducted a survey of the stone-quarries situated in Faridabad District of the state of Haryana and found that there were a large number of labours working in these stone quarries under 93 inhuman and intolerable conditions 94 and many of them were bonded labours. The petition prayed that a writ be issued for proper implementation of the various provisions of the constitution and statutes with a view to ending the misery, suffering and helplessness of these labours, and release of bonded labourers. The court treated the letter as a writ petition and appointed a commission to make an inquiry and ordered the release and rehabilitation of all bonded labourers.

4. LAKSHMI KANT PANDEY VS UNION OF INDIA (1984) 1 SCC 244

A writ petition was filed on the basis of a letter complaining of malpractices indulged in by social organizations and voluntary agencies engaged in the work of offering Indian children in adoption to foreign parents. It was alleged that in the guise of adoption, Indian children of tender age were not only exposed to the long dreadful journey to distant foreign countries at great risk to their lives but in case they survive they were not provided any shelter and relief homes and in course of time they become beggars or prostitutes for want of proper care. Bhagwati (J) laid down principles and norms, which should be followed in determining whether a child should be allowed to be adopted by foreign parents. With the object of ensuring the welfare of the child, his lordship directed the government and various agencies dealing with the matter to follow these principles in such cases, as it is their constitutional obligation under Articles 15(3) and 39(c) and (f) to ensure the welfare of the child.

5. M.C.MEHTA VS UNION OF INDIA AIR (1986) 2 SCC176

In the above-cited case, the Supreme Court directed the company manufacturing hazardous and lethal chemicals and gases posing danger to health and life of workmen and people living in its neighbourhood, to take all necessary safety measures before reopening the plant. There was a leakage of chlorine gas from the plant resulting in the death of one person and causing hardships to workers and residents of the locality. This was due to the negligence of the management in maintenance and operation of the caustic chlorine plant of the company.

6. KHEDAT MAZDOOR CHETNA SANGATHAN VS STATE OF MP AIR 1995 SC 31

In this case, the Supreme Court directed the CBI to impartially investigate and prosecute officers, however high or low, for torturing and handcuffing innocent tribals.

7. INDER SINGH VS STATE OF PUNJAB AIR 1995 SC312

In this case, while deciding a Habeas Corpus petition against alleged abduction of seven persons by senior police officers and sundry policemen, the Supreme Court directed the Director CBI to personally conduct inquiry in the case.

8. NANDINI SATPATHI VS PLDANI AIR 1978 SC 1025

In this case, the Supreme Court upheld the right of an accused to secure the services of a lawyer of his choice at the time of police interrogation. In the first Sunil Batra Case, (AIR 1978 SC1675), putting bar-fetters on, and handcuffing of prisoners was regarded a kind of torture, cruel or degrading treament in terms of Article 5 of the Universal Declaration of Human Rights and prescribed procedural safeguards. In the second Sunil Batra case, (AIR1980SC1559) the Supreme Court considered solitary confinement of prisoners as a human perversity, which should be avoided and issued suitable guidelines.

9. SMT. NILABATI BEHERA VS STATE OF ORISSA AIR 1993 SC 1960

In this case, the Supreme Court while ordering compensation of Rs. 1.5 Lakh by the state to the petitioner for custodial death of her son aged 22 years, reiterated that compensation for contravention of human rights and fundamental freedoms guaranteed in the constitution, is an acknowledged remedy for enforment and protection of such right.

10. On January 18, 1999 (Times of India, Jan.19, 1996), the Supreme Court sentenced a senior Haryana IPS officer to imprisonment for 18 months for perjury and contempt of Court in a case of illegal detection and abduction of two children from Agra in 1992.

11. On May 9,1996 (Times of India, May10, 1996), the Supreme Court in a report to CBI, sentenced another senior IPS officer of Assam to three months' imprisonment for "Covering Up" unnatural death of an under trial prisoner three years ago.

12. On May13, 1996 (Times of India, May 14, 1996) again acting on a CBI report, the Supreme Court ordered the State of Punjab to pay Rs.10 Lakh compensation to the parents for abduction and murder of an advocate, his wife and two year old child and falsely implicating an innocent person, and also pay Rs. 2 Lakh to the latter as compensation for the suffering caused to him due to false implication and remaining in jail since 1993.

There are a few other cases, which are relevant on the issues and values of human rights. They are listed as under.

1. Kishore vs State of Rajasthan, AIR 1981, SC 625.
2. Sheela Barse vs State of Maharashtra, AIR 1983, SC 378.

3. Saheli vs Commissioner of Police (Delhi), AIR 1990, SC 513.
4. Arvinder Singh Bagga vs State of Uttar Pradesh, AIR 1995, SC 117.
5. D. K. Basu vs State of West Bengal, AIR 1997, SC 610.
6. Prem Shankar Shukla vs Delhi Administration, AIR 1980, SC 1535.
7. Sunil Gupta vs State of Madhya Pradesh (1990) 3 SCC 119.

The list of cases is not limited but exhaustive which establishes not only the values of human rights but also enforces the basic human rights. Thus, we find that the Public Interest Litigation for upholding the human rights and values has been entirely initiated and nurtured by the apex court. Being aware of the limitations of legalism, the Supreme Court in the main and the High Courts to some extent, for the last decade did their best to bring law into the service of the down trodden under the banner of Public Interest Litigation. It has covered a wide range of human rights, viz. in sanitary structures, garbage, starvation deaths, bonded labourers, daily wage workers, untouchables, inmates of protection homes, prisoners, provision of toilets of railway stations, nepotism in medical education, discharge of trade effluents, ill treatment children in jail, sexual exploitation, victims of gas leakage disaster, environment pollution and other matters involving human rights. It is often seen that the human rights are being violated not only by the action or inaction of the established authority of the state machinery or by any anti-social activity of some organized groups in a society, but it may also be there due to the hazardous and inherently dangerous activities of different enterprises. Bhopal gas case and the Delhi Olium Gas Leak Case settled the group for Public Interest Litigation. It explains the scope of Article 12 of the Constitution to cover even private companies to bring them within the domain of human rights of Article 21, in the case of hazardous and inherently dangerous activities of enterprises.

The judicial trend in preventing the violation of human rights is prevalent now a days. To save democracy of the country and the democratic rights of the people, the court should always remain vigilant. However, only judicial directives cannot ensure a good government. The judiciary should not only award compensation in proper cases, but it should also see that its directives are properly implemented. The directions are hardly of any effect on the actual violators, since the payments, if any, are to be made from the state exchequer only. It is extremely important that the responsible officers should not only be directed to pay a part of that compensation but they should also be admonished for the gross violation of human rights. If these issues are addressed by the judiciary, then only we can expect a society where there is no willful and deliberate violation of human rights.

16

Justice for Judges: The Bitter Experiences

- *V.P. Srivastav**

There is widespread assumption that the judiciary, who are supposed to keep the people on the straight and narrow path, do not themselves have any scruples or value system. Whether it is a politician who wants the charges against his supporters to be dropped, or the industrialist who wants a trade union leader to be fixed, or a landlord who wants his tenants to be hounded out, or employer who wants that dedicated officer be booked on false allegations an all of them approach the judiciary with confidence. He may understand the plea that his request is politically inexpedient, or that the other side is even more influential, or that the course of action is too risky but he would be flabbergasted if the judiciary raise an objection on the ground that it is unfair or unjust. The first reaction may be that judiciary is pulling his legs.

It is now taken for granted that the administration, including the judiciary, would be available to the party in power to favour its supporters, harass its opponents and do whatever was dictated by the interest of the ruling junta. The judiciary apparently, is more than willing and uses this partnership for its own aggrandizement. Rule of law implies, essentially, that no citizen can be deprived of his life and personal liberty except according to the procedure established by law. Democracy itself is threatened when the administration cease to respect the legal and constitutional rights of the citizens and persistently disregards the due

* Ex. Addl. Public Prosecutor, NCT Delhi, Currently Copyright Information Officer, Ministry of HRD, Department of Education, Shastri Bhawan, New Delhi - 110 001.

process of law. After 1947, there were two areas of functioning, which required urgent and comprehensive restructuring. One was the education system and the other the legal system. Unlike the field of education, the constitution itself provided for a certain mechanism for review and renovation in respect of law and legal procedures. A standing Law Commission was set up. Over the years, it has been submitting reports. One has only to look at the fate of almost 200 reports submitted during this period to see that nobody is seriously interested in reforming the legal system. Indeed, with the passage of time and growth of population, things have become much worse than before.

There are no two opinions that the judiciary has served the country well even in difficult times. It has produced judges of outstanding integrity and ability. The people of India have confidence in the judiciary because it has functioned independently and impartially. Judicial Independence is the foundation on which the whole concept of justice is based. If judges are not independent and impartial, who will have faith in the administration of justice? The concept of independence of judiciary is primarily to appoint the best persons with integrity and a sound knowledge of the laws; persons who will not succumb to pressures of any kind from any quarters. This kind of independence alone secures justice for all and creates confidence of the society in judges. But today the past scenario has been totally changed. There are instances where the judges have succumbed to pressure. In Maharastra, the first major instance of corruption in the judiciary was brought to light in April 1990 when Justice MP Kania of the Bombay High Court expressed his inability to continue his association in the hearing of a multi-crore property dispute case (Mehta vs. Mehta) because of "threats" he had been receiving. It later transpired that the threats came from Thelma Menezes, a travel agent believed to be close to Justice S.K.Desai, the judge with whom Justice Kania was sharing a division bench. Justice Kania 92s revelations and his subsequent protest fast the first in the judicial history led to the transfer and eventual resignation of Justice Desai on June 8, 1990. The controversy did not end here innuendo and mud slinging continued over the earlier mysterious discovery of Rs.1.5 Lakh in Justice

Kania 92s personal toilet. Once the Chief Justice of Supreme Court Justice E.S.Venkataramiah had created a furore with the candid revelation that he had in his possession the names of 90 sitting Judges who were "Entertained" by members of the bar. Surprisingly, there is no provision for judicial control over misconduct of judges. So, let step be taken by judges themselves to formulate a code of conduct. Immediately, the Bar Council of India must painstakingly and creatively, with relevance to the prevalent pathology, draw up a professional code for the Bar and suggest one for the Bench.

Justice V.R. Krishna Iyer, the former Chief Justice of India, recommends the urgency of the need for a disciplinary mechanism, therapeutic and corrective in this domain where the process must maintain confidentiality and retain the judges 92 confidence and the whole disciplinary outfit and operation must be functionally kept at an appropriately high level but assuring that no robe escapes from his wrong-doing. The judicial accountability considering the variety of aberrations or rogue some of which the Judges are guilty of, requires careful and realistic handling because many of the improprieties go unnoticed behind the iron curtain of Contempt of Court. Judges, like other constitutional functionaries, must face the law if they depart from or deceive the law. Justice is no cloistered virtue and the path of criticism, even if exaggerated, must be permissible since freedom of expression is a guaranteed right applicable as much for the judges as against the judges. The procedure for impeachment is very cumbersome which is ultimately not in the hands of judiciary. So, we can say that the quality of justice depends upon independence enjoyed by the judiciary. The principle that judicial independence is a privilege for the protection of the people and not the judges 92 own applies to India and all democracies based on the rule of law. Judicial principles should unite the judiciary, not its men. In the United States of America, judicial independence has developed into a set of institutions that ensure that judges decide according to law, rather than according to their own whims or the will of others, including other branches of the government.

The five components of judicial independence comprise the constitutional protection that judges in the United States have the independent administration of judiciary by the judiciary, judicial disciplinary authority over the misconduct of judges, the manner in which conflicts of interest are addressed and the assurance of effective judicial decisions. India accepted the concept of security of tenure for judges in our constitution. The procedure for impeachment of judges is very cumbersome which is ultimately not in the hands of judiciary. The case of former Supreme Court judge, V. Ramaswamy regarded as a benchmark as far as corruption is concerned. Finally the impeachment was moved in the parliament and debate on its legality, which ensure all came to naught. Despite having said that he would resign in May1993, V. Ramaswamy retired quietly on Feb 2E 1994, surviving the first threatened impeachment of a judge. Judge power is a critical factor of the highest importance in our constitutional order. For that very reason, the law must keep them away from lawless, immoral, unethical and unbecoming conduct. Some cowardly judges and opportunist brethren obligingly bend their judgments when political heavyweights and tycoons with clout happen to be parties. Some leading members of the Supreme Court bar wrote, not long ago, a complaint to a chief justice referring to holiday hearings and nocturnal proceeding where influential persons figured as parties. Even the Bhopal Gas litigation and later settlement with judicial imprimatur have come in sharp criticism, bordering on the needle of suspicion being pointed at five judges. The Indian judiciary is presently in the search of justice for their mena lot of vacancies are available for the post of judges but government is not fulfilling them for reason best known to the concerned authority. Most of the judges are pró-government and they are not pronouncing the judgment against the governmental organization with their vested interest despite the fact that the government is faulty. The reason behind such an act is they may be given the charge of some inquiry commission after retirement. Currently the Chief Justice of India has asked the government to fulfill the vacant post in the judiciary. It is relevant to mention here that there is no independent administration of appointment of judges inside the judiciary. The government has got the supremacy over the transfer of judges keeping in view the relevant provisions of law. When the then Chief Justice of Allahabad High Court Justice Saitsh Chandra had resigned due to his transfer as a Chief justice of Calcutta, this issue of transferring the judges became more sensitive.

The democracy of judicial justices, according to the Justice Iyer, must be founded on the triple pillars of justice, justices and just icing. Inevitably, new thinking is necessary if Indian Justice is to fulfill its peoples 92 promise. The judges, despite their handicaps of monetary resources and legislative authority, have done a great job, inventive, innovative, intelligently adaptive, departing from the adversary process. The court shall keep its promise in terms of Article 39-A, which mandates that the state (which includes Courts) shall secure that the operation of the legal system promotes justice.

In order to get things in right perspective, it should however be seen that the judges must made himself independent in all respect. Without saying anything more about this issue, one has to be less dramatic and more pragmatic. Three things in particular need to be noted. More than 95 per cent of the higher judiciary is functioning exactly as it used to function. Secondly, no questions are being raised in regard to whether the laws enforced are appropriate to our social structures and other conditions of life or whether they require any kind of review or amendment. Thirdly, despite half a century of independent functioning, there is hardly any significant body of thought or research, which would show the inadequacy of the Anglo-Saxon jurisprudence, which has held the field for almost a century and a half. Each of these issues need to be analyzed further with the modernization of fossilized procedures.

Some judges think that disciplinary power over their peers may be left to the chief justices. Unfortunately, there are many instances where complaints have come against chief justices and judges themselves, in private, admit the chiefs to be over-bearing or dubious. Justice V.R. Krishna Iyer have mentioned that it is widely known that Chief Justice even of the Supreme Court have abetted or arranged hearing of bail petitions of VIPs on holidays and after nightfall. A senior mos judge of the Supreme Court, who later became the chief justice, and another senior most judge of the Supreme Court, who also became the Chief Justice later, did hear criminal matters on an abnormal day or at an abnormal hour making a special exception for the accused tycoons. It is also reliably rumoured, perhaps, that a Chief Justice of Punjab and Haryana High Court was not consulted in the appointment of a Judge to his High Court, and likewise a judge of the Supreme Court was appointed even though the chief Justice of that time had not been consented to his appointment. Other instances can be discovered, without much research, about deviances by Chief Justices themselves.

The justice system is our only stable asset. Let us preserve it. What a few of the superior judges are doing is admirable and deserves to be applauded; but can we say that the rest of them have also changed their antenna? The fact of the matter is that they are functioning in their customary, lackluster ways. It is true that the judiciary has to depend on the executive for the implementation of its decisions but it does not mean that the executive or even those who are sitting in the legislature can ignore such decisions. Legal sanctions against judicial delinquency are a necessity.

Bibliography

1. *V.R. Krishna Iyer: Justice At Crossroads.*
2. *Praveen Swamy: Supreme Concern, Frontline, May3, 1996.*
3. *Gurmukh Singh, Sanghamitra Chakraborty and Sabina Sehgal: "The Dishonest Indian", The Sunday Times of India, New Delhi December 17, 1995.*
4. *Sumer Kaul: "Law, Crime and Punishment", The Hindustan Times, New Delhi dated September 30,1996.*
5. *VM Tarkunde: "A Case for Timely Disposal", The Hindustan Times, New Delhi dated August 2,1998.*
6. *Amrik Singh: "Judicial Activism", The Hindustan Times, New Delhi dated October 19,1996.*